Termination and Relocation

TERMINATION AND RELOCATION

Federal Indian Policy, 1945–1960

Donald L. Fixico

University of New Mexico Press
Albuquerque

To
Michelene

Library of Congress Cataloging-in-Publication Data

Fixico, Donald Lee, 1951–
Termination and relocation.

Bibliography: p.
Includes index.
1. Indians of North America—Government relations—1934– . 2. Indians of North America—Cultural assimilation. I. Title.
E93.F52 1986 973'.0497 86-16057
ISBN 0-8263-0908-9

First paperbound printing, 1990

Contents

Illustrations

Maps

Preface

War is a brutal conflict that simultaneously destroys peoples and nations and erodes developing civilizations. Throughout the history of humanity, war has produced change, the only redeeming aspect of its destructive intent, and with each episode of conflict and the clash of ideologies, new ideals are born. Frequently such ideals foster action, and drastic changes occur sometimes in the name of reform—of improvement for all concerned.

Following World War II, a new era dawned for the United States and American Indians. The momentum of Commissioner John Collier's retribalization policy, implemented under the Indian Reorganization Act of 1934, came to a halt. BIA officials, the American public, and even Native Americans were convinced that the IRA plan of reconstructing tribal governments and restoring cultural traditions was outdated. Both Indians and bureaucrats favored a modernized society that would require the integration of the Indian population into the mainstream of modern America. This new direction in affairs between Indians and the federal government spurred a policy of terminating the government's trust relationship over Indian lands and relocating the native residents to new homes in urban areas.

Termination and relocation, however, were not new themes in federal Indian policy. In fact, prior to the founding of the federal government of the United States, foreign governments who occupied parts of the western hemisphere introduced quasi-policies of termination and relocation that seriously usurped the autonomy of the indigenous peoples. These policies advocated paternalistic supervision and, in some cases, the eradication of native populations. The perpetuation of similar policies can be ascertained throughout the history of United States–Indian relations.

In the beginning, a young and precarious national government composed of the thirteen colonies exercised careful diplomacy with Indian tribes who initially had enjoyed military superiority. Over a span of nearly one hundred years, some 389 treaties were negotiated between Native Americans and the United States, until Congress passed a law in 1871 that halted Indian treaty-making.

As the white population grew, the military strength of the United States quickly surpassed that of Indian tribes. Negotiations with tribal groups frequently failed, resulting in misunderstandings that led to the homicidal termination of Indian people by the superior U.S. military. Clashing armies and Indian forces decimated the native populations. Until the mid-1800s the destruction of Indian life on the battlefield assumed an obvious physical form of termination, or, to be specific, genocidal extermination. The establishment in 1824 of the Indian office within the Department of War signified the early hostile relations existing between Americans and Indians. Federal-Indian relations were largely viewed as a military problem, and the federal government dealt with Native Americans as an enemy to be conquered.

In the nineteenth century, American settlers clamored for Indian lands and penetrated into the wilderness, often without protection from the federal government. Simultaneously, the settlers demanded that federal officials remove the native inhabitants from the land, and the continuous pressure of Manifest Destiny forced the relocation of Indians further westward. Congressmen, particularly those of the frontier territories and states, were hard put to support legislation favoring westward expansion in order to save their seats in government. But the paramount question of whether or not to remove Indians from their homelands divided congressmen and other federal officials. The majority of officials supported removal, while a minority of humanitarians objected to the injustice of seizing Indian lands. They believed that Native Americans held superior rights, or at least should possess the same moral rights to the land as whites. Despite the efforts of several congressmen to prevent removal, the Indian Removal Act of 1830 authorized an exchange of lands of those tribes residing in any of the eastern states or territories for lands west of the Mississippi River. In his final annual message to Congress, President Andrew Jackson stressed that removal was necessary for the protection of Indian people.

During the nineteenth century, Americans increasingly intruded deeper into Indian country, thereby forcing the federal government to deal with the tribes more effectively. Relocation became the focus of federal Indian policy, and when this was met with armed opposition the devastation of tribal communities ensued. Military resistance from zealous native patriots like Black Hawk of the Sauk and Fox, Crazy Horse of the Sioux, Chief Joseph of the Nez Percé, Geronimo of the Apaches, and Chitto Harjo of the Creeks led to a nationwide suppression of the Indian population.

Humanitarians who felt that the United States had a responsibility for preserving Indian existence initiated a reform movement to aid the recovery of the defeated red man. Commissioner of Indian Affairs Luke Lea called for implementation of a second major removal period. In an annual report dated 27 November 1850, Lea requested the relocation of western tribes to reservations for their self-preservation. Federal bureaucrats argued that the reservation program would protect Indians from white depredations and that they would receive needed supplies to survive in a sedentary life-style.

Whether or not the reservation program saved the red man, large tribal landholdings were reduced. Surplus lands became available for white settlement, and safe migration routes to the West were guaranteed. Indian relocation opened the West to settlement, as a trans-Mississippi corridor unfolded through the once hostile lands of the Comanche, Apache, Kiowa, Cheyenne, and the Sioux. With the opening of the Santa Fe, Overland, Butterfield, California, and Oregon trails, and the building of the railroads that followed, more settlers pursued the American dream westward.

Congressional erosion of Indian legal rights through legislation represented other forms of termination. In 1887, Congress passed one of the laws that most significantly affected Native Americans and Indian policy in the nineteenth century—the General Land Allotment Act. This legislation, often simply referred to as the Dawes Act, essentially reduced reservation lands by allotting land to individual Indians. From 1887 to 1900, the federal government approved a total of 53,168 allotments, involving nearly five million acres. A parallel can be drawn between the Dawes Act and the termination policy of the 1950s, when many Indians were freed of trust restrictions. The allotments served basically to break up reservations and tribal communities in favor of individualizing Indians and granting them fee-simple lands. Although the reservations were held in trust by the government, individual allotments were not initially held in trust. The Burke Act of 1906 later placed the allotments under trust restrictions.

White assimilationists argued that the Dawes Act would benefit Indians by enabling them to farm and to become civilized for integration into American society. Government officials were convinced that traditional Indian life-styles were no longer practical and would jeopardize the future of Native American people. The bureaucrats believed that Indians should finally realize they could no longer retain their age-old customs, and should adopt the so-called civilized ways of white Americans.

With the turn of the century, the federal government instituted a policy to "save the red man" from the impoverished reservations and rural allotments. Part of this reform can be attributed to Indian interest groups like Friends of the Indian, members of the Lake Mohonk conferences, along with the impact of Helen Hunt Jackson's muckraking book, *A Century of Dishonor,* a shocking exposé of how Native Americans had been severely mistreated.

Federal Indian policy attempted to resolve the Indians' equivocal legal status once and for all in the twentieth century. The allotment program under the Dawes Act provided some Indians with citizenship. Others became citizens by virtue of having served in the military during World War I, after an act permitting this was passed on 6 November 1919. The movement for Native American citizenship culminated in congressional passage of the General Citizenship Act on 2 June 1924—a landmark event in the history of Indian–white relations. Politically, Indians had become a part of the American society.

The General Citizenship Act was considered a major step toward the reform of Indian Americans. Negative implications of termination and relocation were not immediately involved since Native American people were not restricted as stated in the act. Actually, Indians could be citizens of both the United

States and their own tribes. However, the act was an all-inclusive measure that did not give Native Americans the choice of accepting or rejecting U.S. citizenship.

In 1934 Congress passed another landmark act, the Indian Reorganization Act (IRA), also known as the Howard–Wheeler Act, named after its congressional sponsors. Primarily, Indian communities were allowed to restore tribal governments that had declined after allotment. The IRA included the conservation and development of Indian lands and resources. Tribal groups were extended the opportunity to form business organizations and credit systems, while other provisions fostered vocational education for students and encouraged the restoration of native arts and crafts. Commissioner of Indian Affairs John Collier was a primary proponent of the act and encouraged Indians to accept it in spite of the criticism surrounding it.

Passage of the IRA ignited controversy among both government officials and Indians. In sessions of Congress, Representative Abe Murdock of Utah led a protest of anti–New Deal sentiment that voiced opposition to the bill. Among the Indian community at large, tribal members split over the provisions of the measure. Joseph Bruner, the president of the American Indian Federation, and some tribal officials, like Jacob C. Morgan of the Navajo Tribal Council, claimed that the act reversed the progress of Indians, and they denounced the measure as a communistlike attempt to return Indians to communal living. In spite of much opposition, Congress passed the bill, and for those tribes who accepted it the act remains today the basis of their tribal governments.

Federal Indian policy from the 1920s to World War II did not involve deliberate attempts at termination and relocation. Native American communities were pressured to approve organization under the IRA in order to receive federal assistance. When Indians approved inclusion under the Indian Reorganization Act, they sometimes inadvertently initiated the self-termination of autonomous traditional governments. Under the IRA, tribal governments were regulated by federal guidelines. They embraced the political and social norms of white Americans, often without fully realizing the impact that this would have on future generations of their people. During the first half of the twentieth century, federal Indian policy was a sincere effort to reform Indian conditions and to assist Native Americans in developing the confidence and economic improvement for assimilating into the dominant society. It was a reversal of policy from the previous century of U.S. military–Indian wars and treatymaking.

The history of relations between the federal government and the Indians revolved around treaties that were, and are, the mainstay of Indian rights. Treaty provisions staved off termination and relocation, but the government's efforts to serve the Indians' best interests often changed policy and produced damaging repercussions for Native Americans. In essence, Indian rights eroded gradually from total sovereignty to wardship status, until Native Americans were supposedly assimilated by the General Citizenship Act of 1924. In spite of this well-meaning measure, the stronghold of Indian rights existed in treaties negotiated between Indians and the United States government. As long as the treaties are recognized, Indians possess legal rights as sovereign peoples.

Observance of the treaties and the government's fulfillment of their provisions continued until they were reviewed by the Indian Claims Commission and the Hoover Task Force Commission Report of 1948. In the wake of a postwar America entering the atomic age, the new attitudes of a Republican leadership in Congress and an assimilationist Bureau of Indian Affairs rendered a new direction in federal–tribal relations. This crucible of proassimilation ingredients yielded far-reaching laws after World War II, which reversed the federal Indian policy of the earlier 1900s, and renewed termination and relocation.

Acknowledgments

This study of federal Indian policy from World War II through the administration of John F. Kennedy has demanded the attention of numerous individuals at various research institutions throughout the country. I have the greatest admiration for these individuals, all of whom are highly knowledgeable of research materials on Indian affairs. Although the following list is lengthy, I would like to take this opportunity to thank each of these individuals for their gracious services in directing me to pertinent research materials for this book.

I wish to thank Mr. Kent Carter, Chief of the Federal Archives and Records Center at Fort Worth, Texas, and his assistants, Ms. Barbara Rusk and Ms. Jeanette Ford, who were more than helpful during my research on Oklahoma Indians. I am also grateful to Ms. Valerie Foster and Mr. Allen Core, formerly of the Department of Tribal Operations at the Bureau of Indian Affairs in Muskogee, Oklahoma, for helping me gain permission to examine federal records in Fort Worth.

I would also like to thank Mr. Herb Pankratz and Dr. John Wickman of the Dwight D. Eisenhower Presidential Library, Abilene, Kansas; Mr. Allan Perry, Archivist, at the Federal Archives and Records Center in Kansas City, Missouri; Dr. Benedict Zobrist, Mr. Philip Laguerquist, Ms. Elizabeth Safly, Mr. Dennis Bilanger, Mr. C. Warren Ohrvall, and Mr. Harry Clark of the Harry S. Truman Presidential Library in Independence, Missouri. I am also grateful for a research grant from the Truman Library to conduct research there.

Researching this monograph was facilitated by Mr. Glen Burchet, Federal Archives and Records Center in San Francisco, California; Ms. Carmen Facio, Realty Specialist of the Bureau of Indian Affairs in Sacramento, California; Mr. Peter Bunce, Chief of Archives, Federal Archives and Records Center in Chicago, Illinois; and a special thanks to Ms. Elizabeth Trimmer, former Assistant Archivist. Appreciation also is extended to David M. Piff, Archivist, and Joyce Justice, Archives Technician, of the Federal Archives and Records Center in Seattle, Washington, and to Joel Barker and staff members at the Federal Archives and Records Center in Denver, Colorado. Also, I am appreciative for the assistance of Mr. John Aubrey of the Newberry Library and David R. Miller, former Assistant Director of the D'Arcy McNickle Center for the History of American Indians in Chicago.

I am grateful for the assistance of the staff at the National Archives in Washington, D.C., and to Mr. Dennis Petersen, Chief of Tribal Government Services, his assistant, Mr. Michael Smith, and Mr. Robert Pennington, Chief of Tribal Government Services, for sharing their knowledge of federal Indian policy with me. I am also grateful to Mr. Roland Wilson and his assistant Mr. Berney Gardner who directed me to the Federal Archives and Records Center at Suitland, Maryland; Dr. Bill Moss, Chief of Archives, for his advice on research material at the John F. Kennedy Presidential Library in Waltham, Massachusetts; and Mr. John Carver, Jr. for allowing me to examine a transcribed interview with him. A research grant from the Lyndon Baines Johnson Foundation and Director Lawrence Reed was of important assistance while I was researching at the Lyndon B. Johnson Presidential Library in Austin, Texas.

My thanks also go to Judy Pence, Mary McCarthy, and Rose Diaz of the Special Collections, Zimmerman Library, University of New Mexico, Albuquerque. A postdoctoral scholarship at UCLA allowed me to continue working on this book. Support for this work came from Professor Charlotte Heth, Director of the American Indian Studies Center, and staff, Anthony Brown, Velma Salabiye, Lenora Stiffarm and Professor Norris Hundley of the History Department. I am grateful for the assistance of Drs. Floyd O'Neil, Gregory Thompson, formerly, and S. Lyman Tyler of the American West Center at the University of Utah and for the staff of the Special Collections, Marriott Library, University of Utah, Salt Lake City. The staff members of the Oral History Collection at the California State University Library, Fullerton and at the Huntington Park Library in Los Angeles, California, deserve recognition for their assistance.

I am also grateful for the assistance of Guy Louis Rocha, Jim Harrington and June Stevens of the Nevada State Archives, Carson, Nevada, and for Professor Jerome Edwards of the University of Nevada for sharing some of his research information. David L. Snyder of the California State Archives, Sacramento was helpful as well as the staff at Tehama County Library in Red Bluff, California. My appreciation is extended to Kenneth Duckett and Hillary Cummings of the Special Collections, University of Oregon Library, Eugene and Mrs. Wayne Morse who graciously allowed me to research her late husband's papers. I am grateful for the assistance of Thomas Vaughn and Layne Woolschlager at the Oregon Historical Society in Portland and Mr. J. D. Porter of the Oregon State Archives at Salem.

Special recognition goes to close friends Dr. Thomas Holm, Ina and family and to Jay, Sara and Ron McGath whose hospitality enabled me to make extended research trips; to Mr. Philip Lujan, Director of Native American Studies, University of Oklahoma, and his former assistant, Ms. Sherry Carter, who were very helpful and supportive of my efforts to complete my research, and to Dr. Philip Vaughan, Chairperson of Social Science Division and Mr. Tom McMichael, Assistant Chairperson at Rose State College, Midwest City, Oklahoma, who advised me on sources in the early research work.

During my research I spent many days examining papers of Oklahoma congressmen at the Western History Collections of the University of Oklahoma at Norman. I am especially grateful for the assistance and advice of Mr. Jack Haley, Assistant Curator, and Mr. John Windolph, former Assistant Archivist.

I am also grateful for the suggestions and helpful criticism of Dr. Arrell M. Gibson. A special thanks go to Drs. William Bittle, James Goodman, William Maehl, Jr., and Dr. H. Wayne Morgan, for reading this manuscript when it was first put together. A special thanks is for Ms. Josephine Gil, formerly of the History Department, for her assistance.

I am indebted to Dr. Marilyn Affleck, Acting Dean of the Graduate College, University of Oklahoma; Ms. Judith Cole, Secretary of the Association on American Indian Affairs; Mr. John Rainer, Director of American Indian Scholarships, Inc., Congressman Sidney Yates who made special efforts to gain continued funding for A.I.S.I., and Dr. Arturo Madrid, former

National Director of the Ford Foundation, who encouraged the early work on this research project.

During my final revisions on this book, I am most grateful for the suggestions and support from Professors Reginald Horsman at University of Wisconsin-Milwaukee, Donald L. Parman at Purdue University, and R. David Edmunds at Texas Christian University. They took time out from busy schedules to read and comment on my revisions. I am also grateful for the meticulous work of Donna Schenstrom of the cartography services at University of Wisconsin-Milwaukee for drawing the maps in the book.

I am also indebted to Dr. Angie Debo for the loan of her personal papers.

My greatest appreciation is for my wife, Michelene, who morally supported me throughout this work. The completion of this manuscript would not have been possible without her contributing efforts and sacrifices.

Termination and Relocation

1

Warriors in World War II and New Attitudes

As a tropical breeze in the South Pacific began to clear the air after a hotly pitched battle, six weary men stood at the top of Mount Surabachi at Iwo Jima to complete one last task. The marines had defeated a large Japanese force in a tenacious struggle that ended in hand-to-hand combat. To signify the victory, the six men—five marines and one naval serviceman—pulled together to hoist an American flag. This famous scene was photographed and became the rallying cry for American patriotism during the remainder of World War II.[1]

One of the six weary men to raise the flag was Marine Private First Class Ira Hayes, a Pima Indian from Arizona. Hayes became an instant public figure when the United States government hailed him as a hero in an effort to induce Americans to buy more war bonds. In the hands of government officials, Hayes was exploited as the noble warrior who devotedly served his country. Billboards and media reports touted him as the virtuous "red man" whose integrity and traditional dignity symbolized American ideals. Unfortunately, celebrity status prohibited Hayes from fulfilling a personal quest as a soldier in his tribe's warrior tradition. He was removed from combat duty and sent on tours for the express purpose of maintaining the nation's spirit of patriotism. Continuous public exposure led to his ruin. The government had exploited Hayes without realizing the damaging consequences that would befall him.

Upon returning to his desolate reservation in Arizona, Ira Hayes found himself unable to socialize successfully with his own people, nor could he adjust to the mainstream society. Having experienced the world outside his homeland for the first time during the war, Hayes felt uncomfortable in interacting with other Americans; somewhere inside him, his old confidence in socializing had been displaced by self-doubt. Nonetheless, Hayes's heroism convinced his Pima brethren that he was the best person to represent them in Washington D.C. on tribal issues. Bureaucratic pressure on Capitol Hill unfortunately overwhelmed the war hero, and when he failed the Pimas rejected him.

With the hero image continuing to plague Hayes, he soon left the reservation to find work, but everywhere he went people greeted him with a hero's welcome. At the risk of losing his personal identity, Ira left Arizona to work in Chicago for the Indian Bureau's new employment and relocation program. Newspapers in Chicago reported the Pima warrior's arrival, and ran photos of the famous flag-raising scene. He could go nowhere, it seemed, without hero-worshipers offering him a drink for a chance to meet the Indian celebrity. Confusion and loss of perspective led Hayes to alcoholism. But even during his personal struggle to set things right in his mind, the newspapers overpublicized Ira's fight to stop drinking. Tormented, he returned to his reservation to escape the pursuant publicity. During a cold night in January 1955, the Pima warrior died of exposure and alcoholism in an irrigation ditch in Arizona. Ira Hayes ended life as a broken man. In Washington, the government gave Hayes a war hero's burial in Arlington National Cemetery, not far from where the 850,000 dollar, ten-ton war memorial statue stands depicting that famous scene at Iwo Jima.[2]

Other Indian veterans of the war suffered a similar fate. Overall, an estimated 25,000 American Indians served in the armed forces of the United States during World War II. Approximately 22,000 served in the army on the front lines; 2,000 in the navy; 120 in the coast guard; and 730 joined the marines.[3] Drafting American Indians in many instances was unnecessary since they eagerly volunteered, believing that military service in World War II might be their last opportunity to prove themselves as warriors. Even though some did not even understand the draft, a Native American patriotism prevailed throughout Indian country in support of the United States. In the frenzy of the call for men, even old Navajo men hurried to draft board stations, carrying their guns and asking, "Where is the enemy?"[4]

When one questions why the Indians fought and died for the

United States—the same country that cheated them out of their homelands—several intriguing answers are discerned. Living under the domination of another foreign nation like Germany or Japan could have been far worse than living in the United States. More likely, Native Americans felt that it was their solemn duty to serve in the American armed services or in the war industries. During the 1800s, when the United States and the tribes warred against each other, all of the tribespeople, including women and children of the Indian nations, were involved in the fighting. Armed threats made against the tribes and their homelands aroused a strongly felt, native nationalism to protect the people and defend tribal territories. For individuals, World War II presented opportunities for Indian men to fulfill their roles as traditional warriors. Simultaneously, a chance to prove their manhood induced them to volunteer to fight alongside white strangers. Peer pressure from relatives and friends persuaded many to join the armed services, especially the army, which obviously meant combat and meeting the enemy face to face. When death approached, Indian soldiers summoned their courage to confront it in the manner of their ancestors, desiring to die in an honorable manner. When death seemed near, the wailing death songs from the Indian warriors could be heard once again across battlefields amidst the gunfire and shelling.

Indian women strongly supported their men in the service, especially mothers of soldiers who worried for their sons and supported them with prayers. In rural Indian communities and on reservations, they organized War Mothers clubs to write letters and send gifts to sons, husbands, brothers, and uncles in the service. An estimated two hundred to three hundred Indian women joined the nurses' corps, military auxiliaries, the Red Cross, and the American Women's Voluntary Service. Other women assumed the responsibilities that the men had left behind. Approximately fifty women worked at the Menominee tribal sawmill in Wisconsin. In Minnesota, crews of two women and one man planted young saplings to replace trees cut down in the Red Lake Forest. Women worked at fire-lookout stations on the Colville and Klamath reservations in Washington and Oregon. Further northward, Alaska Native women and girls sewed skin clothing, mittens, mukluks, and moccasins, and made snowshoes and other apparel for American soldiers stationed in cold climates. Some women, like "Rosie the Riveter," left their families everyday to work in war factories as inspectors, sheet-metal workers, and machinists. Approximately fifty thousand Indian men and women worked in aircraft factories, in other war industries, and on the railroads. Aside from physical contributions to the war effort, Indian Americans invested more than seventeen million dollars of restricted funds in war bonds.[5]

All of the women's contributions could not prevent the deaths of loved ones. After news of the deceased reached the reservations and Indian communities, the families and tribesfolk prepared to receive the bodies, and in traditional ceremonies, they commemorated the fallen warriors for their bravery. At modified victory and scalp dances, communities honored those who survived and returned home safely. In their personal quest for traditional achievement, they had earned the respect of their tribesmen. It is not surprising that a very large percentage of American Indian men today have military service records of participation in World Wars I and II, and in the Korean and Vietnam wars.

A higher percentage of Indians fought in World War II than any other ethnic minority group. Ironically, this patriotic effort was not always welcomed. In the barracks, other servicemen ridiculed the Indian GI with name-calling. "Chief," "Geronimo," or just "Hey Indian" labeled the Native American serviceman, sometimes with derogatory intent. At first, the native GI enjoyed being called "Chief," which signified to him the distinction of leadership; later, however, he came to despise the name when he learned that he was being ridiculed. Frequently, he was the butt of jokes, and in addition to the enemy on the battlefield, he fought fellow soldiers in the barracks and in bars.

In combat, his relationship with other soldiers improved remarkably. Other GIs believed Indians were effective fighters and spoke of what an assuring feeling it was to be in a foxhole next to an Indian whose ancestors were regarded as fierce warriors.[6] For the Indian soldier, war conditions, aside from combat, differed little from reservation life. Coarse food, long hours, and lack of privacy presented no hardship.[7] One Standing Rock Sioux recalled, "The Marines was a snap. When other people were complaining, I was used to it 'cause I'd been on the reservation."[8] While the privations of war anguished the white American soldier, the Indian GI accepted the oppressive situation. His tribespeople's history of fighting in all kinds of adverse weather conditions ingrained in him an undeterred discipline and an ability to respond alertly with little food or rest while keeping irregular hours.

The performance of Native Americans in World War II was rewarded with praise and admiration. Indian servicemen accounted for a total of seventy-one air medals, fifty-one silver stars, forty-seven bronze stars, and two congressional medals of honor. The congressional medals were awarded to Lieutenant Ernest Childers, an Oklahoma Creek, and Lieutenant Jack C. Montgomery, an Oklahoma Cherokee. Childers earned the medal of honor for his bravery in Italy. With an injured foot and against doctor's orders, he rushed back to the front line to aid his fellow soldiers. In his path, he killed five German soldiers while knocking out two machine-gun nests. With mortar shells exploding around him, he proceeded to capture the mortar observer, which allowed his battalion to advance.

Montgomery was awarded the congressional medal for his incredibly brave deed against the German enemy near Padiglione, Italy. At daybreak, three stubborn German forces entrenched their troops enclosing Montgomery's rifle platoons. Alone, the Cherokee soldier rushed toward the enemy to draw their fire so that his men could spot the enemy. Montgomery's fearless action saved the platoons and resulted in eleven enemy killed, thirty-two prisoners taken, and an unknown number wounded.[9]

More Native American servicemen received medals for their performances during the war, but the Bureau of Indian Affairs could not identify all the Native American troops. Overall, Indian servicemen proved themselves as warriors and drew praise from the Supreme Commander of the Allied Forces. Several years after the war, President Dwight Eisenhower commented on their fighting performance in World War II: "Never did I hear a complaint about the battle conduct of the Native American Indian."[10] This is in face of the fact that Indians were frequently assigned as point or scouts on patrols, and were sacrificed as the first to encounter the enemy. Furthermore, 90 percent of the Indian servicemen enlisted in the army.

Navajo Code Talkers also gained recognition for their outstanding performance in World War II. Initially, the Marine

Corps trained a small group of twenty-eight fluent Navajo native speakers to transmit coded messages in their language. Navajo was one of the few extant Indian languages that Europeans had not yet studied. Other than the Navajos themselves, only a handful of missionaries and storekeepers spoke the language fluently.[11] On the battlefields in the South Pacific, they delivered strategic messages over radios in their native language. For extra precaution, the Navajo messages were also coded. Frequently, their efforts ensured the success of Allied attacks against the enemy.

During the war, the transition from reservation life to mainstream society was a cultural shock for Indians. They faced an additional shock when they tried to readjust to the reservations after the war. Indians found themselves faced with the decision of which world to live in. Mainstream culture and urbanism clashed acutely with tribal traditions. Many Indians who came in contact with members of various other tribes gained comfort through shared experiences associated with these adjustments. This pan-Indian experience allowed individual Native Americans to relate to each other's problems. Dealing with the dilemma of tribal traditions versus mainstream culture was the crux of the maladjustment that Indian veterans experienced. Common problems associated with adaptation served to unite Indian people from different tribes.

The postwar experience of Ira Hayes exemplified the difficulty of the Indian veteran's adjustment to a new life. Military service or work in war industries had thrust Indian Americans into a society that contrasted dramatically with their accustomed life-style. Upon returning to their native communities, veterans found it difficult to fit into their former life-style, and many became estranged from their people. Elders claimed that the outside world had contaminated the returning warriors and that they had to be ceremonially purified. In the Southwest, the Pueblo groups held dances and ceremonial rites for each GI, to exorcise from his being the German or Japanese death spirits. Family members customarily avoided their beloved returned warriors until after the purification rites.

Economic conditions on reservations offered very few employment opportunities for Indian veterans. Extreme poverty pervaded the reservations, and the return of soldiers strained the already limited resources. On the Navajo Reservation alone, in 1946, only an estimated 5,300 of the 11,000 families could farm, and these people averaged only 189 dollars in crops consumed or sold.[12] While the Navajos and other groups encountered poor economic and health conditions, uninformed Americans criticized Indians for not being more independent and improving their impoverished state. When one Navajo applied for aid at a Red Cross office, the worker asked:

> "Why don't you get a job?"
> "I can't. I feel tired all the time," replied the Indian.
> "I can't put that on the record. What do you mean?" the worker asked.
> "Well you see—sometimes I don't eat for two or three days," the Navajo said.[13]

Many returned veterans soon became frustrated with reservation life. Unable to find work on or near reservations, they moved to cities to search for jobs. Indians who had worked in factories during the war and had returned to reservations also began migrating to urban areas for work. After the war boom, the demand for production fell and factories needed fewer workers. Usually, Indian workers were the first to be laid off. Although they had learned the basics, their limited mechanical skills did not qualify them for permanent jobs. Despite the uncertainty awaiting them in urban areas, economic pressure forced the migration of many Indian Americans from reservations to cities. Many of the younger generation were curious about cities after hearing stories from friends and relatives who had returned from relocation. They, too, soon left the reservations to discover and experience the cities for themselves.

Former BIA Commissioner John Collier, in observing the Indian migration, exclaimed that "the war has brought about the greatest exodus of Indians from reservations that has ever taken place."[14] Years later, a news release from the Department of the Interior reported: "World War II demonstrated to many Indians who participated in the various phases of its activities, both in the armed services and in defense industries, the futility of attempting to maintain an isolated system of primitive community life. The outside world did offer to the participating

Indians exciting, desirable and worthwhile possibilities for individual achievement."[15]

While many Indians chose to try urban living, they experienced difficulties in adjusting to working hours from 8:00 A.M. to 5:00 P.M., the noises of the city, and the fast pace of living. N. Scott Momaday's *House Made of Dawn,* a Pulitzer Prize-winning novel, is a classical saga of an Indian veteran who experiences harsh urbanized relocation in a large city. The novel depicts the discrimination, economic hardship, and sociopsychological maladjustment that the migrant Indian character, Abel, encounters. For those individuals who remained on reservations, life was equally depressing, and perhaps worse. Depleted land quality failed to support farming and grazing livestock. The burden on Mother Earth to support human and animal life grew heavy.

To provide an alternative, the federal government under the Truman administration began taking the initiative to succor Native Americans. Like Franklin Roosevelt, President Harry S Truman, a Democrat, advocated civil rights for minorities, especially blacks. His stand upset the public and put him in disfavor with the Republican-dominated Congress. Considered one of the most unpopular presidents in American history, Truman appeared headed for defeat in the presidential election of 1948. His upset victory over Thomas Dewey had an indirect but pertinent effect on Native Americans.

Truman's appointment of William Brophy as commissioner of Indian affairs brought a friend to the Indian people. Many Native Americans believed that Brophy held the same philosophical principles as Truman, who advocated civil rights for all Americans. Brophy firmly believed that American Indians should not be discriminated against, especially Indian veterans who were "entitled to the same benefits, rights and privileges as any other veteran under the bill of rights." As an example, Brophy complained to a senator that many Indian veterans experienced some difficulty in obtaining loans from banks and lending agencies that remained "reluctant to lend money to Indians."[16]

Bankers considered Indians poor financial risks, particularly full-bloods whom they stereotyped as undependable and incompetent in business matters. Mainstream Americans viewed mixed-bloods as more dependable, since they had fewer "Indian" physical characteristics and were more likely to be treated as socially equal. Consequently, many mixed-bloods of little Indian extraction refuted claim to their ancestry to avoid social discrimination. In addition, they were better educated than full-bloods, which helped them in blending more easily into Anglo-American society. During the late 1940s and throughout the 1950s, many mixed-bloods were reluctant to admit that they were part Indian. Such denial of their heritage caused many Indians to develop inferiority complexes, which were fostered by the mainstream society's prejudice and misconception of Indians and their cultures.

Although the mainstream society in general exhibited largely anti-black attitudes, they considered all dark-skinned people as second-class human beings. As a result, physically identifiable Indians experienced open discrimination. A Jemez Pueblo man recalls: "One time I got on the bus in Amarillo, Texas and . . . I sat right behind the driver, I got on the bus, and the driver said, I am sorry, sir, you have to sit back there behind the curtain. And I said, 'Why?' and he said, 'Well it is just that our laws are that way.' And I said, 'What kind of laws?' Well colored people are supposed to sit back there. I said, 'Well, is that rear end of the bus going in the same direction with you?' And he said, 'Yes.' Well it doesn't matter as long as the whole bus is moving in one direction, I will sit back there. So I did, I sat back there with the colored people."[17]

Native Americans faced similar discrimination from personnel in schools and social service organizations. Generally, the traditional full-bloods suffered the most. Indian youth were particularly mistreated in public schools, where they were considered less intelligent than their white counterparts. The staff in hospitals and teachers in schools found the Indians' brown skin, long black hair, and tattered clothing repugnant. Their physical appearance evoked the stereotyped image of the downtrodden Indians of the 1800s. Professionals in public schools and hospitals viewed Indians as poor, dirty, and illiterate in comparison to white Americans, and felt uneasy around them. They performed their duties with an ethnocentric attitude, sometimes acting in a bluntly, discriminatory manner. The traditional full-bloods often avoided utilizing public and social services provided to the mainstream society in favor of government services set up solely for Indians; here, at least, they shared the same treatment with other Indians.

The light-skinned mixed-bloods were more readily accepted in schools and other public places, especially if they tended to act in a nontraditional Indian manner. Their growing numbers and greater success in school and in employment were noted by federal officials, who became convinced that Indians were assimilated enough into mainstream society to handle their own affairs and no longer had a need for specialized government services.

The decision to dissolve such services came from bureaucrats who mistakenly took their cue from the off-reservation experiences of Indian veterans. Concerned citizens like Dr. Haven Emerson, president of the Association on American Indian Affairs, believed that many veterans were not ready to be left completely on their own in mainstream society. Emerson released a statement in opposition to H.R. 1113, a legislative measure to remove trust restrictions over Native American veterans. "Indians are citizens now, though many Congressmen, as well as the general public, seem unaware of that fact," Emerson said. "If they are now denied their full rights of citizenship in some States, and if they are subject to discrimination at the hands of non-Indian neighbors in many localities, these 'disabilities' are not a result of existing Federal law, and cannot be remedied by Congressional legislation of this character. Real emancipation of the American Indian from discrimination and ignorance requires education—education of the non-Indian public and education of the Indians themselves. Meanwhile the provisions of our laws which protect Indian rights and property against injustices and plunder must be maintained."[18]

Educating Indians and meeting their health needs became the focus of congressional concern. Proponents of a bilingual approach to Indian education argued that many Indian children who spoke their native languages during their early years later encountered difficulty in learning because of their limited English ability. Willard Beatty, Director of Education for the Bureau of Indian Affairs, stated that a study of school records for 1948 indicated that only 28 percent of the children entering federal Indian schools came from homes in which only an Indian language was spoken.[19] Therefore, government efforts were concentrated more on those tribes who suffered in the health areas, particularly in Alaska and in the Southwest, and who attracted national attention. Tuberculosis was prevalent in Alaska and common among rural Indians because their homes lacked proper sanitation. In the Southwest, the Navajo and Hopi people suffered from both poor living conditions and disease. In addition, many Indians had endured severe shortages of food and fuel during the severe winter snowstorms of 1947 and in the early months of 1948. The media publicized their critical situation and aroused national concern. On 4 March 1949, President Truman stated publicly, "recently I requested the Secretary of the Interior to report to me on the emergency situation of the Navajo Indians . . . this winter."[20] Several months later, Congress passed an act to start a rehabilitation program for the Navajo and Hopi.

The supportive actions of the Truman administration failed to impress foreign critics of American Indian policy. On 6 May 1948, the Adirondack *Daily Enterprise* reported that Soviet officials questioned current American treatment of Indians and criticized past United States involvement in Indian wars. The Russians cited the past efforts of the dominant American population to eradicate Indians, and stated that American Indian policy after World War II continued to mistreat the country's indigenous peoples.[21]

In her daily column in the Washington *Daily News* on 5 October 1949, Mrs. Eleanor Roosevelt warned the public about the government's mishandling of Indian affairs. She advised that caution was necessary in supervising Indian affairs because of international scrutiny. "One of the Soviet attacks on the democracies, particularly in the United States, center on racial policies," Mrs. Roosevelt said. "In recent months the Russians have been particularly watching our attitude towards native Indians of our country." She then asked: "Are we indifferent to the way our Indians are treated? If not we had better let our representatives in Congress know that we do not like the present trend of legislation."[22] Mrs. Roosevelt, a humanitarian at heart, became a leading spokesperson for Native Americans and other minorities. Her views on measures to guard against the exploitation of American Indians concurred with those of President Truman, who strongly advocated minority civil rights.

American officials asserted that the Soviet attack was unwarranted. In reference to postwar treatment under William Brophy's administration as commissioner of Indian affairs, Truman supported the Bureau of Indian Affairs. Brophy "has been marked by a spirit of humanity and a genuine interest in the progress of the Indians," said the president.[23] The reform measures undertaken by the government, although paternalistic and carried out with little Indian involvement in their design, were requested by Native Americans to meet the economic and health needs of their communities.

American Indian involvement in World War II significantly changed relations between Indians and Anglo-Americans. The crisis of war drew the red and white races in close contact as they worked and fought side by side for the American cause. The exodus of patriotic Native Americans from reservations to war factories and to service in the armed forces caused many Americans to reassess their views of Indians. The war, in effect, temporarily united Indians and whites. A large number of Indian veterans awoke to the challenge of individual progress and expressed a desire to participate in the mainstream society. One young Indian veteran stated: "I was good enough to fight for my country. I am good enough to own property and support my family."[24] In reflecting this attitude, Indians believed that federal trust restrictions hindered their progress toward improved livelihoods, and they wanted the government to do something about it.

Joseph Bruner, national president of the American Indian Federation, supported the emancipation of Indians from federal supervision. On 3 September 1945, he wrote to Congressman William Stigler, asking, "Don't you think World Wars I and II, alone entitle him to the enjoyment of FREEDOM at HOME from government supervision and direction by people less capable than himself, and a final settlement with his guardian-government?"[25] Bruner criticized the federal government for its inefficient handling of Indian affairs. The outspoken leader also requested that the government formally hear Indian claims against the United States, an issue that persuaded officials even more that Native Americans were ready to enter the competing mainstream society.

On 27 September 1945, Montana Congressman Wesley

D'Ewart introduced House Resolution 4196, one of the first serious proposals for ending federal restrictions on Indians and for seeking possible cutbacks in federal spending on Indian services. The proposed measure directed action "to provide for removal of restrictions on property of Indians who serve in the armed forces."[26] From another perspective, the proposed bill sought to satisfy discontented Indian veterans who could not make a living from their government-controlled lands. In effect, the government would no longer have authority over tribal properties and assets, which meant that they could be sold and the proceeds distributed among the tribal members.

Unfortunately, the Indians' dedication and involvement during the war was not an accurate barometer of their readiness for assimilation that later proved detrimental to them. The public supported the view that the war experience had sufficiently introduced Indians to mainstream society, a view that added to the momentum for Native American assimilation. Simultaneously, many Americans argued that the desegregation of reservation communities would enable Indian people to earn their livelihood like everyone else. Despite the beliefs of the public and the government, Indians did not readily assimilate into the mainstream society.

Those Indians who did not fit into the mainstream mold faced public animosity, which was often expressed through acts of discrimination. In 1959, the report, "Discrimination against Indians," submitted by Sophie D. Aberle and William Brophy to a Senate commission, substantiated acts of discrimination against reservation Indians throughout the country.[27] Discrimination was especially prevalent in local areas where townspeople held Indians in low esteem. The local townspeople viewed reservations as impoverished "cesspools," and those who stayed there were deemed indolent.

In spite of the wide gulf which existed between juxtaposed communities of Indians and other Americans, the federal government believed successful assimilation was occurring. Out of necessity, Indians and Anglo-Americans were coming more in contact with each other, and, as a result, government officials concluded that many Indians had been and were assimilating into mainstream society. Many mixed-bloods dressed like white

Americans and imitated their life-style, which reinforced the belief that Indians were assimilated and were ready for trust removal.

Actually, the Indian view on trust removal was divided. Primarily, mixed-bloods concurred with federal officials on removal of trust restrictions, while traditional full-bloods believed that their people still differed considerably from white Americans in their values and their outlook on life. The position of the mixed-bloods and full-bloods who considered themselves as progressives gained attention when they expressed dissatisfaction with government supervision over their properties, and professed that federal trust status labeled them as second-class citizens. They expressed a readiness to join the mainstream society in spite of objections from the traditional full-blood faction. Robert Goombi, a traditional Kiowa from Mountain View, Oklahoma, stated emphatically, "I don't think our Indians are competent to rub elbows with our white brothers."[28] Former Commissioner of Indian Affairs John Collier concurred that many of the Indian people still required federal trust protection to avoid exploitation until they obtained education and skills in crafts that would enable them to work toward independent success.

While working diligently to improve general Indian conditions, Commissioner William Brophy faced a dilemma in dealing with the traditional and progressive factions of the Native American population. Like many bureaucrats who optimistically believed that Native Americans wanted assimilation, he favored the progressives. "The purpose of the office of Indian Affairs is, in my opinion," stated Brophy, "to give the Indians the same opportunities other Americans enjoy . . . [and] the United States is under obligation to provide hospitalization and education for the Indians, and . . . a chance at any occupation they may choose."[29] Brophy added that Indian ex-servicemen should have "full benefit of the loan and other features of the G.I. Bill of Rights."[30] But helping Indian veterans find jobs became a major task for the Indian Bureau.[31] Many lacked marketable skills; and the traumatic transition from reservation to urban society, plus the war experience, had unsettled the inner peace that they had been taught to maintain. These problems were compounded by the American public's failure to accept Indian people.

While Congress sought to rectify the situation by enacting legislation to provide full civil rights to Native Americans, white Americans continued to treat Indians as "second-class" citizens. Furthermore, at least two state governments, New Mexico and Arizona, denied voting rights to their Indian citizens. Lester Oliver, an Indian veteran, wrote to Oklahoma Senator Elmer Thomas to complain: "Since I live in Arizona and am Apache Indian I have no say in the voting and our Senators will not pay any attention to me. Why don't [*sic*] a Veteran of World War II have the right to vote? We also have Racial prejudice here on our Reservation. We have Whites here who don't like Indians but still stay here and make their living on Indian Service."[32] Sporadic protest from individual Indians offered increasing evidence of Native American dissatisfaction with the treatment of Indian people.

Frustrated with mainstream ethnocentrism, Native Americans began to assume more responsibility for their own affairs, regardless of whether they were prepared to do so. Certain groups like the Klamaths, considered one of the more progressive Indian tribes, desired more independence and greater participation in formulating policies that affected them. In early May, Boyd Jackson, while representing the Klamath tribe in a meeting with Commissioner Brophy and Associate Commissioner William Zimmerman, proclaimed his people's support of Senate Bill 794. Also known as the Klamath Welfare Bill, the measure proposed funding for tribal members who needed capital to develop properties.[33] To allow more time for discussion of the removal of trust restrictions from Klamath properties, Congress deferred consideration of the bill.

Other Indians echoed the Klamaths' preference for removal of trust restrictions. A Cherokee, Reed Buzzard, wrote to Congressman George Schwabe on 22 June 1946, complaining about the growing confusion in federal-Indian affairs. In requesting termination, Buzzard stated: "I am Republican and an Indian, interested in the success of the Party and final settlement with the Indians. This idea of going on forever with this Indian business is both silly and expensive."[34] Schwabe replied that he thought it was a good idea "to get rid of the Indian Bureau as fast as possible. It is a drain upon the taxpayers and . . . a poor guardian for the Indians. I think it tends to encourage paternalism and socialistic and . . . communistic thinking."[35] Schwabe's reference to communism exemplified the legacy of postwar patriotism and his personal conviction that anything outside the norm must be un-American. Similar bias in the 1930s had charged Commissioner John Collier with attempting to foster "socialism" when he pushed for traditional Indian communal economic activities.

Responding to the controversy, President Truman took the initiative in enacting changes. In a report to the Seventy-ninth Congress entitled "Aspects of Indian Policy," the chief executive suggested recommendations to dissolve the Indian Bureau:

> The original purpose of the Indian Bureau was to help the Indian to become a citizen and it was intended as a service rather than as an administrative agency. Thus we see that although the original aim was to make the Indian a citizen the present aim appears to keep the Indian an Indian and to make him satisfied with the limitations of a primitive form of existence. The Bureau . . . had been concerned with building up a system instead of a service and to make itself self-perpetuating, and in accomplishing this purpose it has segregated the Indian from the general citizenry, condemned him to an indefinite if not perpetual wardship, tied him to land in perpetuity, and forced a system of Bureau-controlled education and land use upon him.[36]

The report also called for the elimination of the Bureau of Indian Affairs at the end of three years. In coming from the president's office, such a statement endorsed Truman as a terminationist, but one who truly believed that assimilation into the American mainstream would be best for Indians. Actually, President Truman was an assimilationist who believed that all Americans should enjoy the constitutional rights that the United States guaranteed, although he realized that the dominant society excluded Native American people from exercising their civil rights.

Yielding to the requests of progressive Indians and to presidential pressure, Congress entertained measures to lift trust restrictions. In February 1947, Congressman Schwabe introduced House Resolution 2148 in the House of Representatives. This resolution sought "to enable Osage Indians who served in World War II to obtain loans under the Servicemen's Readjustment Act of 1944."[37] Actually, Schwabe viewed the Osage as one of the progressive tribes who needed restrictions removed to allow them to pursue economic opportunities.

Three days later, House Resolution 2165 was introduced during the first session of the Eightieth Congress as another attempt to assist Indians. Again, reform was targeted at Indian veterans: H.R. 2165 proposed to "emancipate" certain Indian individuals who had served in the armed forces during World Wars I and II. While campaigning in the 1946 election, Republican-elected congressmen had promised a reduction in federal services, including the usual appropriations earmarked for Indian services. By focusing first on the Indian veteran population, the congressmen reasoned that other Native Americans would also seek federal assistance to liberate them from the grasp of government control. The congressmen could then trim other costly programs. Accordingly, they now set out to honor their original promises by pledging to cut appropriations "making it necessary not only to terminate appointments of some employees but in some instances to abolish entire bureaus."[38]

Congress believed that Indian war veterans were the best candidates for leaving the reservations and that services to them should be discontinued. On 25 June 1947, a report in the House of Representatives discussed the removal of restrictions on those veterans' properties. The report referred to a previously entertained bill, H.R. 1113, in which some changes had been made. Indian citizens who wanted trust limitations removed could do so with a writ from a court of law, if they were over twenty-one years of age.[39]

In commemoration of the patriotic service of Indians in World War II and in recognition of their progress as citizens, Congressman William Stigler of Oklahoma introduced House Resolution 2085, which proposed a "National American Indian Day." The Indian Council Fire, an associate of the Illinois Federation of Women's Clubs, heartily agreed that Native Americans should be recognized for their patriotic performance in both wars and for their contribution to American culture in general. Although other organizations supported this idea, the attempt to establish an Indian holiday failed.

Both Indians and whites, and especially the latter, deemed that a new era had dawned for American Indians. They were convinced that the Native American population, or at least a large portion, was ready to assume responsibility for their own lives without intervening government trust restrictions. Such sentiment sowed the seeds for the termination policy that called for liquidating the federal trust relationship. Bureaucrats became convinced that both the public and Native American population wanted the Indians to be assimilated into the mainstream.

The melodrama of the postwar aftermath swept both Indians and other Americans in pursuit of a modern America. As the country rejoiced over winning the war, feelings of patriotism revitalized the people's spirits. The nation enjoyed an improved standard of living that would broaden middle-class America. Unfortunately, the assimilationist movement overlooked the traditional Indians' needs and protests against assimilation. For the duration of the postwar optimism, the traditionalists would experience criticism and discrimination until they finally gained support against the destruction of their tribal existence.

2

The Indian Claims Commission and the Zimmerman Plan

The pressures during World War II to thwart German and Japanese aggressions compelled the United States to decrease funding for social service programs in favor of war industries. In overshadowing all domestic issues, the war effort impelled Congress and President Truman to work fervently with the Allies to defeat the last enemy resistance. The need to reduce spending on domestic programs, including those in the Bureau of Indian Affairs, intensified as the United States prepared to launch a final assault against the Axis powers. Although government officials voiced their genuine concern for Indian Americans, they emphasized that Bureau services and other programs had to be sacrificed as a means to win the war.

Other federal efforts to reform Indian affairs also called for cutbacks. Two central efforts—the Indian Claims Commission and the Zimmerman Plan—called for drastic changes to decrease governmental intervention in the Indians' lives. And by happenstance, the strategy of cutbacks and the redirection of appropriations coincided with the legislative instigation of the termination policy that flourished during the next decade. While Indian affairs slipped into obscurity during the war, Congress began recklessly entertaining a rash of minor bills and major legislation to terminate Indian services. Although the BIA naturally assumed responsibility for Indian affairs, Congress played an increasing role in plans designed to make Native Americans independent of the government. The Bureau of Indian Affairs also tried to reduce government responsibilities by selecting certain Indian schools and hospitals for closing. Maintaining federal trust responsibilities over Indian properties was too expensive and time consuming.[1]

Envisioning the reorganization of Indian services as a threat,

Native Americans formed a new alliance that would voice the concerns of the Indian population. Across the nation, Indian Americans began to identify common problems. In response to the evolving termination policy and other pertinent issues, delegates from twenty-seven different states and fifty-five tribes met in 1944 at the Cosmopolitan Hotel in Denver, Colorado, to organize the National Congress of American Indians. After so many pan-Indian efforts had failed in the past, this movement grew in membership and developed into a defender of Indian rights in the following decades.

Legislative threats to abolish services provoked opposition from tribal groups. In Oklahoma, a concerted effort by the Five Civilized Tribes opposed Senate Bill 1311, an omnibus measure proposing the removal of trust restrictions over Native Americans. The bill prompted concern from the superintendent of Indian affairs at the Muskogee area office, who disclosed a collective view among the tribes. "It was a general feeling that . . . it would be a very short time before they lost all their property," he said.[2]

During the immediate postwar years, the Indian community at large became increasingly vulnerable to federal changes and congressional actions. The absence of two central figures who had previously supported Native American citizens aided the bureaucrats who favored the new Indian policy. After serving twelve years as commissioner of Indian affairs during the 1930s and early 1940s, John Collier resigned from the Bureau of Indian Affairs in 1945. During his tenure in office, western congressmen had often opposed his reform ideas because of his protraditional scheme to reconstruct tribal governments. The Indian people suffered another loss, as did the entire nation, when President Franklin Roosevelt died suddenly near the end of the war. The president had supported Interior Secretary Harold Ickes, who had backed Commissioner Collier's reform policies.

The war years had focused government activities on the country's survival, and the resulting neglect of Indian affairs had discouraged Collier, who grew frustrated with "inept" federal officials. The commissioner would not compromise his positions on Indian reform, and he was often annoyed with those congressmen whom he perceived as too conservative. His efforts to improve conditions for Indians were further hindered when he disagreed with President Truman's Cold War policy.[3] Collier's liberal ideals drew criticism from federal officials outside the Bureau, who attacked him for attempting to initiate Indian reform programs too quickly. His dismissal of BIA workers, whom he deemed incompetent, fueled the steady barrage of criticism from his enemies. Rumors on Capitol Hill depicted Collier as a dreamer whose reorganization of tribal governments retrogressively impeded Indian progress. Critics alleged that Collier's administration promoted idealism; some Indians even disagreed with the commissioner's views. Collier's conflict with Congress reached its apex when other Indian Bureau officials had to represent the BIA before congressional committees.

Collier's resignation represented a serious loss for Native Americans, and his few friends in Congress knew that he would be missed. After witnessing substandard living conditions on reservations, Representative Karl Mundt of South Dakota endorsed Collier's reform efforts: "Mr. Collier has stimulated considerable improvements in the living conditions of the Indians . . . he genuinely had the interest of the Indian at heart."[4] Many Indian people conveyed their gratitude to John Collier for his years of dedicated service. Now, they wondered whether the next commissioner would be as genuinely concerned with their affairs. In a final message to the BIA, tribal councils, Indian leaders, and pro-Indian supporters, Collier insisted that there would be no fundamental change or weakening of his policy under the new commissioner. He praised his successor, William A. Brophy, and stated that Secretary Harold Ickes of the Interior Department and Assistant Commissioners William Zimmerman and Joseph McCaskill supported Brophy. Collier declared emphatically that Brophy was "utterly loyal to the Indians and their interests."[5]

With the exception of some Indian people from the Southwest, the majority of Native Americans supported Brophy's appointment. Although Brophy lived in New Mexico and had become well acquainted with the Southwestern Indians, his appointment made the United Pueblos uneasy. The Gallup *Independent* reported that Brophy's marriage to Dr. Sophie Aberle disturbed the native people because her actions as the superintendent of the Pueblo groups had sometimes opposed the wishes of the people.[6]

Brophy's sincerity toward Indian Americans won over many doubters who had argued previously that an Indian should have been selected as commissioner. The Albuquerque *Tribune* reported that some apprehensive native people feared that Brophy might even invoke a paternalistic policy.[7] A few congressmen like George Schwabe of Oklahoma also asserted that an Indian should have been chosen as Indian commissioner. One citizen voiced a popular notion that Oklahoma Congressman William Stigler should have been chosen since he was part Choctaw and familiar with Indian affairs. Critics asserted that Brophy might have more political influence in Washington, but others were more qualified to be commissioner of the Bureau of Indian Affairs.[8]

A native New Yorker transplanted to New Mexico, Brophy had acquired a broad experience from working closely with local Southwestern Indians. For nine years he served as an attorney for the Pueblo Indians. His other experiences included work as a special representative for the Secretary of the Interior on Puerto Rican affairs. A youthful, sincere-looking, dark-haired man of Irish background, Brophy presented a handsome impression. Highly intelligent and exuding charm, the new commissioner remained dedicated to his work.[9] Upon assuming office, he stated, "I hope that I shall perform my duties with wisdom and in a manner to advance the interest of the Indian people."[10]

With Collier and Roosevelt no longer on the scene, bureaucrats began promoting the idea that the Indian experience in World War II indicated that Native Americans were capable of assimilating into urban life. Some members of Congress were receptive to such proposals. During mid-July in 1945, Congressman William Stigler wrote to a friend that committees on Indian affairs in the Senate and in the House of Representatives were entertaining the assimilation concept: "We have some very outstanding men on the committees of each body—men who recognize the need to do something about the emancipation of the Indian."[11]

On the same day, the Albuquerque *Tribune* reported that Brophy planned to restructure the BIA administration. After studying the supervision of Indian affairs, Brophy believed that maximum efficiency could be achieved if he delegated more responsibility to field-workers who dealt directly with native communities.[12] This adjustment would expedite resolution of local problems and would be more effective.

Commissioner Brophy wanted to see the reservations first-hand and meet the people, so he scheduled a series of visits throughout Indian country. On each trip the people welcomed him as he won their confidence. While visiting the Blackfeet at their reservation in northwestern Montana, the commissioner was adopted by the tribe as one of them. They honored Brophy with gifts and bestowed upon him the name "Mountain Eagle."[13] During his visits, Brophy praised the military record of American Indians, adding that they had gained valuable off-reservation experience while fighting in the war. The commissioner stressed that Indian citizens should use their newly acquired training and skills to better their livelihoods.[14]

In late 1945, Commissioner Brophy completed his visitations of reservations throughout the United States and Alaska. The Albuquerque *Journal* reported on 24 August that the commissioner had noted that maintenance of roads and other facilities for Indian communities had been neglected during the war. Despite Bureau staff reductions during the war and decreased federal funding, Brophy asserted that the Indian service had done a respectable job.[15]

After observing the reservations first hand, Brophy believed that the Indian Bureau could provide more effective services to American Indians. He planned to reorganize the entire Bureau of Indian Affairs in Washington and restructure the field offices. He planned to streamline the BIA to dissolve bureaucratic channels and to extend maximum services to the Native American population.[16] Other parts of his reform proposals included serious consideration of legitimate Indian claims against the government and the removal of trust limitations on Indians.

In early September, Brophy's ideas gained the attention of the Seventy-ninth Congress when the lower house entertained House Resolution 237 during its first session. The measure proposed to establish a "congressional committee to study the claims of Indian tribes against the United States and to investigate the administration of Indian affairs."[17] Originally, reform measures during the Indian New Deal era included the establishment of an Indian Claims Commission as a part of the Indian Reorganization Act of 1934, but Congress disapproved the provision. The concept of expending millions of dollars to compensate tribes for treaty violations failed to obtain congressional approval until the rising number of claims forced Congress to deal with the matter. In essence, H.R. 237 stated that tribal groups would be compensated for the government's past unfair dealings in seizing Indian lands. Simultaneously, by settling all tribal claims the government could once and for all "get out of the Indian business." Consequently, remaining tribal-federal relations would likely be terminated.

In late October, Congress entertained a similar measure when Washington Representative Henry M. Jackson introduced House Resolution 4497 "to create an Indian Claims Commission, to provide for the powers, duties, and functions thereof . . ."[18] Like the previous resolution, this measure also attempted to establish a governmental agency to hear tribal claims presented against the United States. While Congress considered Jackson's measure, the congressman prepared materials to secure its approval. Later in December, he submitted a favorable report to the Committee on Indian Affairs to substantiate the need for creating such an Indian Claims Commission.[19] He stressed that tribes deserving claim settlements could provide their members with economic opportunities for better lives, although the process appeared to be a very expensive solution.

Jackson's efforts won support from Commissioner Brophy, who firmly believed that Indians should have the right to present claims against the United States. On 17 January 1946, in an address before the Indian Rights Association, the commissioner stated, "For years many Indian tribes have been claiming that the United States, either by violation of treaty or agreement, or by mishandling their resources or money, has become indebted to them, and that they have just claims against the United States Government." Brophy noted that the existing procedure for handling claims wasted enormous amounts of time in going through bureaucratic channels. Each claim was presented before Congress as a bill to be reviewed according to the jurisdiction of the United States Court of Claims. Brophy warned, however, that some Indians hoping to get rich would meanwhile become docile, thus hindering their progress towards self-improvement.[20]

Theoretically, the creation of an Indian Claims Commission

to settle all tribal claims against the United States would financially liberate Native Americans from dependency on federal programs implemented during the Collier years. Such compensation would grant them important revenue to invest for developing their own programs and properties.

As Congress debated the creation of an Indian Claims Commission, they also had to consider procedures for hearing the cases. In a memorandum to President Truman, Harvey Smith, director of the Bureau of the Budget, recommended a format for the Indian Claims Commission. Smith explained that Jackson's resolution would establish a "fact-finding commission to determine the merits of all outstanding Indian claims, subject to appropriate legal review by the Court of Claims."[21] Congressional Indian committees could then concentrate on other serious matters in Indian affairs.

In mid-July, Wyoming Senator Joseph O'Mahoney submitted a positive report to the Senate Committee on Indian Affairs for supporting and designing the Indian Claims Commission. He outlined the commission to "be composed of three commissioners, appointed by the President with the advice and consent of the Senate and would be equipped with the usual powers of a fact-finding commission to hold hearings and to examine the witnesses."[22] The schedule for the commission allowed tribes to submit their cases during the first five years of its existence. At the end of a second five-year period, the commission was to have completed its study and judgment of claims.[23]

Until Congress could vote on the Jackson resolution, tribal claims continued to be presented in the form of bills before the House of Representatives and the Senate. Interest groups, who became aware of the Indian plight and were knowledgeable of the historical wrongdoings to the red man, supported the Indian Claims Commission bill. Organizations like the General Federation of Women's Clubs agreed that Indian Americans should be allowed to present claims against the United States. In a letter dated 6 August 1946, leaders of this group reminded President Truman that a statute in 1863 barred all Indian treaty claims substantiating discrimination against Native Americans from coming before the U.S. Court of Claims. Except for those Indian claims that were already in Congress as special legislation, Native Americans had no access in presenting legitimate cases;

therefore, Jackson's H.R. 4497 became imperative for creating the commission.[24]

In a hearing before the Senate Committee on Indian Affairs, the bill was presented as an attempt to "facilitate and simplify the administration of Indian affairs."[25] In this light, streamlining the Indian service via a commission to hear Indian claims represented another attempt in a series of postwar termination efforts that seemed to be anti-Indian. By concluding all obligations to Indians, Congressman Jackson and other federal officials hoped to rid the government of its longtime responsibilities to Native Americans. During the discussion of the commission bill in Congress, attention focused on the likelihood that much federal money would be spent to compensate tribes, a realistic possibility that impeded congressional members from enthusiastically supporting the bill. Yet, during the second session, both houses of the Seventy-ninth Congress approved the bill as Public Law 726.[26] Ironically, earlier in the first session, two similar bills failed to pass; one was H.R. 1941, sponsored by Senator Elmer Thomas of Oklahoma, but neither was approved "due to budget cutbacks."[27]

President Truman signed the Indian Claims Commission bill, stating optimistically, "I am glad to sign my name to a measure which removes a lingering discrimination against our First Americans and gives them the same opportunities that our laws extend to all other American citizens to vindicate their property rights and contracts in the courts against violations by the Federal Government itself." He thought that the new law would "mark the beginning of a new era" for Indian American citizens. The president believed that Indians had earned their right to such legislation for having "valiantly served on every battle front" and having "proved by their loyalty the wisdom of a national policy built upon fairdealing." Enacting the commission enhanced the next step after "the final settlement of all outstanding claims," as Indians could now "take their place without handicap or special advantage in the economic life of the nation and share fully in its progress."[28]

In reality, the Indian Claims Commission Act represented a major legislative reform affecting Indian affairs during the postwar period. More importantly, it provided direction for federal Indian policy. Reform for assimilating American Indians into the mainstream society became the policy under the early Truman years—a concept that was not at all new. On 24 August, the Oklahoma City *Times* reported Commissioner Brophy's assessment of the federal administration of Indian affairs and his comparison of it with the Collier administration. Although Commissioner Brophy sought the same general reform of independence for American Indians as Collier, he approached Indian affairs differently. While Collier urged Indians to reorganize tribal governments, to become self-sustaining, to grow in confidence, and to integrate with other Americans when they were prepared, Brophy believed that many Indians, veterans especially, were ready to assimilate. Furthermore, he encouraged Native Americans to use more of their own resources and to concentrate on improvements in areas of conservation, health, and education.[29]

More significantly, Brophy claimed that federal supervision of Indian affairs under Collier was superfluously bureaucratic. He criticized Collier for creating too many offices within the Bureau and proposed to revamp the Indian service.[30] Brophy worked to dissolve district offices, thereby reducing costs for personnel and program expenses. Simplification of the Indian Bureau complemented the congressional retrenching guidelines. Further reductions were considered with plans to eventually dissolve the Bureau itself.

In early August, President Truman signed a bill to "facilitate and simplify administration of Indian Affairs." Reorganization of the BIA permitted the commissioner to set up five geographical areas with headquarters in Minneapolis, Minnesota; Billings, Montana; Portland, Oregon; Phoenix, Arizona; and Oklahoma City, Oklahoma. This move eliminated over forty offices and empowered area offices with more authority. In addition, the new law cut the budget structure from 116 to 29 titles of appropriation to streamline administration. Such revisionary actions reduced the bureaucracy that had been created during the Collier years, and substantiated the early enactment of the termination policy to dissolve parts of the Indian service.

Faced with an enormously inflated national debt, Congress sought the elimination of certain government programs and a reduction in the number of federal employees. Interestingly, the creation of the Indian Claims Commission contradicted the government's policy of reduced spending, but supporters believed that by settling with the Indians now they could save millions of dollars in the long run. Federal officials also believed that the commission's decisions for compensatory awards would help the red man to assimilate into the mainstream society. On 23 August 1946, Congressman Stigler wrote to a friend, "I think this is one of the most important bills, as far as the Indian is concerned, that Congress has passed in the last quarter of a century, and it will go a long way in emancipating the American Indian and permitting him to take his place with the white brethren."[31]

Not all members of Congress supported the bill. Possible repercussions impelled several congressmen to criticize the creation of the Indian Claims Commission. Republican Senator Ed Moore of Oklahoma stated that it "looks to me like just another useless bureau."[32] In a statement before the Subcommittee on Indian Affairs of the Senate Public Lands Committee, Moore argued that the commission was a "wasteful duplication of government expenditure" and that the act should be repealed. He declared that the commission's purpose was inconsistent with procedures for filing claims against the United States government; that it would lead to "graft, fraud and corruption at the expense of the public treasury"; and that the Indian Claims Commission Act furnished "an excuse for continuation of the Indian Bureau." Moreover, the Bureau of Indian Affairs cost 40 million dollars a year, and Moore asserted that it should be abolished.[33]

Other Republican congressmen made similar arguments, alluding to the astronomical cost that the Indian commission would entail. They asked, "Why must we buy America from the Indians all over again?"[34] Furthermore, these congressional members charged the tribes with hiring prudent lawyers who would swindle the federal government out of enormous sums of money. Such an assault on the federal treasury would impede the country's progress in recovering from the war. In spite of the budget-minded congressmen, the tribes soon began to present their cases before the new commission.

Oscar Chapman, then the Acting Secretary of the Interior, wrote to President Truman, strongly recommending that Felix Cohen be named as chief of the commission.[35] A native New

Yorker, Cohen held a doctorate in Ethics and Jurisprudence from Harvard and a law degree from Columbia. He had taught at Yale Law School, and had written extensively on law pertaining to Indians. His *Handbook of Federal Indian Law,* published in 1942, established him as a leading authority on Indian law. In spite of Cohen's expertise, President Truman selected Edgar E. Witt, a former lieutenant governor of Texas, as the chief commissioner. Louis J. O'Marr, a former attorney general of Wyoming, and William M. Holt, a prominent Nebraska lawyer, were chosen as Witt's associates.

Upon receiving their appointments, the three commissioners began hearing claims against the United States. Within the first five years the commission heard 852 cases.[36] Numerous claims forced the extension of the Indian Claims Commission until 1961, and similar circumstances forced the approval of an additional five-year extension until 1966. Again, Congress granted additional time and increased the number of commissioners to five members to expedite the hearings. After granting extensions and adding two more commissioners, Congress finally dissolved the commission in September 1978.

Meanwhile, a steady stream of bills, all purporting to be in Indian interests, followed the Indian Claims Commission bill. It is important to note that each legislative measure became another step toward terminating federal services to Indians. During the first week in January 1947, Senator Pat McCarran introduced Senate Bill 30 in the first session of the Eightieth Congress. The bill authorized "the Secretary of the Interior to issue patents for certain lands to certain settlers in the Pyramid Lake Reservation, Nevada."[37] Certain non-Indians would be granted ownership over the properties that they had developed on the Pyramid Lake Paiute Reservation. The bill escaped attention until several months later when Congress endorsed the McCarran measure, provoking a vehement Indian response. The tribal council of the Pyramid Lake Indians telegraphed Senator George Malone, declaring that "every member of the Pyramid Lake Tribe together with all Indians of Nevada vigorously protested the passage of S–30," which was later defeated.[38]

Another anti-Indian measure, Senate Resolution 41, was heard in the Eightieth Congress on 8 January 1947. The bill proposed to reduce staff levels in the government. After several hearings, the Senate Committee on Indian Affairs reported "that the Bureau had ceased to be of utility." Senator Dennis Chavez of New Mexico stated emphatically, "I think we ought to abolish the Indian Agency entirely. It is absolutely unnecessary."[39] Another attempt to terminate Indian services resulted in Senate Bill 405, which was introduced on 27 January 1947. The bill sought to repeal the Indian Claims Commission; Republican congressmen endorsed it on the basis that it would make the government vulnerable to a barrage of tribal claims, with the Indians expecting to be paid.

Federal officials asserted that Indians should not be penalized by maintaining trust status; they contended that during the war Native Americans had proven without doubt that they deserved the same privileges and rights as other Americans. In early April, Congressman Francis Case of South Dakota proposed a measure to remedy what he called the Indians' second-class status. The Case bill proposed "to emancipate the Indians of the United States and to establish certain rights for Indians and Indian tribes."[40] Congress held hearings on the bill throughout the rest of April. Two similar bills, H.R. 2165 and H.R. 1113, followed which also advocated emancipation from federal trust restrictions for Native Americans. Wade Crawford, a concerned Klamath, testified that "with regard to the Indians—there are different groups—different classes, throughout the United States. It is impossible to draw legislation . . . that would correct all the wrongs and give the Indians what they want and need on the different reservations throughout the United States to bring the Indians into full citizenship."[41] Crawford did note that a legislative study might be made of Indian age-groups for trust removal. He suggested that those from eighteen to thirty-five or forty years old would seem the most advanced of the Native American population.

The drive for total emancipation of Native Americans provoked controversy between proassimilation congressional members and Indians and their supporters. Many concerned citizens criticized the federal government for its plans to reduce services to Indians. Continued Indian-supported opposition coalesced into a sporadic movement to restore funding to Indian programs. One supporter, Alice H. Rossin, vice-president of the Association on American Indian Affairs, was quoted in the New York

Herald-Tribune as having said to the House Indian Affairs Subcommittee: "Give the bureau the tools to properly educate our Indian minority; money for more and better schools, money for more and better hospitals, housing and land development. Only by spending sufficiently NOW can the ultimate goal of full citizenship-integration of our American Indians become a certainty in this country."[42]

In spite of popular concern, federal officials continued to seek methods to undercut Indian programs. Such retrenchment convinced pro-Indian supporters like Rossin that a termination movement was gaining momentum to dissolve Indian services, especially after Commissioner Brophy became ill with pneumonia and then developed tuberculosis following his tour of native communities in Alaska during early 1947. The responsibility of the BIA fell upon the shoulders of Assistant Commissioner William Zimmerman, who caused some discomfort among Indians and their supporters. While they trusted Brophy, skeptics questioned how Indian affairs would fare under Zimmerman. They were soon to find out when the actual plan for the termination policy was presented. On 8 February, at the request of Congress, Zimmerman proceeded to divide the tribes into three categories, depending on his perception of their readiness for withdrawal of federal trust status.[43] This became known as the infamous Zimmerman Plan, which laid the foundation for identifying which tribal groups would be terminated in the 1950s and early 1960s.

Without doubt, the Zimmerman Plan served as the blueprint to abrogate the federal-Indian trust relationship. Congress soon passed termination legislation which followed the Zimmerman Plan. On the second day of May, Undersecretary of the Interior Oscar L. Chapman offered a cautious opinion on a newly introduced measure, Senate Bill 598, in regard to Indian trust lands. Chapman warned that granting of fee patents or removal of restrictions would complicate the status of Indian properties. Many Indian trust lands would encumber several heirship owners upon the deaths of original allottees. With the removal of trust restrictions, multiple heirs would be subject to taxation upon receiving new lands. Multiple landowners would make the collection of inheritance taxes more complicated.[44] Previously, federal regulations had required Indian citizens, who desired to obtain unrestricted titles on their properties, to make written applications to the Secretary of the Interior, who reviewed individual cases for approval.

On the same day, Senator Wayne Morse of Oregon introduced Senate Bill 1222 "to remove restrictions on the properties and monies belonging to the individual enrolled members of the Klamath Indian Reservation . . . to confer complete citizenship upon such Indians."[45] The Klamaths consisted of Modocs, Klamaths, and the Yahooskin Band of the Snake Indians living on the timber-rich reservation in Southern Oregon. Morse was convinced of Indian self-initiative and proposed that the Klamath be "permitted as rapidly as possible to assume all the rights and prerogatives, the privileges of all other citizens."[46] Of all Indian groups, the Klamaths seemed one of the few who could probably assume control of their own affairs. Many Klamath members were as educated as the whites who lived near their reservation, and they appeared assimilated within nearby communities.

In determining federal appropriations for 1947, Congress took its cue from the financially wealthy Klamaths and planned to reduce funding for Indian schools and other facilities. The House of Representatives approved the decreased appropriation, claiming that the management of Indian affairs consumed more time and cost to the taxpayers than was necessary. In addition to appropriating fewer dollars, Congressman Schwabe reported to an Indian leader that members of Congress "believed that the Indian Office should be given less and less jurisdiction and supervision over the Indians, instead of more. But the Bureau insists upon authority for more supervision rather than less. This is where the conflict lies."[47]

In explaining the shortage of federal money, Schwabe stated that the government was still operating on the budget established from the previous fiscal year and would continue to do so until 30 June 1947. He explained that the appropriations for the 1947 fiscal year were inadequate, but that Congress had provided approximately all of the funding that local officials had requested for their Indian schools and hospitals. The congressman blamed the insufficient funding on school and hospital administrators who had not estimated their budgets high enough to meet their operating costs. Rising inflationary costs for supplies and labor had not been calculated correctly. By using this information from the commissioner of Indians Affairs, Schwabe tried to clear Congress of the blame for the funding shortage.[48]

If erroneous budgeting did indeed occur, the retrenchment policy of the federal government was the actual culprit in reducing the Interior Department's funding for the Bureau of Indian Affairs by 50 percent. In Oklahoma, the Bureau officials slated seven and possibly eight Indian schools for closure, and they intended to reduce the budgets of Indian hospitals.[49] Speculation, much of it correct, insinuated that Congress would also sharply curtail funding of other services and withdraw BIA supervision over Indian affairs. Such actions indicated that the Bureau would be dissolved in the near future, but the correct course had yet to be decided. Because of the government's past blunders in Indian affairs, it was imperative that officials select the right method for dissolving the Indian Bureau and prepare Indians for adjustment to the dominant life-style.[50]

Congressional intentions in reducing BIA services disturbed Native Americans who no longer passively accepted federal actions. One Oklahoma Indian wrote Senator Elmer Thomas that he was aware the Republican Party controlled Congress, but he lobbied for Oklahoma tribes who needed the Indian hospitals, their own schools, and the Indian Bureau.[51] Congressional members who supported the closing of Indian schools and hospitals claimed that state-supported institutions could supply the same services to both non-Indians and Indians. Indians asserted that they were discriminated against in public schools and in hospitals. Reportedly, officials in charge of public hospitals ignored Indian patients, and Indian children were harassed by other students in public schools. Thus, Indians preferred Indian hospitals and schools.

Federal efforts to assimilate Indians by terminating their services and special status under trust became a collective endeavor. On 21 July, Senate Bill 1681 was introduced during the second session of the Eightieth Congress as another bureaucratic attempt to abolish federal responsibilities. The proposed bill provided for final settlement of federal obligations to certain New York Indians by abrogating trust restrictions with the Six Tribes of the Iroquois League. During a discussion on Indian affairs in the Senate on the same day, Senator Hugh Butler exhorted immediate removal of such trust restrictions. He argued that they should be removed "as rapidly as it can be done, [and] the Indians should be emancipated from Federal wardship and control."[52] At this point in his remarks, he introduced Senate Bill 1684, a measure pertaining to the Osage Indians, which would remove restrictions on tribal properties and monies belonging to "enrolled tribal members in Oklahoma." Proceeds from selling properties would then be distributed to the Osage members on a per capita basis.

Butler was part of a small but growing bloc of westerners in Congress that condoned termination and believed that American Indians should assume control over their own destinies. Butler and his associates in Congress advocated the dissolution of federal services to Native American citizens, but they did not become effective as a terminationist faction until the Eighty-third Congress. Until then, the root of the issue lay in the question, "When should Native Americans be terminated of trust status?"

On 25 July, officials in the Department of the Interior announced the reorganization of Indian services in Oklahoma. A 50-percent reduction in appropriations meant that BIA offices in the state would need to be streamlined.[53] Principal changes involved the establishment of the Western Consolidated Agency of field offices at Anadarko, with additional supervision of affairs for the Quapaw Agency performed at the Muskogee Agency. This gradual withdrawal or simplification of the Bureau of Indian Affairs, along with reform legislation for certain tribes to improve their conditions for financial independence, became the first phase of the termination policy. Federal officials deemed that it was important for all tribes to assume responsibility for their own members.

On 4 August 1947 Congress approved House Resolution 3064, making members of the Laguna Band of Mission Indians in California independent of trust regulations. Enacted as Public Law 335 with President Truman's approval, the act authorized the Secretary of the Interior to issue patents in fee to the Lagunas. William Brophy and other federal officials believed that trust status had hindered the California Indians, who were considered to be progressive American citizens. For all of Commissioner Brophy's work, this case of freeing the California Indians represented one of his achievements. In his brief term in office during the early Truman years, Brophy set the tone for Indian freedom from trust restrictions—the well-intentioned goal of the termination policy that began to unfold.

While Brophy battled tuberculosis, he stayed in contact with Native American people and encouraged their progress. During September 1947, the commissioner wrote to Ruth M. Bronson, secretary of the National Congress of American Indians, to thank the NCAI members for conveying their good wishes for his recovery. While touring native villages in Alaska, the commissioner noted that the native peoples needed supplies to combat tuberculosis and other serious ailments. Responding to a report of a tuberculosis outbreak among Indians near Sitka, Alaska, Commissioner Brophy informed Mrs. Bronson that federal funds had been appropriated to finance treatment of the disease. Furthermore, the government allocated additional funds for a new hospital, sanitarium, and equipment to detect tuberculosis. As a preventive measure, government workers educated the Alaskan inhabitants in preparing healthy diets, practicing sanitation methods to prevent tuberculosis, and improving general living conditions. "But all of this is not enough," a concerned Brophy wrote. "This siege has dramatically brought home to me the necessity that we increase our assaults on all fronts [for Indians], the medical, educational, economic and social."[54]

Brophy's comments reflected the destitute living conditions and generally sad state of affairs on many reservations. Frustrated with the environment on desolate reservations and in rural Indian communities, Native Americans began to protest. *The Daily Oklahoman* reported on 21 September that Indians wanted at least 7 billion dollars from the United States. The astronomical figure was projected by Louis Allen Youpe, a dissatisfied Oklahoma Indian who announced that "250 tribes will hand Uncle Sam a bill for real estate they claim he didn't pay enough for in the first place."[55] The outrageous claim registered one of the first public Indian protests against injustice during the postwar period.

Disgruntled Indian sentiment and complaints by interest groups produced some reform action for Native American assistance. In response, the government established an Indian Credit

Association to improve living conditions for Native Americans. On 18 October, Congressman Stigler wrote a concerned friend that he believed the association to be "one of the greatest instrumentalities for rehabilitating our Indian people."[56] As early as 1945 Congress had considered legislation that would aid Indian-owned organizations and businesses, and extend an education program to the Native American population.[57] When more citizens inquired about federal assistance to Native Americans, the government showed greater concern.

In a public report dated 2 December 1947, President Truman summarized the needs of all Indian people, and especially those of the Navajo Tribe, which was starving during severe winter blizzards. "Our basic purpose is to assist the Navajos—and other Indians—to become healthy, enlightened, and self-supporting citizens, able to enjoy the full fruits of our democracy and to contribute their share to the prosperity of our country."[58] At Truman's request, Secretary of the Interior Julius Krug proposed a ten-year federal program for the rehabilitation of the Navajo and Hopi tribes, since both groups had suffered heavily and received national attention from the media.[59] Krug's proposed program involved vocational training and development of reservation resources to improve the tribes' economy and health conditions. Shortly afterward, Congress approved the program, and the Navajos and Hopis embarked on a shaky road to gradual recovery. Interestingly, while the federal government cut back overall funding for Indian programs, the Alaskan Natives and these two groups in the Southwest received increased federal assistance.

Indian uncertainty over the future increased when an ill William Brophy resigned as commissioner of Indian affairs on 31 December 1947. Native Americans had indeed lost a sincere friend and a supporter in the federal government. Brophy wrote to President Truman, "It is with deep regret that I am compelled to inform you that my health will not permit me to carry on fully the vigorous work that must be done by the Commissioner of Indian Affairs if the Indians are to be protected in their treaty, civil and property rights."[60] Brophy urged Secretary of the Interior Krug to maintain a "policy of preserving Indian resources, of assuring the people the right to live . . . in their own way."[61] He stressed that the natural dignity of the people be nurtured by respecting their heritage, protecting their civil and social rights, and extending to them public services.

Brophy's departure, plus the lack of sufficient current data on Indian conditions and needs, hindered federal officials in efficiently supervising Indian affairs. Indians and interested white organizations, which believed Native Americans were not ready to supervise their own affairs, objected to termination legislation. The Osages adamantly opposed Senate Bill 1684, which called for the removal of restrictions on property and monies belonging to enrolled tribal members. Considered one of the wealthiest tribes on a per capita basis, the Osages had faced continual harassment and exploitation from grafters since the 1920s. Oil found on their lands provided huge royalty payments which, in turn, lured swindlers. During the 1920s and 1930s, opportunists cheated and even murdered several Osages for their money and properties, indicating that wealthy Indians, although economically self-sustaining, were not experienced enough to defend themselves. Osage Chief Fred Lookout opposed the Senate bill because he feared that his people would experience further exploitation.[62] While many Osages were educated and had served in World War II, tribal members expressed concern for elders, who were the most vulnerable—a concern that most tribes expressed.

The Agua Caliente Band of California Indians also opposed termination. On 2 February, their attorney, Eugene L. Graves, wrote to Senator Elmer Thomas: "These Indians are very much opposed to the so-called Butler Bill which proposes to sell all of the Indian land in California to the Government and to divide the proceeds."[63] It is likely that some California Indians had inadvertently encouraged termination when the Siletz Tribal Council requested the Department of the Interior to release all of their funds from timber sales for per capita distribution.[64] Such action implied that the Siletz were confident of being able to assume their own affairs without federal supervision. However, Congress delayed action on the bill to allow further consideration.

The proposed termination of the Siletz's trust restrictions focused attention in Congress on the Butler Bill and similar measures. House Resolution 1113, calling for the emancipation of Indians from individual trust restrictions, especially caused disagreement among Senators Elmer Thomas, Burton Wheeler, Carl Hatch, Joseph O'Mahoney, and Dennis Chavez, all of whom opposed the bill; and all signed a petition to substantiate the concurrent unreadiness of Native Americans to assume full responsibility over their own affairs. Interestingly, they were all western congressmen who were protective of Indians, whereas their other western colleagues were insensitive to Indian interests.

At the federal level, at least two types of bureaucrats took interests in Indian affairs: insensitive terminationists and concerned pro-Indian supporters. In the White House, President Truman expressed concern for Native Americans when he vetoed a bill for the disposal of submarginal lands within Indian reservations. During a lengthy drought period from 1932 to 1938, the government had acquired 245,000 acres of drought area for the Secretary of the Interior to use for the Indians' benefit. This new legislation, House Resolution 3153, proposed the sale of barren lands on reservations in North Dakota, South Dakota, and Montana. By vetoing the bill, President Truman permitted the affected tribes to continue using the submarginal lands under the auspices of the Department of the Interior.[65] Although the Interior Department intended to assist them, Native Americans found that the department actually restricted their activities, and they objected to this so-called paternalism. Evidence for this charge can be found in the case of the Sac and Fox. The Interior Department supported S. 1820, which would place the Iowa Sac and Fox under state jurisdiction.[66] The federal government implied that the tribe's members needed direct protection from the state of Iowa to prevent their exploitation.

The termination of trust protection during the postwar period forced many incompetent Indians to literally surrender their lands to opportunists. Their economic situation compelled them to sell to obtain revenue to develop their properties. The mid-1940s represented a period of hardship for the majority of Native Americans. Perhaps the only positive aspect was the provision of cash settlements to tribes by the Indian Claims Commission. On 24 March 1948, P. L. 451 authorized payment to certain enrolled members of the Seminole Tribe, a small and impoverished tribe. The distribution of funds to the Seminoles indicated the usual attempt to improve a tribe's economic livelihood via a claims settlement that had little overall affect on the tribe's economic development.

Five days later, President Truman signed House Resolution 2502, authorizing payments of five hundred dollars to each Klamath Indian. The Treasury Department disbursed the per capita payments from the tribe's capital reserve fund, with an additional two hundred dollars allowed for each veteran of World War II. The total amount withdrawn from the Klamaths' account concerned President Truman, who expressed an interest in the tribe's ability to spend the money wisely: "I urge the Klamath Indians to give deep thought to the use of their resources, both individual and tribal, in ways that will insure their future security and progress. I say this because it will not be possible for them to recover these resources if they are once lost through unwise transactions."[67]

Frequently, members of tribes who won claims awards received per capita payments in amounts of thousands of dollars, and then frivolously squandered their money. Merchants easily persuaded the recipients to spend their windfalls on new cars, trucks, television sets, and other material goods that they never had before. In areas where newspapers and the media reported that Indians would be receiving money, merchants commonly inflated their prices and extended credit to every "soon to be rich red man."

Federal officials perceived the claims settlements as ending the tribes' dependency on the government. By dispersing per capita monies among tribal members, the Indian communities would have sufficient income to pay for services they needed instead of relying on federal programs. While enticing the people with money, the administration worked to free itself from the remaining obligations to Native Americans. On 20 September, Theodore H. Haas, chief counsel for the Indian Bureau, addressed a conference of field staff in Billings, Montana, on Indian affairs.[68] In his speech, entitled "Trends and Portrends in the Indian Bureau," he attempted to clarify the reasoning behind the federal withdrawal policy. Haas explained that transferring supervision from the Bureau of Indian Affairs to the tribes would make them more independent. This would result in the dissolution of the BIA and in the eventual assimilation of Native Americans into society.

Haas failed to mention the potential repercussions from ending federal involvement. Some tribes did not possess the competency to handle Bureau functions, and states lacked experience in assuming the responsibility for supervising business affairs. A memorandum from the file of the Secretary of the Interior, dated 26 October 1948, listed the properties and incomes of the largest tribes, indicating the state of their financial preparedness to handle their affairs; but socially the majority of the tribes remained unfit for immediate assimilation. While some states refused to take responsibility for their Indian citizens, Congress was considering three bills: H.R. 4725, H.J.R. 269, and S.J.R. 162. The bills would empower the states by giving them more authority over Indian affairs. The first measure extended state jurisdiction over Indian criminal offenses committed on reservations. The last two measures authorized the Secretary of Interior to establish reservations in Alaska Territory.

The first Truman administration and Indian policy during the postwar years ushered in a new era in federal-Indian relations. Truman advocated protection of minority civil rights, while he continued implementing federal services of the New Deal through the war years. But due to congressional cutbacks in funding, such services were offered at a reduced scale. In fact, a subtle change in Indian policy occurred in the war's aftermath, which helped the oppressed Indian minority, even though the Republican Congress advocated decreased Indian services. When the views of the president and the Congress clashed, Truman retreated. He chose not to support Indian policy by restructuring tribal governments, as had his predecessor, Franklin Roosevelt. Even more, President Truman lacked an effective leader as Indian commissioner, while the Congress lacked firm direction from the BIA. Although Truman's views on Indian policy sometimes differed with the Republican Congress, he too believed that Indians should take their place in American society.

In addition, large claims settlements were intended as means toward tribal independence. The largest settlement for an Indian claim made prior to 1950 was awarded to the Utes. The claim involved three bands of Utes on the Uintah-Ouray Reservation in Utah, numbering sixteen hundred members, and two bands of twelve hundred tribespersons on the Consolidated Ute Reservation in western Colorado.[69] Ernest Leroy Wilkinson, the Utes' attorney who had worked on the Ute claim since 1935, finally achieved successful results.

Wilkinson announced the U.S. Claims Court's decision at the Utes' annual bear dance. Standing before the Indians to tell them the good news, the attorney paused before the jubilation he expected to occur in the next few seconds. Then, with the aid of an interpreter, he announced that the U.S. Court of Claims had ordered the United States government to pay the Utes 31.7 million dollars! But not a single Indian flickered an eyelid. Wilkinson asked the interpreter to repeat the good news, but again the people accepted it in dead silence. They took the news in stride, and it is very likely that many had no comprehension of the huge amount of money to be given to them. The settlement was compensation for six million acres of land that had been taken from the Utes in western Colorado in 1868.[70]

Rather than distribute per capita payments of ten thousand dollars to each tribal member, and then try to prevent exploitation and wasteful spending, the Utes planned to spend the money through the BIA on schools, livestock, and hospitals. President Truman later congratulated the Uintah-Ouray Indians for their sound planning, stating that "the native peoples of the United States have proven that once they are given the opportunity and tools to work with, they can contribute to the stability and betterment of our civilization."[71]

The early Truman years had produced two important elements for altering the course of federal-Indian policy. As the immediate postwar years came to a close, the Indian Claims Commission and the Zimmerman Plan became guiding factors that brought about termination in Indian affairs. In brief, the seeds of termination were planted. Ironically, some Indians supported termination of trust status, and this unexpected support encouraged a congressional movement that promoted the termination policy. In large part, this native attitude was due to the Indians' experience during World War II, which gave them a new perspective on reservation life. Furthermore, their traditional livelihood seemed no longer practical as America entered the atomic age. The war had revitalized a nationalistic spirit of patriotism and modernization as Americans were temporarily drawn together. At the same time, nontraditional Native Americans identified with American patriotism. They adopted the new materialistic values of the mainstream society and left reservations and allotted lands to become a part of the urban scene. World War II had, in fact, altered the life-style of many Indians, and federal officials were convinced that Native Americans as a whole were ready to assimilate into the mainstream.

3

The Truman Fair Deal and the Hoover Task Force Report

After incumbent President Harry Truman shocked the nation by defeating the popular Thomas E. Dewey in the election of 1948, his Fair Deal program took root in coalescing the American people toward the economic improvement of their lives. Truman continued his "holistic" endeavor to mold the American populace according to his democratic principles. His Fair Deal to help the poor sought to recreate a better America with equal treatment for all citizens, including minorities. In the eyes of the federal government, Indian Americans had little choice but to become a part of the general populace and to share the same rights and privileges as other citizens.

This attitude of national conformity permeated Congress and the various departments of the federal government. Objections from Indians and opposition from pro-Indian organizations failed to distract Congress and the Bureau of Indian Affairs from continuing to purvey this philosophy during the second Truman administration. Ironically, while BIA policy attempted to pursue equality by assimilating Indians into American society, other areas of the government impeded Native American progress. On 13 January 1949, the executive board of the Association on American Indian Affairs requested social security benefits for Indians in New Mexico and Arizona. For fourteen years since the passage of the Social Security Act, the two states had refused to allow American Indian citizens to receive benefits for their aged, their blind, and their dependent children.[1] In 1949 Arizona and New Mexico possessed the second and third largest Indian populations of all the states. Of a total estimated Indian population of 350,000 in the United States, 56,000 lived in Arizona and 43,000 resided in New Mexico.[2] People from all over the country petitioned Secretary of the Interior Krug and President Truman to halt discrimination against Indians, particularly those living in Arizona and New Mexico.

Oliver La Farge, president of the Association on American Indian Affairs and chairman of its American Indian Fund, emphatically criticized the practices of the two state governments. "This callous and illegal treatment of thousands of American Indians," said La Farge, "intensifies their suffering, is responsible for deaths from starvation and malnutrition, and increases their need for emergency relief and public charity."[3] Furthermore, the executive board of AAIA charged government officials of Arizona and New Mexico with racial prejudice, and demanded President Truman's immediate action to end the discrimination.

Discrimination, coupled with federal cutbacks of Indian services, created anxiety among Native Americans. The closures of Indian hospitals and clinics meant that Native American citizens would lose services and have to apply to county health departments for medical care. In Oklahoma, one concerned citizen wrote to his congressman, Carl Albert, that Indians of half-blood and over would not endure the red tape involved in applying for medical care, and would die.[4] Fearing humiliating discrimination, Native Americans often remained stubbornly reluctant to mingle with non-Indians and therefore elected to face the consequences of avoiding professional health services. Instead, they opted to depend on their medicine men and traditional healing practices.

In Oklahoma, the federal government attempted to turn over the Indian hospitals at Talihina and Pawnee to the state. Choctaw Principal Chief Harry J. W. Belvin claimed that Oklahoma impeded Indian health care and that it had requested the federal government to relinquish its control of the two hospitals to state supervision.[5] Such jeopardy of Indian health moved Senator Elmer Thomas to respond to the Indian Bureau's decreased appropriations for the past several years. In fact, federal economizing had created a shortage of funds sufficient for the Bureau of Indian Affairs to carry out its work satisfactorily. Thomas explained to concerned Indians that passage of special legislation was necessary before the state could gain control over the Indian hospitals; and none, he said, was pending in Congress.[6]

Mistreatment of Indians and government abuse of their rights provoked an emphatic demand for federal reform measures from the Association on American Indian Affairs. Such attention also spurred an inquiry from the president. On 4 March, President Truman wrote to Secretary of the Interior Krug to ask about the progress of the proposed ten-year program to assist the Navajo and Hopi Indians in Arizona and New Mexico.[7] Truman wanted the Indian Bureau to assist the suffering native groups, but the AAIA charged both the president and the Bureau of Indian Affairs with procrastination. Of all organizations concerned about American Indians, the AAIA undoubtedly voiced the most demands for immediate action.

In an article in the New York *World-Telegram*, Eleanor Roosevelt added her disapproval of Indian–white relations in Arizona and New Mexico. The former first lady stated that a hidden provision in House Resolution 2632 excluded Native Americans from receiving social security benefit payments in the two states.[8] Other people could even have the rates of their social security benefits increased, but not Indians. More important, American Indian citizens had been excluded initially from the social security rolls in the two states. Mrs. Roosevelt charged that this action amounted to blatant discrimination. In closing her commentary, she asked her reading public: "Why is it we cannot seem to treat the first citizens of this country with decency and justice? It makes one ashamed."[9]

Instead of rectifying the discrimination against Native Americans in New Mexico and Arizona, the federal government opted to improve civil rights for the entire Indian population. In February 1949, during the Eighty-first Congress, House Resolution 2724 was introduced as a measure to improve general living conditions for Indian Americans by trust removal. The bill actually duplicated another measure, H.R. 1113, which stated the same objectives of Indian assimilation via trust termination; therefore, Congress had a choice of two measures affecting Native Americans who wished for freedom from trust restrictions and wanted to live in the mainstream. Upon reaching the age of twenty-one, any restricted Indian could apply to a court of law for a "decree of judgment of competency." Pro-Indian supporters claimed that this resolution provided just another way to thrust unprepared Indians into a competitive American society and was simply another effort to solve quickly the "Indian problem." Furthermore, they charged the BIA with manipulating Native Americans, especially when Commissioner William Brophy fell ill. Subordinate Bureau officials assumed responsibility over Indian affairs and pushed for rapid Indian assimilation while claiming to be sensitive to the governmental restrictions that confined the lives of Native Americans.

Brophy's inability to return to his position and the nomination of a new commissioner of Indian affairs intensified federal-Indian difficulties. President Truman's designation of Dr. John R. Nichols of New Mexico as the next BIA chief provoked protests from Indians and their supporters. Senator William Langer of North Dakota argued that the new commissioner should be an American Indian. "Roughly 3 years ago I was a member of the Committee on Indian Affairs, when the nomination of . . . William A. Brophy to be Commissioner of Indian Affairs came before the committee. I protested that appointment," noted Langer. "Nevertheless, we were told . . . that would be the last time when a man would be nominated for the office of Commissioner of Indian Affairs who did not have some Indian blood in him."[10]

Senator Langer firmly believed that an Indian would provide valuable insights into Indian problems and would be more familiar with Native American affairs than a non-native. Interestingly, a number of Indian graduates from leading universities possessed the general qualifications to be the commissioner of Indian affairs. In spite of this, President Truman appointed Nichols. Although the new commissioner lacked Indian blood, Truman believed that he was the person best qualified for the job. Nichols held a doctorate in educational administration and had participated in the Hoover Commission study. Native Americans, who wanted an Indian as commissioner, viewed the appointment as an insult. To them, once again a non-Indian had been selected to supervise their affairs.

Since World War II the general progress of Native Americans had convinced the rest of society that Indian people possessed ample competence to supervise their own affairs. Some federal officials were even more sure of the progress Indians had made. In New York on 8 April 1949, Assistant Secretary of the Interior Bill Warne met with members and guests of the Association on American Indian Affairs to discuss self-government for American Indians. In his address, Warne reemphasized self-determination on the part of Indians to direct their progress away from federal supervision. Warne favored the development of self-governing bodies whose members would be less traditional, well-educated, and employable in the work force alongside other citizens. Such a position was incongruent with self-governing tribal bodies proposed years earlier in former Commissioner John Collier's policy, which stressed preserving cultural traditions that would produce autonomous governing communities on the reservations. Cooperation between Indian people and the government, Warne argued, represented a key asset for solving Indian problems. He noted, "What we need most is the knowledge which will enable us to awaken in our Indian fellow citizens a desire to move away from the past of their fathers into the future we have arranged for every youngster."[11]

At the twelfth annual meeting of the Association on American Indian Affairs on 4 May, the new commissioner urged the independence of Native Americans. Nichols expressed the importance of the Indian people's future as American citizens, commenting that one day they would not be treated as a special people. All tribal designations and treaty responsibilties would become impractical.[12] Nichols avoided the discussion of any possible repercussions resulting from immediate independence following the termination of trust restrictions. By stressing the impracticality of Indian people who were dependent on future government services, he was justifying the BIA's move toward termination procedures, which began shortly afterward.

On 26 May, the Department of the Interior recommended transferring the Bureau of Indian Affairs to a new department more related to social security and education. The Hoover Commission suggested a "Department of Natural Resources" for handling Native American affairs as well as for developing natural resources on Indian lands. Indian affairs would only be an integral part of the duties of the agency, which would primarily emphasize national conservation and development of forests, water, and other natural resources.

During this time, one Indian person expressed frustration with the large federal bureaucracy in Washington that dealt with Indian affairs. Robert Goombi, a Kiowa, remarked that another department would be superfluous. In May, he wrote to Senator Thomas about the difficulty of paperwork in the Bureau of

Indian Affairs. "Pass the buck [is] all they do at our Agency they send the Indian to the land department, them [sic] they are sent to the Land Committee, and round and round the poor Indian goes. I tell you Senator I just hate to kick about things but it is just a shame the way they do business in our Land Department."[13]

Goombi's complaint, like those from others, did little to distract Congress from entertaining more of the so-called reform measures. Supposedly intended to aid individual Native Americans in assimilating into the mainstream society, House Resolution 5099 was introduced in Congress on 9 June. The bill proposed to appropriate 25 million dollars to the Secretary of the Interior to purchase restricted individual Indian lands, including water rights and improvements, at not more than the appraised value of the real estate. The acquired land would belong to the federal government, thus disallowing anyone else from obtaining Indian land, and revenue from the sales would benefit American Indian citizens. No further action on the bill occurred, but it represented the protective intention of the federal government to conserve and develop natural resources. Unfortunately, such a safeguard also meant that Indian landholdings would be reduced.

Land development constituted only one of several service areas where the government attempted to aid Native Americans. The Department of the Interior released a report at the end of June, stating that the Indian Bureau was making significant progress in developing more effective tribal self-governing bodies and establishing economic stability for the country's 400,000 Indian populace.[14] Simultaneously, Congress recognized the additional economic, social, and educational needs of Indians that had to be met if Native Americans were to attain a standard of living comparable to that of their white neighbors. In particular, Congress took pertinent legislative action pertaining to the ten-year rehabilitation program for the Navajos and Hopis. A similar development program costing 23 million dollars was started for the Papagos. On 30 June 1949, government loans totaling 29,933,000 dollars became available to tribal corporations, Indian credit associations, and cooperative groups in twenty-three states. These organizations then loaned funds to individuals or tribal enterprises. In health services during this period, the BIA operated sixty-four hospitals. The most noticeable progress was made in education, where public schools enrolled an estimated 92,000 Indian children. All of these services were aimed to help those Native Americans who wanted to become integrated into the dominant society.

Undoubtedly, American Indians experienced difficulty in assimilating because of their special trust relationship with the federal government. Senator Patrick McCarran of Nevada viewed this relation as "lawful" discrimination and claimed that in regard to Indians the United States Constitution should be amended to eliminate special treatment for America's indigenous peoples. On 20 July McCarran introduced Senate Joint Resolution 120, which would strike out the phrase "and with the Indian tribes" in the commerce clause of the Constitution. McCarran charged that the phrase "to regulate commerce with foreign nations and among the several states, and with the Indian tribes" had been used to justify federal control of Indians. The senator claimed that federal supervision actually impeded their progress toward assimilation.[15]

Senator McCarran's actions in dealing with the Pyramid Lake Paiutes of Nevada contradicted his statements. In fact, he had a long history of troubled relations with the Paiutes. He favored the white ranchers living on Pyramid Lake Reservation, who were his constituents. His lead in advocating that the Secretary of the Interior should issue patents on the reservation to certain residents indicated his anti-Indian position. Furthermore, McCarran remained a constant threat to the Indians while he remained in Congress. He served on the appropriations committee which handled the budget of the Interior Department, which included the budget of the Bureau of Indian Affairs. His influence increased when he became chairman of the Senate Judiciary Committee, a committee in which he was known to assert his power. Prior to his death in 1954, McCarran introduced in Congress a total of nine bills to issue patents to "certain residents" on the Pyramid Lake Reservation in Nevada. Fortunately for the Paiutes, none of the measures passed that would have given absolute title of ownership to white residents on Paiute land.[16]

Each time McCarran introduced his bills, the Association on American Indian Affairs opposed them and any other threatening legislative measures. Opposition from the AAIA also focused on Senator Joseph O'Mahoney's S. 17, which was aimed at the Pyramid Lake Tribe. The AAIA blasted the O'Mahoney bill for being "in the worst tradition of anti-Indian legislation. It would strip Indian owners of their lands in the interest of non-Indian trespassers and squatters, against the expressed and determined insistence of the Indian that they want to retain their lands."[17] Several months later, the National Congress of American Indians expressed a similar sentiment in a news release intended to protect the interests of the Pyramid Lake Paiutes. Overall, the landholdings of Pyramid Lake families averaged less than the holdings of white ranchers.[18] The Paiutes then took action of their own. Backed by endorsements from NCAI and AAIA, the Paiute tribal council passed a resolution to buy out "squatter" interests on the Pyramid Lake Reservation.[19]

In an attempt to justify his own actions, Senator McCarran cited several reasons why the Indian population was not able to exercise full citizenship rights. Approximately one-half of the Indian children had to attend Indian schools rather than public schools, and they received an inferior education. For health treatment, Native Americans were directed to seek medical care at Indian hospitals, rather than utilizing public services available to other citizens. In business, restricted Indians could not buy, sell, or lease their lands without permission from the federal government. More importantly, Native Americans could not withdraw personal funds deposited in the U.S. Treasury without permission. McCarran's arguments included the existence of reservation Indians who remained under tribal jurisdiction and depended totally on the BIA for federal social services. Furthermore, he falsely claimed that Bureau regulations prevented Indian veterans from obtaining GI loans. Their rights as citizens, he said, were also violated by restrictions placed on purchasing alcoholic beverages. Finally, and perhaps most important, McCarran maintained that the tribes and the BIA regulated businesses on reservations, thereby disallowing free enterprise. A special act of Congress was necessary to free individual Native Americans from restrictions on their property. In summarizing the effect that the commerce clause had on American Indians, the Senator stated, "The retention of this power in the Constitution makes for continuance of paternalistic Federal control over Indians indefinitely in the future," and should be amended.[20] Allegedly, McCarran actually desired to control Indian lease lands in Nevada to further his personal economic interests. But opposition to his land schemes came from Secretary of Interior Oscar Chapman, who refused to go along with McCarran's proposals, thus causing a mutual animosity between the two men.

McCarran's actions were typical of blunt federal efforts aimed at assimilating Native Americans into the mainstream. The constant bombardment of arguments from bureaucrats extolling the virtues of assimilation eventually convinced some Indians that integration into the mainstream would be best for them. In August, another measure, H.R. 4510, aimed at dissolving special Indian treatment was introduced during the Eighty-first Congress. Approved by the House on the nineteenth, the resolution provided funds to the school board of Klamath County, Oregon, for construction, extension, and improvement of public school facilities which would be available to all Indian and non-Indian children without discrimination. The measure signified that Oregon Indians had consented to cooperate with county officials in combining school facilities, henceforth eliminating segregation of Indian students and simultaneously initiating the closing of most Indian schools in Oregon.

Increased federal efforts to help Native Americans particularly involved the president when he took a special interest in the Navajos and Hopis. On 17 October, President Truman vetoed a potentially harmful bill, S. 1407. The proposed measure authorized 88,500 dollars for a ten-year program to aid the Navajo and Hopi Indians. Although the bill was intended to help the two tribes, provisions within the bill threatened their sovereignty by extending state civil and criminal laws and court jurisdiction to the Navajo and Hopi reservations. Their homelands would be subject to both federal and state laws. Several months later, however, President Truman signed a similar bill, providing for a ten-year rehabilitation program for the Navajos and the Hopis. Senate Bill 1704, enacted as Public Law 474, did not contain the extended law provision found in Senate Bill 1407.

At the end of October, Truman signed another bill that provided hospital care for Indian patients in New Mexico. Senate Bill 2404 appropriated 1.5 million dollars for the purpose of collaborating with Bernalillo County, New Mexico, for the construction in Albuquerque of a hospital with at least one hundred beds for Indian patients. The time had arrived when Indians and other citizens would share services.

Since World War II federal officials had entertained termination legislation to bring about the desegregation of Native American communities and to assimilate Indians into the mainstream. In another attempt to achieve this end, Montana Senator George Malone introduced Senate Bill 2726 during the first session of the Eighty-first Congress. The bill would abolish many BIA functions and remove trust restrictions over their lands. The measure also attempted to repeal the Indian Reorganization Act of 1934, the legal foundation of tribal governments. Senator Malone cited the enormous operating costs of the Indian Bureau and noted that the budget for fiscal year 1950 amounted to 58 million dollars.

In an attempt to gain support for his bill, the senator argued that American Indians should be given the same status as other citizens. "Indian blood is good blood," he said. "If I had any Indian blood in my veins, I would be very proud of it." He claimed that Native Americans possessed an inferiority complex and that the government was partly responsible for creating it. Indians were "born of the fact that they do not have equal opportunities and privileges, as compared to other American citizens."[21] Malone automatically assumed that removal of guardianship and trusteeship would give Indians an opportunity to exercise their abilities and build their confidence, thereby removing their inferiority complex.

Soon afterward, Oklahoma Senator Mike Monroney succeeded in having a resolution approved in both the House and Senate to abolish the Committee on Indian Affairs. The Public Lands committee became responsible for handling Indian land cases. When a sufficient number of bills had accumulated, the cases went to a subcommittee for review, and then to the larger committee. Overall, the Monroney reorganization bill reduced the cost and time spent on Indian affairs, bringing expenditures in line with congressional budget guidelines.

The Hoover Commission study had recommended such a reduction of federal supervision in Indian affairs. While addressing the Oklahoma–Kansas Superintendents' Association in

Oklahoma City on 17 November, Commissioner Nichols insisted that Indian services would be reduced at the federal level and that area offices would assume more obligations. Nichols pointed out that since the publication of the Meriam report in 1928 a large number of highly qualified professional and technical personnel had entered the Indian Service, providing, until World War II, a widespread concern about federal services to Indians. He added that the lack of sufficient funds in recent years would result in a reduction of staff levels to serve a growing Indian population.[22]

The troubled financial status of Indians and their impoverished living conditions presented a grave problem for federal officials. Members of the Eighty-first Congress, who met in session during March, included the substandard living conditions of the Indian population on the agenda for discussion. Wisconsin Senator Alexander Wiley suggested an investigation into the progress of Native Americans and their affairs. He then proposed Senate Resolution 245, a measure that would review the government's Indian policy. While introducing the bill, Wiley declared "that our Federal Government has bungled the job of enabling the Indians to become self-supporting independent citizens in keeping with the noble traditions of the Redskins."[23]

The increasing focus on the needs of Native Americans and the federal administration's supervision of Indian affairs spurred the involvement of other congressional members. In a speech to the Eighty-first Congress, Nebraska Senator Hugh Butler asked, "Does the Indian desire to be considered Uncle Sam's stepchild forever?" The senator then declared, "No. Wardship with all its paternalistic trappings is increasingly distasteful to him."[24] Butler recommended that the United States should determine what its debt to the Indian amounted to, individually and collectively, and pay such debts. Then, Native Americans should take their place in the community with other citizens.

Congress was interested in desegregating Native Americans, thereby reducing the need for the Bureau of Indian Affairs. In order to document justification for decreasing Indian services, Senator Reva Beck Bosone, a Democrat from Utah, introduced Joint Resolution 490. The measure proposed directing the Secretary of the Interior to study tribes, bands, and Indian groups to evaluate their qualifications for managing their own business affairs. Basically, Bosone believed that Indians possessed the same inherent intelligence and capacity for handling their affairs as other Americans.[25]

In July, Secretary Chapman reacted to the Bosone resolution in a letter to J. Hardin Peterson, chairman of the Committee on Public Lands in the House of Representatives. After warning that Native American rights should not be violated, Chapman stressed that full consideration should be applied to H.J.R. 490 to thwart disastrous consequences that could affect native groups.[26] He warned that withdrawal of guarantees protecting Indian property rights or the termination of federal services before state services were made available to Native Americans would surely damage the economic status of Indian groups. Preventing such potential disaster was Chapman's main concern. Despite Chapman's warning, BIA Commissioner Dillon Myer, who had succeeded John Nichols, believed that immediate passage of H.J.R. 490 would be a major step in assimilating Indians.[27]

Former Secretary of Interior Harold Ickes also expressed concern for preventing potential harm to Native Americans. He contended that the proposed Bosone resolution jeopardized entire tribes, and he hoped that President Truman would veto the bill.[28] The resolution had already passed in the House of Representatives and was favorably recommended to the Senate. The basis of optimism for this termination bill rested on the fact that some Indian groups were already independent, and they no longer required federal assistance.

On the last day in August, Oscar Chapman wrote to former BIA Commissioner John Collier to inform him that the Department of Interior could finally support Bosone's bill. The department had been cautiously critical in studying the bill, and Chapman assured Collier that there were no hidden threats in the bill that would exploit Native Americans. "It has been thoroughly and carefully considered by the Department, as indicated by its report," Chapman declared. "I have full confidence in the key staff of the Bureau of Indian Affairs, and am quite sure there is no malicious intent on their part to liquidate the Indians or to do anything other than aid them to assume their rightful place in the American pattern." In his letter, Secretary Chapman confided his optimism that Indians and concerned individuals had nothing to fear.[29]

Certainly, many Native Americans seemed ready for termination of federal supervision and the removal of trust restrictions from their properties. In reality, however, these people represented a small segment of the Indian population. They found wardship status overly restrictive, and they set out to prove their independence. Thus, a false impression existed that all Native Americans were willing to become a part of mainstream America, and by coincidence this view was given additional credence when the conflict in Korea broke out. As in the first two world wars, when much of the American Indian population joined the U.S. war effort, many Indians enlisted during the Korean conflict. By 27 December 1950 more than 2,500 Indians had joined the military service. Again, the Forty-fifth Thunderbird Division contained a large number of young Oklahoma Indians, and, as in World War II, it soon became famous for its successful combat performance.[30]

Truman's strong stand against communism in North Korea and his position on the Cold War antagonized the Soviet Union. Not too long afterward, Truman was pressured to commit American military aid against the communist forces that took North Korea and thrust southward beyond the Thirty-eighth Parallel, forcing the South Korean forces to retreat to Pusan. The Korean War demanded President Truman's utmost attention, eclipsing domestic concerns, including Indian affairs.

Beginning in 1949, during Truman's second administration, federal Indian policy tended to work against Native Americans. Truman was unpopular with members of Congress, particularly for his stance on civil rights. Unable to influence an antagonistic Congress and faced with larger problems, Truman allowed subordinate federal officials and Congress to shape Indian policy. Nevertheless, Truman considered himself as "President of all the people [including] white, black, brown, red, the working man [and] the banker"; but the early years of the Korean War and national concerns kept him from overseeing Indian affairs.[31]

In general, Truman was a strong president and did not hesitate to act. This quality was reflected in an incident involving an Indian casualty of the Korean War. Sergeant John R. Rice, a Winnebago Indian, was killed in battle in Korea while leading a squad of riflemen against a desperate enemy assault. He had arrived in Korea with the First Cavalry Division only two weeks earlier. The Winnebago Indian had also won honors while serving as a scout with the Thirty-second Infantry Division during World War II. His body was sent back home for burial, but unfortunately his remains were denied admission to a private cemetery near Sioux City, Iowa. A clause in the cemetery's article of incorporation forbade the burial of non-Caucasians. Cemetery officials stopped the funeral when they discovered that the casket contained the body of an Indian.[32]

Commissioner of Indian Affairs Dillon Myer called the incident most detestable. He telegraphed Sergeant Rice's widow, stating his condemnation of the people in charge of the cemetery: "I want you to know that I regard the refusal of Memorial Park Cemetery of Sioux City, Iowa to accept burial of your husband as most deplorable. Any cemetery in America should be proud to honor one of our first Americans who died in the service of his country."[33] Next, President Truman took immediate action and arranged for Sergeant Rice's body to be buried in Arlington Cemetery with full military honors. Surviving members of the Rice family were flown from their reservation home at Winnebago, Nebraska, to Arlington at government expense.

With the Korean War at hand, only congressional members who were devoutly interested in Indian affairs took up the legislative cause of Native Americans. In fact, this small number inherited the responsibility of shaping federal Indian policy calling for Indian assimilation. A rash of bills soon appeared. In early January, Senator Butler introduced Senate Bill 485, a measure that proposed a decree of competency for United States Indians in certain areas. The bill proposed that any twenty-one year old Indian person who was a United States citizen and wanted to be freed of government restrictions could apply for a "decree of judgment of competency."[34] The proposed legislation reflected the general opinion of Congress, which was guided, of course, by a handful of assimilationists who deemed Native Americans had progressed sufficiently to accept full responsibility for their own affairs.

The first step toward Indian self-sufficiency lay in taking responsibility for improving their standard of living. The Indians could not do this while their land and assets were under the government's trust control. On 10 August 1951, a conference of district agents met to discuss new and more liberal Indian money regulations recently announced by the Bureau of Indian Affairs. W. O. Roberts, area director of Oklahoma, anticipated a positive Indian reaction since he knew that the Indians were frustrated with current federal restrictions. He stated that the Indians generally complained, "The Government holds me down," or, "We can't do anything; we have to get approval."[35]

In September, Senator Malone introduced a bill in Congress that contained many of the ideas of Commissioner Dillon Myer, who wanted immediate Indian assimilation into the mainstream society. Senate Bill 2167 sought to establish equal rights for American Indians and emancipate them, once and for all. At the same time, the Malone bill proposed to abolish the Bureau of Indian Affairs. When Malone argued in favor of the bill, considerable debate in the Senate arose over the legislation. Although passage of the bill appeared favorable, it met defeat when it came up for a vote. This incident was unusual since Indian affairs did not usually capture widespread congressional attention during this time.

With the increased possibility that the Bureau of Indian Affairs might be abolished, the move to terminate federal trust over Native American properties gathered momentum. Congressman Toby Morris of Oklahoma advised President Truman about the need for an aggressive program of termination that he believed would benefit Indians. As chairman of the Indian Affairs subcommittee in the House of Representatives, Morris stated that the government had failed to appropriate sufficient funding to administer Indian affairs and that rehabilitation of Native Americans should occur once and for all. He stressed that increased expenditures would be worthwhile in comparison to the previous longer range programs with inadequate funding. In fact, Morris predicted that if 100 million dollars were spent annually over the next few years the Indian problem would be entirely solved—a sound investment in the long run.[36]

In his next annual budget address, President Truman requested Congress to authorize 121,350,000 dollars for the Bureau of Indian Affairs during the fiscal year beginning 1 July 1952. This amount was 50 million dollars more than the 70,370,912 dollars spent on Indian affairs in fiscal year 1951.

Congress refused the request, based on its interpretation that increased federal supervision meant more personnel.

The pursuit for solutions to assist the Native Americans in achieving their liberation from federal trust persisted. In November 1951, an article in the New York *Times* bluntly asked how the federal government would free Native American citizens from wardship status. Although a "withdrawal" federal policy of government services had begun to take shape, no definite program or timetable had been established for liberating Indians. During the same month, an article in *The Commonweal* also noted the lack of definite methods for liberating Native Americans. Some conflict existed within the Bureau of Indian Affairs regarding the Zimmerman Plan of gradually withdrawing obligations to Native American people and categorizing tribes into three groups based on their readiness for termination.[37] Such a policy seemed to be a pick-and-choose method that relied on information from hearings on the various Indian affairs bills which had been introduced during sessions of Congress. The information which Brophy had compiled while visiting the reservations during his tenure as commissioner was not used in deciding which tribes were to be terminated. After the tribes were set free of federal trust regulations, the next step involved the dissolution of the BIA.

During the middle of March, Ohio Representative Frank T. Bow introduced before the House Committee on Insular Affairs a resolution to conduct an investigation into the activities of the Bureau of Indian Affairs and the tribes. Bow particularly sought to study Indian groups to determine if they were qualified to manage their own affairs. After collecting the reports, a list would be compiled of those Indian tribes, bands, and groups who were deemed qualified to be relieved of all federal supervision and to manage their own affairs. Specific legislative proposals would then be designed for terminating federal supervision over the Indians at the earliest possible opportunity.[38]

Congresswoman Reva Bosone of Utah supported the Bow Resolution because it appeared to be analogous to her House Joint Resolution 8. She explained that the latest resolution represented a basic change in the congressional attitude toward the Indian. For the past one hundred years the federal government had endeavored to care for the Indian, she said, although some periods of inadequate service had occurred. She believed that in the future the federal government should attempt to prepare Native Americans to take care of themselves.[39] In explaining the resolution to Business Manager R. D. Curry of the Uintah and Ouray Tribal Business Committee, Bosone wrote: "The resolution provides for the Indian Bureau to set up a program of education, health benefits, etc., for those tribes that are not yet ready to be taken off of wardship in order to prepare them for the day when they will be taken off."[40]

On the first day of July 1952, another resolution in the House of Representatives called for an overall study of Indian progress. Congressman James J. Delany of New York submitted House Resolution 706 "to authorize and direct the Secretary of the Interior to study the respective tribes, bands, and groups of Indians under his jurisdiction to determine their qualifications to manage their own affairs without supervision and control by the Federal Government."[41] Representative Bow, who had introduced a similar resolution in March of the previous year, explained that such legislation was necessary to continue the withdrawal of federal supervision. Actually, the new withdrawal proposal complied with the Zimmerman Plan of 1947. Bow stipulated, however, that Congress, rather than the BIA, should study the tribes to determine their readiness for termination. Such a measure possessed a double meaning, possibly inferring that the Indian Bureau should be investigated for incompetency, especially since several introduced bills and reports had already called for its liquidation.

During the debate in the House of Representatives over the Bureau of Indian Affairs, Delany introduced House Resolution 698. This proposed measure authorized the Committee on Interior and Insular Affairs to act as a whole or by subcommittee in conducting a full study of the activities and operations of the BIA. After considerable discussion on the floor, the resolution was tabled. Federal-Indian relations began to receive increasing attention with the numerous legislative measures introduced in Congress to assimilate Native Americans via termination of trust status and dissolution of the BIA. For the present time, both the tribes and the Indian service remained the same while an ominous termination policy began to take shape.

During the years of the second Truman administration, Native Americans probably would have fared better if the president had had sufficient time to take a more active part in Indian affairs. Certainly, he advocated independence and individualism for American Indians and was compassionate toward minority peoples. However, national and world problems forced Truman to rely on subordinate officials. The Cold War dominated the international scene, and the president was concerned with developing the Truman Doctrine, the Marshall Plan, and other Cold War efforts.

Domestically, President Truman's Fair Deal program occupied the remainder of his time. He endeavored to improve the general social and economic conditions of America's poor in an effort to solidify society during the postwar years. Most of this concern focused on improving the livelihood of minorities through the recognition of equal civil rights. Truman believed that all Americans should be self-sufficient, but for Native Americans this often meant the termination of trust relations and a reduction in federal services.

By this time, the Bureau of Indian Affairs had become "a slothful and lethargic bureaucracy," in the words of former Assistant Secretary of the Interior Warner Gardner (when he was interviewed much later).[42] The ineffectiveness of the bureaucratic Indian service prevented the prompt handling of Indian affairs, apparently due to the Bureau's transitory state of development that kept it somewhere between the Collier legacy and the streamlined Bureau that officials wanted it to become. Without Truman's personal supervision, Bureau officials exercised absolute control over the direction of Indian affairs, and an increasingly unpopular commissioner of Indian affairs, Dillon Myer, began to arouse opposition from Indian and pro-Indian interest groups. During the second Truman administration, federal Indian policy began to take shape as the Hoover Task Force Commission Report and the Zimmerman Plan laid out a new policy very different from the previous Collier policy. Recommendations for assimilating Native Americans into the mainstream inspired congressional legislation for a policy of termination which would mature during the 1950s. Efforts to withdraw services for Native Americans and attempts to dissolve the Bureau of Indian Affairs provoked Indian criticism and public disapproval—hardly a "Fair Deal" for the Native American populace who still needed federal assistance.

4

Commissioner Dillon S. Myer and Eisenhowerism

General Dwight D. Eisenhower's victorious leadership in World War II made him an idol in the eyes of the American people, a champion of the western "free world." As commander in chief of the Allied forces, Ike rose to celebrated-hero status. He exuded an aura of strength and honesty that captured the hearts of the American public. Even several years before his election to the presidency in 1952, he held a mesmerizing, magnetic effect over the people. Americans viewed Ike with such loyal admiration that they followed his lead in a crusade to reshape a better society. Ike symbolized a strong America, a unified patriotism in defense of its democratic principles. His popularity persisted throughout both of his terms as president, making him the most popular figure in government.

The aura of Eisenhowerism enveloped the nation, and men with political leanings similar to those of the president began entering various levels of the federal government. Unexpectedly, on 22 March 1950, President Truman casually announced that Dillon S. Myer would be appointed commissioner of the Bureau of Indian Affairs. The current commissioner, John Nichols, appeared surprised at being replaced, but submitted his resignation to the president on 23 March without public complaint. Immediately, the Department of Interior reassigned the former commissioner as a special assistant to the Pacific trust territories under the Interior's jurisdiction.[1]

Although Nichols's brief term as commissioner lasted only eleven months, he did not escape criticism. James Curry, an attorney for the Pyramid Lake Paiutes, wrote to Paiute Tribal Chairperson Avery Winnemucca about Nichols and the need to replace him. The leader of the Paiutes credited Nichols with having learned about Indian affairs, especially when he served on the Hoover commission, but felt the former commissioner frequently had failed to make his own decisions and "make them stick in the face of conflicting opinions of those who should have been his subordinates."[2] Attorney Curry attributed Nichols's ineffectiveness to inexperience in supervising a government bureau like the Indian service. Curry was quick to criticize Nichols because the Indian Bureau had disputed Curry's contract with the Paiutes.

With Nichols ousted, Curry endorsed Dillon S. Myer as the new commissioner, pointing out that he "had extensive experience with the management of a government bureau." The Paiutes' attorney suggested that Myer would work favorably with Native Americans, and that "the general impression here [in Nevada] is that his appointment will serve the interests of the Indians."[3]

Recently appointed Secretary Oscar Chapman of the Department of the Interior echoed the support for Dillon Myer to President Truman. Before coming to the Indian Bureau, Myer had served as director of the War Relocation Authority. In his recommendation, Secretary Chapman spoke optimistically about Myer. He had done "an outstanding job in the maintenance and relocation of the Japanese evacuated from the Pacific Coast," and the secretary believed that Myer's experience qualified him for the position of commissioner of Indian affairs.[4]

Considerable opposition arose against Myer's appointment, particularly from outspoken Indians like Bob Yellowtail, a Crow Indian who had served at one time as an Indian superintendent to his people. Former Commissioner of Indian Affairs John Collier concurred with the opposition to Myer's appointment. The critics generally believed that Myer would cause harm to Indian people by running the Indian Bureau with the same iron hand that he had used to direct the War Relocation Authority.

Originally from Ohio, Dillon Myer graduated from Ohio State University and earned a master's degree at Columbia University. Myer then served in various positions in the Department of Agriculture during the 1920s and the 1930s. His most important position until the Indian Service was as director of the War Relocation Authority from 1942 to 1946. When he entered the Bureau of Indian Affairs at the age of fifty-nine, Dillon Myer personified stern forcefulness. While carrying out his duties as

Indian commissioner, Myer soon antagonized several colleagues and subordinates. Part of his unpopularity derived from his discharge of officials who held the same views on Indian affairs as John Collier.[5] The Collier bureaucracy had planted many social scientists and protraditional Indian humanitarians in federal programs, and Myer quickly moved to eliminate them. Collier and Myer undoubtedly disagreed in their philosophies on administering Indian affairs, which led to a reciprocal animosity between them.

During September 1951, criticism against Commissioner Myer mounted to a climax. This time, former Interior Secretary Harold Ickes charged in the *New Republic* magazine that the commissioner had purposely neglected to protect the rights and interests of Indians by allowing Senator Patrick McCarran to abuse the Pyramid Lake Paiutes in Nevada. The Indians' patron and superintendent of the reservation at Carson Agency, E. R. Fryer, assisted the tribe in retaining their land and in obtaining irrigation water. Allegedly, McCarran, who favored his non-Indian constituents, demanded that Commissioner Myer remove Superintendent Fryer. Fryer was pressured into leaving his position with the Paiutes, and Myer transferred Fryer after the superintendent asked for a post in foreign affairs. Then, Myer quickly left Washington to avoid the immediate outcry that would follow his actions. Upon the Paiutes' request, President Truman restored Fryer as superintendent to the Paiutes.[6] For his intervention on the behalf of the Paiutes, the National Congress of American Indians expressed its gratitude to the president.[7]

Without Fryer the Paiutes stood to lose portions of their most valuable land in Nevada. Through generations of having lived in the basin area, the Paiutes had developed a deep attachment to the land. They viewed themselves as part of the land, and non-Paiutes violated this relationship. Several people familiar with the situation charged McCarran with engaging in dishonest practices to exploit the Paiutes. The Washington *Post* reported that the senator had attempted on several occasions to cheat the Indian group out of land. News of the charge, whether true or not, generated attention and angered interested people who sought the protection of Indian rights.[8]

Several weeks later, Myer responded to Secretary Harold Ickes's innuendos, while describing Fryer as "an intelligent, alert, aggressive, articulate man with many admirable qualities and with a long history of public service." The commissioner explained that despite Fryer's qualities he had felt compelled to remove Fryer as superintendent at Carson Agency because Fryer had proved to be ineffective in administering Indian affairs. "Unfortunately, I found him to be impetuous and given to snap judgments, with a strong proclivity for ignoring administrative lines. The consequence was a series of embarrassments and headaches for the agency that should have been avoided," Myer said.[9]

In addition to the Fryer episode, Ickes charged that Commissioner Myer had removed officials in the BIA who did not agree with his termination policy.[10] Ickes claimed that shortly after his appointment as commissioner, Myer had recruited H. Rex Lee to replace William Zimmerman as his top assistant. Other Myer appointees possessed very little experience with Indian affairs. In addition, Willard W. Beatty resigned as director of Indian education after Myer had interfered with his administration of Indian education. Beatty had been in Indian education since 1936. Undoubtedly, Myer felt that pro-Collier officials in the Indian Bureau might jeopardize his way of operating, and so he wanted his own people. Naturally, Myer favored officials who shared his philosophy of immediately assimilating Native Americans into the mainstream and dissolving the BIA as soon as possible. At every opportunity, Dillon Myer offered platitudes on Indian assimilation and argued dogmatically that this was in the best interest of Native Americans.

On 12 December 1951, Commissioner Myer addressed the combined assemblies of the Division of Christian Life and Work of the National Council of the Churches of Christ in Pennsylvania on "The Needs of the American Indian." He emphasized the importance of a harmonious relationship between Indians and the federal government, stating that the main problem in Indian affairs was the land issue. The commissioner claimed that the federal government was partially responsible because over the years officials had always tried to convert Indians into farmers, ranchers, or stockmen. In an effort to convert Indians, the government tried to break up tribal holdings into individual allotments. Myer then posed to the audience the question,

"What if Indians had no desire to be in one of these occupations related to land?"[11]

In order to help the Indians break out of the vicious cycle of poverty, paternalism, and despair, the commissioner said that the Bureau of Indian Affairs was implementing two major steps. First, a basic program of training and placement assistance was being organized for those who wanted to leave the reservations. Second, the Bureau was consulting with Indians who preferred to remain on reservations to start developing industrial programs so that they could run their own affairs. In concluding his address, Myer stressed the need for Native Americans to make fundamental improvements in three essential areas: health, education, and economy. He did not believe that a better Indian future was in the land. The Indian-land relationship had not enabled Native Americans to meet the standards of the dominant society, thus it had to be dissolved.

Myer expressed his concern about the best interest of Indians, but many people remained skeptical because of the imprudent manner in which he performed his duties. A straightforward individual who avoided compromise, he sought to get things done despite differing opinions and opposition. Throughout his administration, Myer received criticism that created a negative image of the Indian Bureau.

Some of the criticism pelting the BIA related directly to the Bureau's imposed procedure for hiring tribal attorneys—a controversy confronting Myer throughout the early 1950s. In a statement before a subcommittee of the Senate on Interior and Insular Affairs on 21 January 1952, the commissioner maintained that the effort to prevent disreputable lawyers from obtaining tribal contracts and overcharging for legal services remained a constant concern. As a precaution, he recommended legislation to authorize the commissioner of Indian Affairs to terminate attorney contracts at the tribes' requests. Other safeguards included a maximum length of three-year contracts for legal services, to protect tribes unable to free themselves from binding contracts with attorneys, and periodic reports on contracts between attorneys and tribes, which would also protect Indians from exploitation.[12]

Two months later, before the annual meeting of the Association on American Indian Affairs in New York, Commissioner Myer stressed the danger of questionable attorneys obtaining contracts for legal services with tribes: "I know of nothing more reprehensible than the malicious practice of frightening and confusing Indians by means of out-and-out falsehoods, distortion of facts or half truths for whatever purpose the perpetrators may have in mind. If ever there was a group of people who deserve to be dealt with fairly, forthrightly, and truthfully, it is the American Indian."[13]

Because of the heated protest over the suggested protections for tribal contracts and the criticism directed at Commissioner Myer, Secretary Chapman withdrew the proposed regulations. An earlier editorial in the Washington *Post,* dated 30 January 1952, suggested that perhaps some of the protests originated from attorneys who had lost tribal contracts rather than from Indians. The writer added that Commissioner Myer's efforts were justifiable since exploitation of vulnerable tribes remained quite possible, and only safeguards enacted into the law by Congress could protect the Indians. The editorial concluded that the hiring of attorneys by tribes was another step toward self-sufficiency for Indians: "Perhaps the best way to end paternalism is to free the Indians to learn their own lessons, even though these lessons may be expensive. Certainly they will have to stand on their own feet when governmental safeguards are withdrawn."[14]

Some Native Americans desired removal of trust restrictions or, at least, partial modification of trust limitations over their properties. In a letter to Superintendent Theodore B. Hall at the Osage Agency on the first day of February, Commissioner Myer said that if the Osages were disturbed about limitations on mineral reserves he would recommend changes to the Secretary of the Interior. He would ask for full removal of trust restrictions or modifications, subject to the wishes of the Osages. Myer stressed that the Bureau of Indian Affairs had no intention of injuring the Osages in any way. He emphasized, however, the need for the tribe to reach a consensus to avoid any discontent that might arise later. He also insisted that the Osages should take stock of their situation, and the sooner this began the better able they would be to protect their interests.[15]

In brief, Commissioner Myer attempted to withdraw federal

supervision from the tribes in preparing them for termination. The irony is that by doing so the Indian commissioner would work himself, plus other BIA personnel, out of a job. By preparing Indians for assimilation into the mainstream citizenry, a *fait accompli* would also end special federal recognition of "Indians." Myer unequivocally stated that federal policy deemed Indians to be museum pieces whose life-styles remained no longer viable in the atomic age.

In July, and during the following months, Myer visited various Indian communities throughout the country, reiterating the philosophy of the "immediate assimilation" policy. While meeting with the tribal business association at Red Lake Reservation in Minnesota, the commissioner offered federal assistance, but advised the community members to strive for economic independence in the future. Myer said that he wanted to work with the Indians, but he would not do their work for them. They would have to plan their programs accordingly for the time when there would no longer be an Indian Bureau.[16] In Myer's mind, time was running out for the Indians and they needed to catch up with the rest of society. The commissioner's view, however, was not shared by all the Indian people.

Numerous Indians and their supporters criticized Myer's position on dissolving the Bureau and the sudden termination of trust relationships. His unbending and tyrannical attitude, which advocated swift action and quick results, sometimes unleashed anger from a previously passive native populace. Indians charged him with increasing unnecessary BIA control over the tribal hiring of attorneys and with placing new restrictions upon tribal delegations who traveled to Washington to submit grievances. Furthermore, they claimed that the Bureau curtailed their individual rights regarding land use and denied them the authority to spend their funds and to hold free elections.[17] Undoubtedly, Myer ruled federal-Indian affairs with a heavy hand and was blinded by a passion to dissolve the Bureau of Indian Affairs, and, as he put it, to liberate Native Americans to enjoy the privileges and rights guaranteed in the United States Constitution.

Throughout the presidential election year of 1952, Republican candidate Dwight D. Eisenhower voiced similar sentiments in urging full justice for all American Indians. During a campaign visit to the Southwest, the Gallup *Independent* reported that Eisenhower solicited the Navajo vote. He recalled Indian heroes of his childhood, saying that he admired them, and he also commended the Indian soldiers who had served courageously under him in World War II. The Republican nominee noted that Indians were citizens of the United States and should not be denied their constitutional rights. But Ike wanted to eliminate the wasteful dollars and energy expended by the BIA, which he claimed obstructed national responsibility for improving the conditions of Native Americans. He pledged to undertake programs that would provide Indian Americans with equal opportunities for education, health protection, and economic development. He added that "the next Republican Administration will welcome the advice and counsel of Indian leaders in selecting the Indian Commissioner."[18]

The presidential election year provided the stage for Myer's opponents to urge the selection of a new BIA chief. Felix Cohen wrote to John Collier to urge that Indian resolutions or petitions concerning the need for fresh leadership in the BIA be directed to the two presidential candidates.[19] Once again, a sentiment arose for an Indian to be named as commissioner. The Colvilles endorsed Alva A. Simpson, Jr., chairman of the Governor's Interstate Council of Indian Affairs in Oregon. In Minnesota, Edward Rogers, a Chippewa, gained popularity and backing for the position of commissioner.

While Eisenhower and Democratic candidate Adlai Stevenson campaigned on political issues like the Korean conflict, Myer continued to dominate Native American affairs. In August, Commissioner Myer sent a memorandum on "withdrawing programming" to all Bureau officials. He highlighted the need for cooperation and stressed the coordination of programs with tribal groups. The commissioner wrote that Bureau administrators should encourage Indian initiative and effective leadership. Indian participation was stressed with respect to negotiations between tribal groups and political subdivisions of states and federal agencies whenever such discussions related to federal "withdrawal."[20]

Native Americans who supported Eisenhower for the presidency did not anticipate any repercussions that might occur from his plan to free them of second-class citizenship. Certainly,

Stevenson's lackluster effort to gain the Indian vote in the Southwest helped Eisenhower. While passing through New Mexico, Stevenson spoke in Albuquerque, just as the Navajo Fair was taking place at Window Rock, two hundred miles away. A short plane flight to speak to the Indians gathered there could have easily gained him votes and made him familiar with their concerns.[21] Winning the confidence of the general Indian population was essential for gaining Native American cooperation with the incoming leadership in the federal government.

The lengthy experience of living under the government's paternalism had inhibited most Native Americans, and they feared total withdrawal of federal supervision and the abrogation of trust protection. In mid-September 1952, in the Columbia Plateau area, Commissioner Myer met with Indians from the Nez Percé and Coeur d'Alene reservations to discuss their relationships with the federal government. The two tribes believed that they were operating their tribal affairs efficiently, but continuous local pressure for dissolving the BIA frightened them into believing that their reservations would be liquidated. In response to the federal policy directive to absorb Indians into American society, one speaker voiced his opinion vehemently: "For anyone to say that soon we are going to have all Indians in the society of the white race doesn't go over very good with me. I am proud to be an Indian."[22]

Myer attempted to allay the listeners' fears. "I just want to say, I never expect to state that we are out to liquidate reservations," the commissioner replied. "I feel strongly that the lands that are held in trust by the government belong to the Indians, and what is done with those lands should be determined by the Indians, rather than by me or anybody else, and even though I think the time has come when there will be no Indian Bureau, I hope that those Indians that want to continue to own tribal or individual lands can continue to do so."[23]

Responding critically to the current withdrawal plans, former Commissioner John Collier again vehemently criticized Dillon Myer for his dictatorial control over the tribes. Collier charged that Myer had transformed the Indian Bureau into an instrument dedicated to his single purpose of termination. He alleged that Myer held multiple administrative controls over Indian groups and their personal lives, and had gone so far as "to seek the power to make arrests, searches and seizures without warrant for violation of any of his administrative regulations."[24]

Undoubtedly, Collier opposed Myer's handling of Indian affairs since the incumbent commissioner was striving to dissolve the very programs that Collier had established during the 1930s and 1940s. According to Myer, tribal governments, Indian schools, clinics, and hospitals for Native Americans stifled their development toward independence. Such institutions segregated the Indian population from the rest of society, thereby hindering their progress toward becoming middle-class Americans. Commissioner Myer envisioned Indians earning their way according to the "self-made man" concept rather than depending on the BIA, which he continued to dissolve. Essentially, he wanted to abolish all programs that were created under the Indian Reorganization Act of the Collier New Deal period.

In order to gain tribal approval of his termination policy, Myer sought cooperation from the tribes. On 5 August, he sent a memorandum to all reservation governments to clarify the BIA's position. Calling for tribal cooperation with the BIA in analyzing economic progress in communities, he recommended a step-by-step transfer of federal responsibility either to the people themselves or to other government agencies.[25] Unfortunately, Myer's hard-line approach and his right-wing conservatism only undermined Indian confidence in the BIA. The tribes felt threatened by the commissioner, and termination took on a negative image of usurping Native American traditionalism in Indian communities.

The firm approach of the Bureau, under Myer's leadership, called for continual efforts to clarify the government's position on federal-Indian relations. In early November, Commissioner Myer responded to Marion Gridley, editor and publisher of *The Amerindian,* concerning her questions about termination of trust legislation involving California Indians. Three bills had been submitted that proposed to facilitate termination of federal supervision over Indian affairs in California. Hearings on H.R. 7490 were conducted three times before a subcommittee of the House Committee on Interior and Insular Affairs; and H.R. 7491 was tabled as a matter of convenience, with consent from its sponsor, Norris Poulson of California. A companion bill, S. 3005, which Senators Clinton Anderson and Arthur Watkins introduced, remained pending when Congress adjourned before further action could be taken on them.

Gridley specifically asked the commissioner what would happen to Indians with health problems in California if supervision was ended. Myer assured Gridley that Johnson O'Malley contracts between the federal government and counties in the state would provide medical services to the Indians. Gridley also questioned the granting of additional power to the Secretary of the Interior, as proposed in the termination legislation. The commissioner explained that additional power was necessary to prepare Native Americans gradually for termination. Indians who were fifty years or older at the time when a land patent was issued would be granted a lifetime tax exemption. For persons less than fifty years old, tax exemptions would be extended for a period of five years.[26]

Myer's unpopularity with American Indians did not interest the general public, who remained more concerned with the Korean War, the presidential election, and domestic life in general. Of more importance, the commissioner found only limited support from other federal officials for his continuance as the BIA chief executive. On 7 December, 1952, Myer campaigned for reappointment as commissioner of Indian affairs at the Western Governor's Conference in Phoenix, Arizona. When several governors accused Myer of paternalism in Indian affairs, he explained that Native Americans preferred such a relationship with the federal government.[27] He then spoke optimistically on "Indian Administration: Problems and Goals." His efforts gained the support of Governors Earl Warren of California and Arthur Langlie of Washington. Myer based his campaign upon his two and one-half years of experience in the administration of the "withdrawal" of federal supervision in liberating Native Americans from their trust status wardship and in transferring federal services to the state level.

Former Commissioner Collier severely criticized Myer and adamantly opposed his reappointment. He declared that Myer's campaign statements about effective leadership and reducing Indian services to cut costs were misleading, citing the fact that Myer had almost trebled annual expenditures of the Indian Bureau to 122 million dollars.[28] Collier asserted that Commissioner Myer's withdrawal activities had the effect of "(1) enormously increasing Indian controls while (2) seeking, regardless of Indian consent, the demolition of Federal services to Indians, and (3) destroying the protections which enable the Indians to stay in possession of their own lands, water rights, etc."[29] Collier's indictment of Myer led to further opposition to the Indian commissioner's reappointment, and depicted him as a troublemaker. The campaign against Myer very likely reduced his chances of remaining in office.

In November, Dwight Eisenhower was easily elected president of the United States. The majority of Indians regarded him as a friend and immediately asked for his assistance. Governor Juan de Jesús Romero of Taos Pueblo congratulated Eisenhower on his victory and requested that he act in the best interest of Indian people.[30] Spokesmen for groups supporting Indian rights suggested that one of the newly elected president's first acts should be to replace Myer as commissioner of Indian affairs.

Amidst criticism and pressure to have him removed from office, Myer pushed on with the termination program. Area offices, in particular, revealed that Myer's zealous efforts to decentralize the BIA had begun to materialize. The transfer and recruitment of personnel, as well as the rearrangement of office space and the general expansion of facilities, signified a new distribution of federal obligations and services to Indians throughout the area offices. According to Myer's plan, a skeletal staff at the Bureau of Indian Affairs in Washington would supervise Indian business in a "housekeeping" manner. But the area offices lacked adequate preparation for the transition. For example, the Portland area office stated that the lack of adequate personnel would create serious problems in supervising withdrawal programs involving the tribes.[31]

The severe problems of the changeover were compounded by the stern attitudes and insensitive actions of Myer, Associate Commissioner H. Rex Lee, and Senator Arthur Watkins of Utah. These "immediate terminationists" worried most Indians who feared that their tribes would be the next to be terminated. Native American concern was voiced for replacing Myer as commissioner with someone more sensitive to Indian needs. In early January, Juliet Saxon, president of the Santa Fe branch of the American Association of University Women, wrote to Eisenhower to declare that the commissioner's post played a vital role in the advancement or retrogression of over 400,000 Indian citizens.[32] Mrs. William Hudnut, Jr., chairperson of the Indian committee of the Council of Church Women, also wrote to Eisenhower, stating that if he kept his campaign pledge it would be the first time in history that Indians would be consulted in naming the commissioner of Indian affairs.[33] An article in the New York *Times* supported the possibility of this unprecedented action. The significance of such a consultation meant that an individual who was sensitive to and understood the unique and complex problems of federal-Indian relations would be selected.[34]

The Blackfeet Tribal Council assured Eisenhower of their people's support, while expressing their readiness to be consulted in the naming of a new commissioner: "We feel that your declaration . . . in your inaugural address was reassurance to us that you intend to carry out your pledge to allow minority groups a voice in the determination of their destiny and especially that you allow America's oldest minority, the American Indian, a voice in the selection of a Commissioner of Indian Affairs."[35]

Unfortunately, other pressures intervened. In the following month, the acting secretary to the president, Thomas E. Stephens, wrote to Secretary Douglas McKay of the Interior Department that Eisenhower had inquired anxiously about planned activities to fulfill this plank in his campaign platform.[36] The president's interest stopped there. For the next several weeks, Eisenhower was preoccupied with winning a peace in the Korean conflict. In short, he had little time to settle the issue of a new commissioner of Indian affairs.

When it appeared that a new commissioner would be named, the study of termination in Congress and Myer's actions prompted considerable public debate by those interested in Indian affairs. Meanwhile, Indian reform organizations and tribal groups remained frustrated with the Indian Bureau. Myer allegedly was the chief instigator for liquidating Indian services, and his critics called for his immediate resignation. To offer some defense for Myer, although both he and Congress advocated termination, Myer's office actually represented a liaison for federal-Indian relations. Congressional committee members on Indian Affairs and new statutes actually decided federal Indian policy, but Myer was condemned because the termination policy was implemented through his office. Furthermore, he supported termination enthusiastically while indicating little concern for the negative repercussions affecting Indians. This insensitivity toward Native Americans justified his critics' efforts to oust him from office.

The Bureau of Indian Affairs' rush to dissolve needed Indian programs aroused concern among Christian organizations as well. Three years later, John Collier's article in *The Christian Century* cited the past wrongs of the federal government in dealing with Indians since the 1800s: violations of treaties with Native Americans, denial of Indian community rights, and forced allotment. Collier argued that the termination program during the Eisenhower years had reverted to past wrongs, and had gained momentum under Myer. He charged Myer and his assistant, H. Rex Lee, with influencing congressmen to introduce termination bills to end federal-Indian trust relations as rapidly as possible. This had resulted in at least ten trust removal bills being considered and enacted in Congress. In response to rash congressional termination activities, Collier continually appealed to American citizens to act on behalf of Indian Americans by opposing the abolishment of tribal trust status and services.[37]

A week after Collier's article appeared in print, Oliver La Farge also condemned the termination policy in a piece published in the same magazine. He accused the federal government of not acting in the best interests of Indians by breaking the trust relationship. In one instance, he stated that desire for oil and other minerals under Paiute land represented the true motive for terminating the Paiutes.[38] In a later article in *The Nation,* Collier pointed out that 177 full-blood Paiutes, who possessed 45,000 acres of poor land in Utah, would lose land because of subsurface oil and other rich minerals that likely existed below the earth. He concurred with La Farge that greed was the actual motive for termination, and he blamed Myer for initiating the destruction of Indian life. "Beginning with Dillon S. Myer as Indian Commissioner in 1950, the ruling purpose, harshly intensified by the present administration, has been to atomize and suffocate the group life of the tribes—that group life which is their vitality, motivism, and hope," Collier stated.[39]

Key individuals like Commissioner Dillon Myer, Assistant

Commissioner Rex Lee, Nevada Senator Patrick McCarran, and Utah Senator Arthur Watkins represented the bureaucratic higher echelon that followed the Eisenhower philosophy. An undaunted devotion to conforming all segments of society into a unified nation verified the federal advocation of a revitalized, patriotic America. These subordinate Eisenhower men supported the chief executive's belief in a conservative, nationalistic, and strong America. And American Indians were to become simply Americans.

Anything or anyone who represented something different immediately became a target for criticism. "Un-American" became a much-used phrase to describe anyone who was deemed to be disloyal to the United States. The extreme phenomenon of McCarthyism illustrated the paranoia of patriotic citizens. Simultaneously, public indifference swept Native Americans toward the Eisenhower melting pot in which everyone would be just an American.

Ike's 1953 appointment of California Governor Earl Warren to the position of Chief Justice of the Supreme Court illustrates an indirect attempt to assimilate Indians into the mainstream by extending full civil rights to all minorities. Historical cases involving civil rights for minorities, especially blacks, made it difficult for Native Americans to live in coexistence with non-Indians. The postwar presidential administrations enforced civil rights in the best interests of all minorities—including Indians, whether they wanted them or not. Meanwhile, the Congress and BIA pursued efforts to de-Indianize Native Americans and to immerse them in the mainstream society. Such leadership in the federal bureaucracy, in the name of civil rights issues and assimilation, strove to strip Native American people of their heritage and prepare them for mainstream conversion under the guise of termination. The Eisenhower dream of creating an America of one people enhanced the federal policy to assimilate American Indians, but the reality was a nonreceptive mainstream that harbored prejudices against Native Americans and other minorities. Fortunately for Native Americans, Eisenhower took little time to select a replacement for Dillon Myer. Myer was controversial and had perhaps acted too hastily in pushing termination. Now, the newly-elected president wanted a man whom the Indians could trust—Glenn L. Emmons.

Senator Arthur V. Watkins of Utah (Courtesy Archives and Manuscripts, Harold B. Lee Library, Brigham Young University, Provo).

Senator Patrick A. McCarran of Nevada (Courtesy Nevada Historical Society, Reno).

Senator Richard Neuberger of Oregon (Courtesy Oregon Historical Society, Portland).

Senator Clair Engle of California (Courtesy California State Library, Sacramento).

Congresswoman Reva Beck Bosone of Utah (Courtesy Special Collections, Marriott Library, University of Utah, Salt Lake City).

Opposite, above: William Brophy, Commissioner of Indian Affairs (Courtesy Harry S. Truman Presidential Library, Independence, Missouri).

Opposite, below: Glenn L. Emmons, Commissioner of Indian Affairs (Courtesy Special Collections, Zimmerman Library, University of New Mexico, Albuquerque).

Private First Class Ira Hayes, Pima (Courtesy Special Collections, University of Wyoming Library, Laramie).

Entrance to the Menominee Reservation, Wisconsin (Author's collection, 1985).

Menominee tribal sawmill, with logs in a holding pond in the foreground (Author's collection, 1985).

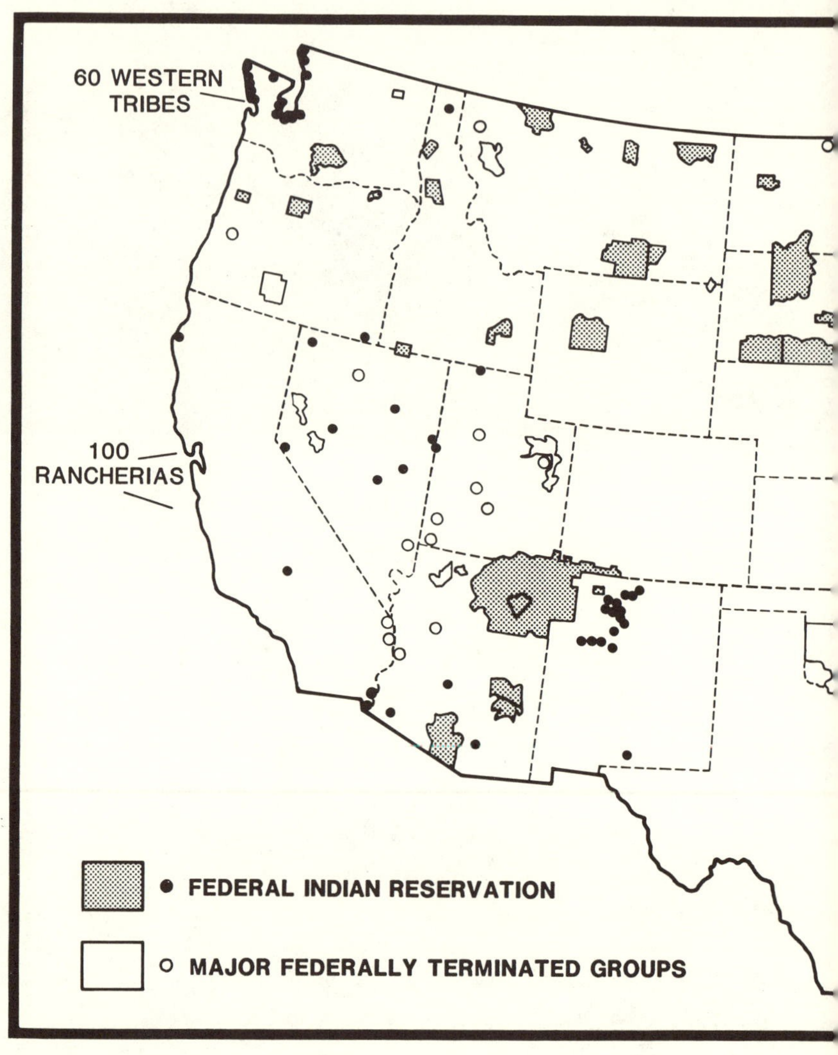

Indian Lands in the United States

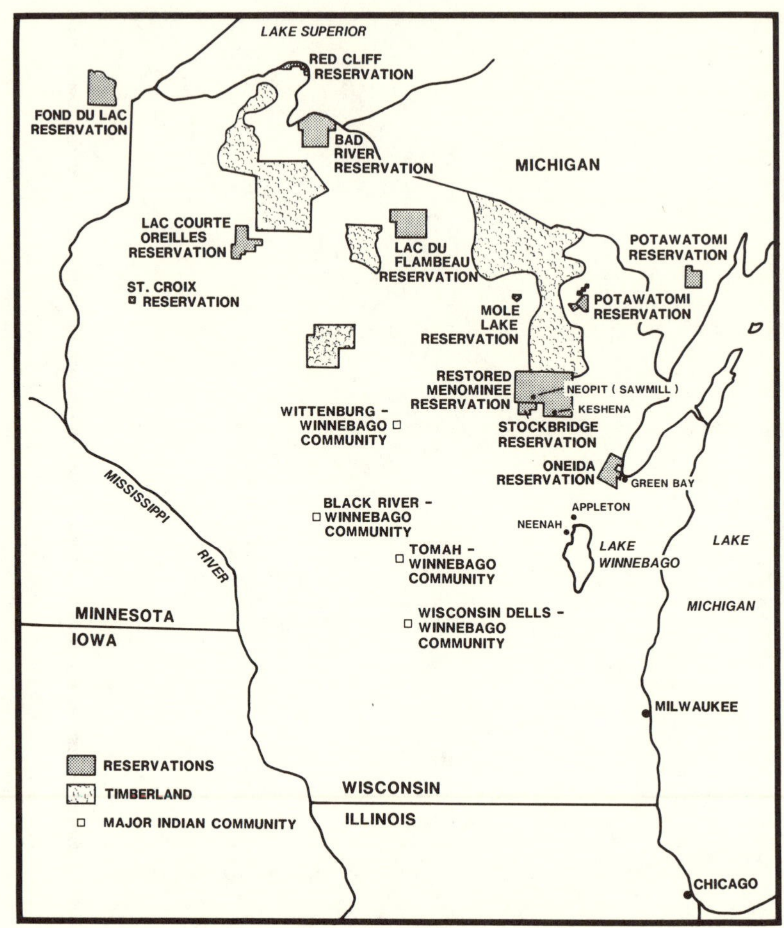

Indian Communities and Lands in Wisconsin

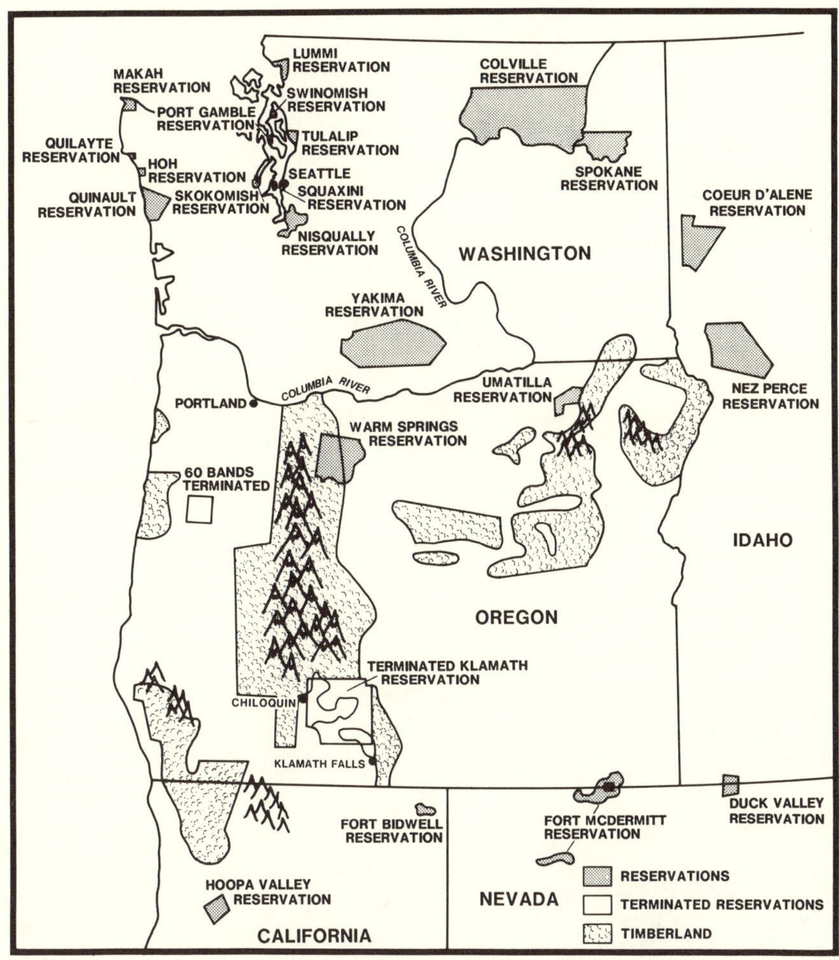

Indian Communities and Lands in the Pacific Northwest

5

House Concurrent Resolution 108 and the Eighty-third Congress

The early 1950s were trying years for Americans and the federal government. War in Korea confronted the new Eisenhower administration, and the challenge to stop the spread of communism tested the patience and support of the American people. Public loyalty was simultaneously scrutinized when a bold Wisconsin senator, Joseph R. McCarthy, accused over one hundred Americans of being communists during a chaotic period that became known as McCarthyism. Any citizen suspected of entertaining liberal ideas ran the risk of public condemnation, loss of job, and ostracization from friends and relatives. A dangerous, superfluous patriotism had gripped postwar America, spreading paranoia among the people. Suspicion bordering on hysteria fueled McCarthyism until the televised army hearings, lasting thirty-five days, ended the Red Scare in 1954.

One group, Native Americans, remained loyal without question. Again, they had served admirably on the battlefield for the United States. Indian off-reservation experiences, while serving in Korea and in World War II, had mistakenly convinced the federal government to push on with the termination of federal-Indian trust relations. Optimistic reports from the BIA on Indian progress prompted Congress to pass additional legislation affecting Indian Americans. A plethora of legislation came out during the first session of the Eighty-third Congress, which earned a degree of infamy for its passage of numerous termination bills. In theory, Native Americans had proven their capability for adopting mainstream qualities. But the real circumstances of terminating trust relations set the stage for scrutinizing the Indian ability to exchange traditional life for that of dominant middle-class values.

Federal Indian policy remained rigorously aimed at quickly

assimilating Indians into American society. While area offices worked with local Indian people, the Eighty-third Congress studied and entertained bills to integrate Indians among other people. In early January 1953, Senator Everett Dirksen of Illinois introduced a measure to establish a federal commission on civil rights and privileges. The proposed bill called for assessing the civil rights of all citizens as a means of eliminating discrimination in employment. From this point, the quest for minority equality initiated a subtle legislative trend that grew until it culminated in the civil rights legislation of the turbulent 1960s.

At the same time, Congress wanted to negate any special treatment afforded minorities, and Senate Bill 132, introduced on the same day as Dirksen's bill, proposed to transfer the administration of health services for Indians and the operation of Indian hospitals to the United States Public Health Service. The bill became law, implementing a major move in streamlining the Bureau by removing its responsibility for Indian health. Federal officials argued that Indians would be better served by more adequate facilities, thereby improving the general health status of Native Americans. The passage of the bill awakened Indians to the reality of threatening bureaucratic changes. They opposed the legislation, fearing that this would lead to the termination of remaining health services. Commissioner Myer and other federal officials who supported the legislation drew criticism from Native Americans and their supporters. On the other hand, government officials viewed Senate Bill 132 as a measure that would halt special treatment of Native Americans by enabling them to apply for regular public health services.

A later hearing before the Senate subcommittee on Indian affairs during February 1954 focused on the Indian health transfer. During the discussion, some interesting insights were revealed about Subcommittee Chairman Arthur Watkins's personal views on termination:

> Mr. Maytubby [Governor of Chickasaw Nation]: This can be on the record or off the record, but there are many qualified Indian boys and girls in Oklahoma that would make fine physicians and surgeons if they had the money to go to school and be educated.
>
> Senator Watkins: Why can they not do the same as the white man does, like my family's physician, for instance? I wanted to be a lawyer.

The Government did not come around and offer to pay my tuition and pay my board and lodging and other expenses while I went to college. I had to get out and work long, hard hours for it. I know some fellows, who had rich dads, and they did not turn out so well.[1]

Arthur V. Watkins, a sixty-six year old Republican senator from Utah, had lived most of his life in that state as a farmer, a lawyer, a devout member of the Mormon Church, and a local political figure. After winning a seat in the Senate in 1946, Watkins established a reputation as an old guard conservative of the Republican Party.

Watkins believed that everyone should achieve their goals without government assistance, regardless of circumstances. From his struggle-to-success viewpoint, he failed to understand the controlling influences of cultural values and background, which persisted in guiding the course of Indian lives as Native Americans attempted to adapt to a white American life-style. His paternal approach in negotiating with the Menominees and other native groups exemplified Republican thinking in Congress during the early Eisenhower years: Indians needed firm supervision in preparing for termination and financial independence. The senator's Mormon tradition of industry and hard work, combined with Republican ideas about free-enterprise, convinced him that Indians had it too easy. Whatever his specific reasons, the impetuous Watkins sought to eliminate federal services to Indians in order to put them on a competitive basis with other Americans.

The Republican Eighty-third Congress favored termination legislation for several Indian tribes. In early June, a busy Congress entertained a resolution that later proved to threaten all tribes with termination. Wyoming Representative William Harrison introduced House Concurrent Resolution 108 in the House of Representatives, and Senator Henry Jackson sponsored the bill in the Senate.[2] Their actions attempted to define the policy of the federal government for Indian affairs. The first part of the resolution reads as follows:

Whereas it is the policy of Congress, as rapidly as possible, to make the Indians within the territorial limits of the United States subject to the same laws and entitled to the same privileges and responsibilities as are applicable to other citizens of the United States, and to end their status as wards of the United States, and to grant them all of the rights and prerogatives pertaining to American citizenship; and

Whereas the Indians within the territorial limits of the United States should assume their full responsibilities as American citizens.[3]

Several weeks later, H.C.R. 108 was placed on the consent calendar for congressional consideration; finally, it reached the floor of the House on 27 July. This paramount piece of Indian legislation, which would establish termination policy during the 1950s, aroused little discussion. It was a great irony that legislation of this magnitude concerning Indian affairs passed without serious debate, while cloaked among a series of minor bills.[4] Korea, racial desegregation issues, and McCarthyism obscured the resolution, giving it minimal attention at best.

Congressional focus on more popular issues permitted a handful of federal officials to monopolize federal-Indian relations. On 22 June 1953, the Shawano *Journal* reported on a confrontation between the imperious Senator Watkins and Menominee leaders at Keshena, Wisconsin. Watkins, chairman of the Senate's Indian subcommittee, Commissioner Dillon Myer, and Associate Commissioner Rex Lee tried to convince the Menominees that the federal government had mismanaged their business affairs. Watkins argued that they could run their own affairs more effectively without federal intervention and that Congress would relinquish full control of their reservation, including tribal assets, plus a per capita payment of 1,500 dollars.[5]

Senator Watkins believed that the federal government should expedite the dissolution of federal trust restrictions because they impeded Indian desegregation. Earlier in February, the senator had stated in a joint hearing on Indian affairs that Native Americans were well acquainted with the American mainstream, and he criticized them for selfishness. "They want all the benefits of the things we have, highways, schools, hospitals, everything that civilization furnished," Watkins argued, "but they don't want to help pay their share of it." He added that when he had twice been chairperson of congressional committees he had "never heard of many objections by an Indian about being an American citizen except in two or three cases."[6]

In late February, Watkins met with Representative William

Harrison and Assistant Secretary Orme Lewis to plan immediate procedures for proliferating the termination of federal responsibilities to American Indians. Transferring federal services to the proper public agencies represented one method for relinquishing obligations. Other suggestions included distributing tribal land assets to individual Indians or groups. As a follow-up after the distribution of assets, rehabilitation legislation was recommended; occupational training for Native Americans would diminish long-term federal responsibilities for Indians. In short, Watkins believed termination to be a liberating opportunity for Indians, and he compared it with the Emancipation Proclamation.[7]

The Menominee tribe was viewed as a sound prospect to undergo termination. They were considered by many to be the wealthiest of all tribes. The Menominees possessed abundant timberlands, and in June 1952, the 3,059 members owned 233,902 acres in trust.[8] In the eyes of federal officials, the Menominees had already achieved financial independence, and many of their tribespeople had integrated into nearby white communities. Therefore, federal services for them appeared to be unnecessary. Watkins felt that they needed to be convinced that federal assistance was no longer applicable to them. During the Menominee General Council meeting on 20 June 1953, Senator Watkins described the progress of the Menominees after having observed the homes, farms, growing timber, and the Menominee sawmill. He was impressed with their state of progress, and he compared them favorably with small, white communities throughout the country. While persuading the Menominees that termination was best for them, the senator tried to flatter the Indians by claiming that they were "destined to take a great part in the future of this country." He assured the Menominees that they possessed the confidence and ability to take care of themselves and should demand independence because "only then can you develop as God intended you to develop."[9]

After Watkins spoke, Gordon Keshena, a Menominee, rose to his feet and gingerly addressed the issue of termination. He pointed out that the Bureau of Indian Affairs had been in business for 125 years and had controlled all Menominee tribal activities. "Everything we wanted to do, we had to go to the Bureau and ask them," said an implacable Keshena; "Can we do this? Can we do that? You cannot ask the people to go on their own and govern themselves now when for all those years they have not been permitted to do anything for themselves."[10] In spite of his statement, Keshena agreed with Watkins that his people would be able to manage their own affairs someday. But he remained convinced that removal of their trust relationship with the federal government should be a gradual process.

Watkins replied, "All you have to do is to agree now to grow up—that you are no longer children; and that you are able to look the world in the face as free Americans, and ask to be regarded as first class citizens."[11]

Watkins continued to urge the Menominees to vote for termination, and when persuasion failed, he unabashedly threatened that the tribe would receive the per capita payments *only* if they agreed to termination. Even the per capita payments were not without controversy. Assistant Secretary of the Interior Orme Lewis opposed the payment, stating that the Menominees were already financially self-sustaining. He pointed out that approximately two-thirds of the tribal members were employed in the tribal forests or in the sawmill, and the other one-third worked off the reservation.[12] Without considering the possible consequences, and perhaps unable to comprehend the effects of abrogating federal relations, the Menominees eventually succumbed to Watkins's pressure. Many Menominees voted yes, thinking that they were only voting on receiving per capita payments of 1,500 dollars. Others approved termination because they feared that the federal government would halt other services to them unless they did.[13]

While Watkins had worked to obtain Menominee approval, the termination policy was increasingly applied to other tribal groups. The Muskogee area office reported on 30 June that withdrawal programs would be implemented for the Five Civilized Tribes, certain Indians of the Quapaw Agency, the Seminoles of Florida, and the Mississippi Choctaws. In addition, withdrawal programs were being studied for the Coushattas and Chitimacha groups in Louisiana, the Cherokees on the Kenwood Reservation, and the Thlpothlocco Creek Tribe Town. BIA staff members, tribal officers, and other Indian leaders of the Muskogee area office's region would participate in the studies and present their findings to Washington for decisive action.[14]

On the same day, the Department of Interior reported that tribal groups in western Oregon and California, the Klamaths of Oregon, the Alabama-Coushattas of Texas, and the Prairie Island Band of Minnesota had approved removal of federal supervision. Next, the Interior Department planned to initiate preliminary termination programs for the Osages of Oklahoma, the Colvilles and Spokanes of Washington, the Flatheads of Montana, and the Menominees of Wisconsin. During the termination momentum, the BIA closed three Bureau hospitals. Local public school authorities took over the operations of sixteen Bureau day schools and assumed the academic work at three boarding schools, all of which affected approximately eleven hundred students.[15] These activities were superseded within a few weeks when termination officially became federal policy.

In July 1953, Congress finally approved House Concurrent Resolution 108, thereby initiating a termination policy movement in the 1950s that lasted through the early 1960s. After receiving a favorable report from the Indian affairs subcommittee and the Interior committee, the resolution moved easily through the channels of Congress.

On the first day of August, Congress adopted House Resolution 108 as a routine order of business. Although the measure was not enforceable as law, it expressed congressional approval for the federal government to redefine imperative, fundamental changes in the Indian policy.

The resolution included removal of federal supervision and the dissolution of BIA control over certain tribes located in California, Florida, New York, and Texas. The termination resolution specifically listed the Flathead Tribe of Montana, the Klamaths of Oregon, the Menominees of Wisconsin, the Potawatomis of Kansas and Nebraska, and the Chippewas located on the Turtle Mountain Reservation in North Dakota. In addition, federal offices of the BIA serving Indians in California, Florida, New York, and Texas were to be abolished. The resolution also authorized the Secretary of Interior to examine existing legislation affecting these Indian groups and review their treaties with the United States government. A follow-up report was expected, with recommendations made, no later than 1 January 1954.[16]

The Department of Interior gave whole-hearted support to

H.C.R. 108. Secretary of Interior Douglas McKay and Assistant Secretary Orme Lewis believed that trust termination of certain already semi-independent tribes would reduce federal paternalism; but opponents of the resolution argued that increased federal assistance required to prepare tribes for termination would actually result in more paternalism.[17]

Some of the more dependent Indian groups objected, but they lacked legal expertise and congressional influence, making them easy targets for termination. Instantaneously, Congress approved additional legislation to abolish federal recognition of more tribes, and called for transferring a portion of government responsibilities and services to the states.[18] Overtly, freeing tribal groups of their federal trust restrictions was the official intent of the termination policy. More importantly, however, termination essentially implied the ultimate destruction of tribal cultures and native life-styles, as withdrawal of federal services was intended to desegregate Indian communities and to integrate Indians with the rest of society.

Some Native Americans, however, personally desired the withdrawal of federal supervision and trust restrictions, claiming that wardship had hindered their individual progress in business and that they desired to live as non-Indians. Trust status as a protective device, they complained, had prevented them from selling portions of their lands to raise capital for investing and developing the remainder of their holdings. These nontraditionalists disliked being wards even more, simply because they resented federal officials directing their lives. But in deciding to accept termination of trust relations, each tribe, like the role-model Menominees, encountered varying degrees of intertribal factionalism. Unfortunately, termination was blanket legislation that did not account for varying degrees of "readiness" among individual tribal members. Equally important, termination created new factionalism or deepened existing factionalism.

In July, after several official meetings and numerous informal discussions, the Menominee Advisory Council approved a tribal resolution calling for termination and asked Congressman Melvin Laird of Wisconsin to introduce a bill requesting withdrawal of federal supervision over the tribe. The results of the voting on the resolution indicated 197 Menominees favoring termination and none opposed.[19] Since many did not fully comprehend English, some confusion occurred later about what the termination resolution actually entailed. Many of these people were elders who would likely suffer financial consequences when the termination of trust protection over their properties left them vulnerable to exploitation and mismanagement. Overall, the Menominee rank and file began to fear termination and felt threatened by the possible ramifications of federal withdrawal. While speaking during a General Council meeting, which Senator Watkins attended, tribal member John Folsum angrily asserted that the government exploited Menominee people as guinea pigs for the termination program: "I do not think you yourself would like to see half of these people die of starvation."[20]

House Concurrent Resolution 108 and complementary legislation proposed to set a new direction in federal-Indian policy by liquidating program applications made under the Indian Reorganization Act of 1934, such as the abrogation of tribal constitutions and the abolition of Indian corporations. More importantly, the measures threatened treaties that had been fundamental to tribal rights for many decades. While the Republican Congress declared that it assisted Indians and improved their livelihood, Indians became increasingly convinced that the federal government "was out to get them." A cursory check of the record reveals government intent to assist Native Americans, but there was only minute success in Americanizing Indian people.

Originally, H.C.R. 108 singled out thirteen tribes for withdrawal of trust status, but Congress initiated termination procedures for only six groups. One concerned BIA official admitted the Bureau knew very well that H.C.R. 108 shocked Indians across the nation, and he hoped Congress would not enact any more termination legislation until it had studied what had happened to the six.[21]

Two weeks after adopting H.C.R. 108, Congress contemplated passing another termination measure, House Resolution 1063. This proposal endorsed the extension of state jurisdiction over Indian reservations. Red Lake Reservation of Minnesota and Warm Springs Reservation in Oregon were to be exempted.[22] The new resolution would authorize any state to amend its constitution to assume both civil and criminal jurisdiction over Indian country within the state, thus laying the groundwork for

Public Law 280. Strong protests from all Indian groups and organizations arose because the proposal did not provide for "consultation" with Indians or "consent" from Indians whose reservations would be placed under state jurisdiction. Anger at this possibility, and especially with H.C.R. 108, was prevalent throughout Indian country.

An irate reaction came from the Chippewas of Turtle Mountain Reservation in North Dakota, who vehemently opposed House Concurrent Resolution 108 and took action. During October 1953, eleven Chippewas signed a petition and sent it to the House of Representatives, the Senate, and the Secretary of the Interior. They petitioned Congress to refrain from enacting any legislation for liberating the Chippewas from federal supervision and control. If federal ties were severed, the Chippewas believed that untold distress and suffering among their people, as well as substantial economic damage, would occur.[23]

Although the Turtle Mountain Indians adamantly opposed termination, they failed to escape its grasp. Several months after the legislation was passed to abrogate their trust relationship with the United States government, a Chippewa woman of the Turtle Mountain Reservation pleaded, "We can't make it without the Federal Government, a few of us have made it maybe, but not whole tribes."[24] Obviously, termination was carried out regardless of whether some tribes and their members were prepared for it, especially affecting those people who could not stop their tribes from being listed for liquidation of federal-tribal trust relations.

Terminationists like Senator Arthur Watkins and Congressman E. Y. Berry of South Dakota displayed little patience in dealing with Indian objections. At one time, Watkins had asserted that Indian treaty rights obstructed the federal government's plenary power in handling Native American affairs because of the country's prevailing recognition of international law, which was the basis of Indian treaty rights. On various occasions, Watkins tried to discount the legal weight of the treaties. During a speech, he informed an Indian group that they were American citizens now and the United States did not enter into treaties with any of its citizens. He found firm support from Congressman Berry, who attended more hearings on Indian affairs than any other member. "Indians are just like white people," said Berry. "They do not advance unless they do the advancing themselves, and you do not advance unless you try, do you?"[25]

Despite the movement to reduce expensive Indian services and the efforts to decentralize the Bureau of Indian Affairs, the president's budget message for fiscal year 1954 called for increased expenditures in services to Native Americans. The budget included funding to provide essential improvements pertaining to hospitals and schools and to increase employment services for the estimated 400,000 American Indian population. One recommended program, which was later funded, would provide Native Americans with training for employment in industry and agriculture, and help Indians make adjustments after relocating to urban areas.[26]

Early January 1954 marked the climax of the termination years when a deluge of termination bills, affecting many tribal groups, flooded Congress. Assistant Interior Secretary Orme Lewis submitted drafts of three bills to President Eisenhower on January 4, with his recommendation for the termination of several tribes. House Resolution 8365, which was approved during cloture in Congress, called for the issuance of fee patents for properties of Indian tribes, bands, and groups in California, plus the end of federal supervision over their properties. Another bill proposed termination of federal supervision over the property of the Confederated Salish and Kootenai Tribes of the Montana Flathead Reservation. Of the 4,213 reservation members, nine-tenths of the Flathead families were considered fully self-supporting, and this fact deemed federal supervision of them no longer necessary. The third bill recommended termination of federal supervision over the property of the Florida Seminoles. Without reason, the Seminoles were listed for termination although the majority of the 870 members were inexperienced in handling their own business affairs and lived under extreme substandard living conditions.[27]

Four other Indian groups—the Sac and Fox in Kansas and Nebraska, the Iowa of Kansas and Nebraska, and the Kickapoo and Prairie Island Band of the Potawatomi of Kansas—were listed in another proposed termination bill. Of the 2,415 members from the four tribes, 600 did not work while the rest lived in nearby towns or on small farms. Although they were considered self-supporting, the bill failed to pass.[28]

Two related bills passed into law, affecting approximately 2,100 members of certain tribes and bands of Indians located in Western Oregon. Public Law 588 terminated federal supervision over the Indians' property, and Public Law 715 authorized the preparation of tribal rolls for the distribution of tribal assets to members.[29] The Indians would receive per capita distribution of funds from claim settlements, which theoretically would make them economically self-sufficient. In all, sixty Indian groups of Western Oregon were slated for termination.

Passage of another measure, Senate Bill 2745 into Public Law 587, terminated federal supervision over the property of the Klamath Tribe, which also included the Modocs and the Yahooskin Band of Snake Indians. The law released all tribal properties from federal trust status. A large portion of the trust property contained rich timberland, consisting of some 590,000 acres capable of producing 3.8 billion board feet of commercial lumber. Klamath landowners would undoubtedly be prime targets for opportunists when the tribes' trust relation was terminated. In preparation for removal of trust restrictions, P. L. 587 allowed the Klamath Tribe a period of six months to compile a tribal roll of its members. Tribal property would then be distributed to enrolled members only.

The impending termination of the Klamaths disturbed the Association on American Indian Affairs (AAIA), who adamantly opposed all termination bills introduced in Congress. However, Oliver La Farge, the association's president, cautioned against automatically rejecting all such termination measures. He warned that opposition should be carefully considered first, if it was to be valid and if they hoped to gain public support to thwart termination. Dr. Alexander Lesser, AAIA executive director, wrote to Professor Philleo Nash, an expert on Indians and later BIA commissioner, stating that while some tribes appeared ready for withdrawal of trust relations others like the Florida Seminoles, the Turtle Mountain Chippewas, and certain California groups were definitely not ready. He argued that termination of trust would not seriously improve the welfare and progress of these groups.[30]

A BIA inspection of Indian country revealed that Indians had not progressed significantly since Commissioner Brophy's tour after World War II and the investigation conducted by the Hoover Task Force. For a short while, the Bureau's report slowed the flow of termination bills, and officials became more concerned with ameliorating the economic state of the Indian populace, especially when criticism from tribes and watchful Indian supporters grew heavier. At the Muskogee area office in Oklahoma, Bureau officials reported to principal Indian spokespersons that House Resolution 1381 had been introduced in Congress to promote rehabilitation of the Five Civilized Tribes and other Eastern Oklahoma Indians.[31] Reportedly, the government began to make similar efforts to assist other tribes through federally funded programs.

Although the effort to assist Native Americans appeared to be sincere, some people questioned the true motive behind rehabilitation actions. Opponents of termination believed federal officials would temporarily placate Indians, but would soon end trust relations with the tribes before they were ready. In mid-February, John Collier, president of the Institute of Ethnic Affairs, presented a speech on "Terminating the American Indian." He warned Native Americans, friends of Indian rights, and citizens concerned with national honor that the Eighty-third Congress was entertaining ten bills to liquidate tribes of their trust status without their consent; and this, he declared, violated Indian rights.[32]

Under public scrutiny, the Bureau of Indian Affairs worked out a program for every tribe listed for termination. Each tribe had two options for disposing tribal properties: (1) to organize into a corporation for continued management under a trustee of their choice, or (2) to sell all properties and assets with the proceeds to be distributed among tribal members. If a tribe failed to exercise either option, the Secretary of the Interior had authority to transfer titles of properties to a trustee of his choice, who would then assume temporary ownership for liquidation purposes. Furthermore, the government mandated that certain procedures be followed for the withdrawal of federal supervision. First, tribal rolls were updated and submitted to the Department of the Interior for publication. The Secretary of the Interior would then review the rolls, but no changes would be implemented. Once termination of the federal-tribal trust relationship occurred, enrollment entitled tribal members to tribal assets. Enrolled Indians would also receive fee patents to their individually owned trust properties. If any individuals remained unable to manage their own affairs after termination, the Secretary of the Interior would protect their rights. Ordinarily, the tribes had two to five years for completing termination programs, but this time period varied, depending on problems that had to be resolved.

One complex case involved eight tribes in northeastern Oklahoma who owned no substantial tribal lands. In fact, members of the Eastern Shawnee, Miami, Modoc, Ottawa, Peoria, Quapaw, Seneca-Cayuga and Wyandot tribes owned few individual properties in trust. Preparation of final tribal rolls were necessary, however, for the distribution of personal assets, including cash and tribal lands held in trust in other states. These tribes, small in population and already integrated into local communities, willingly prepared for termination. Members of the eight tribes presumably believed that wardship status impeded their livelihoods and they would benefit from abrogation of trust status. If the tribes had opposed withdrawal of trust relations, it is likely that they would not have been influential enough to effectively resist it. Their lack of large populations, funds, and legal expertise, as well as the absence of support from powerful friends, especially in Congress, made them prime candidates for termination.[33]

One of the eight tribes, the Quapaws, requested an investigation into the proposed discontinuance of the Quapaw field office. For years the small office had served their people and other tribes in northeastern Oklahoma, an area congested with tribes from the old Northwest Territory who remained unrelated culturally and politically separate from the Five Civilized Tribes and Plains groups in Oklahoma. The BIA assured the Quapaws that no proposal existed to close the field office, but that limited funding had forced the BIA to reduce staff and maintenance offices throughout the country. Furthermore, the Department of Interior mandated that tribes and Indian groups would be terminated soon and that Native Americans should be preparing to assume complete management of their own affairs. The Interior Department drafted several bills that were "discussed fully with the affected Indian people and modified in accordance with their suggestions," before submitting them to Congress.[34]

The final preparation and closing of a tribal roll concerned the Quapaws, who called a meeting with Bureau officials in Muskogee to discuss the matter. Over the years the tribe had maintained open membership—until now. Three years earlier, the United States Court of Claims had approved a claims settlement for the Quapaw, but members, by blood, did not want new "adopted" members to share in any per capita distribution. Walter King, Jr., chairman of the Quapaw Business Committee, reported that the tribe wanted to close the roll, limiting distribution of settlement money to an estimated 757 members.[35]

Tribes like the Quapaw, whose successful and respected citizens were impeded by trust restrictions, complicated efforts to reach a workable Indian policy that would include them as well as those members who were against termination. While most of the tribes were not prepared for termination, several progressive groups spoke out in favor of lifting trust restrictions. Dissolving trust relations remained a difficult issue for all those interested in Indian affairs, especially for federal officials.

Sometimes they disagreed. Florida Senator George Smathers and Senator Arthur Watkins, for example, debated the topic, "Should The American Indian Be Given Full Citizenship Responsibility," on Dumont Television, a Washington station. Watkins, chairman of the Indian subcommittee of the Senate's Insular and Interior Affairs Committee, supported termination. Senator Smathers, a member of the Insular Affairs Committee, had originally supported House Concurrent Resolution 108, but later reversed himself after becoming familiar with the problems of termination and the poor living conditions in Indian communities.[36]

The debate climaxed when Senator Watkins declared, "May I point out also that what the Indian really wants; he wants representation without taxation. He can tax all the rest of us and vote for people who do tax us; but he doesn't want to pay taxes himself even though he is able to do so."[37] Smathers retorted, "Now I wouldn't go that far because every Indian that leaves the reservation and goes out and lives like the rest of us live, he is paying his fair share of taxes; he's in the service; he's doing everything everyone else is doing."[38]

Senator Smathers sympathized with Native Americans for he believed they lacked the capability to take advantage of the federal government and did not yet have the capacity to live successfully among other Americans. In contrast, Senator Watkins held the view of many who sincerely believed that termination would abrogate legal discrimination against Native Americans. Trust status deprived Indian people of full citizenship rights, and therefore should be liquidated.

During the first two years of the Eisenhower administration, Indian affairs received considerable congressional attention, but a handful of members monopolized Indian affairs in the House and Senate. According to a memorandum written by recently appointed Commissioner Glenn L. Emmons and dated 24 September 1954, the Eighty-third Congress introduced 288 public bills and resolutions on Indian affairs and 46 were to be enacted into law. In addition, the Bureau of Indian Affairs submitted 162 reports on Indian affairs to committees in Congress.[39] In the history of federal-Indian relations, the Eighty-third Congress probably dealt with more legislation on Indian affairs than any other Congress.

According to Sherman Adams, Eisenhower's assistant, the policy of the president stipulated that the Interior Department would consult with Indians during drafting of legislation and incorporate their ideas when there was agreement. Disagreements were also to be reported to Congress.[40] Adams stressed that the BIA would try very hard to cooperate with both Congress and the tribes in preparing the Indians for independence.

In January 1955, Congressman Ed Edmondson of Oklahoma introduced House Resolution 1563 during the first session of the Eighty-fourth Congress. Edmondson's bill proposed to extend time for cases to be presented before the Indian Claims Commission.[41] The bill would provide tribes with further opportunities to prepare claims against the United States, and it would afford the federal government with more time to finalize its compensatory treaty obligations regarding Indian lands. Such compensation would provide tribes with a monetary base to invest in business ventures or to provide loans to members. With the claims awards, the government would end forever their treaty obligations to the Indian groups.

Concerned citizens felt that the government was abandoning tribes who were still in critical need of assistance. One person wrote to President Eisenhower to say that the federal government should not ignore the necessary needs of Native Americans. Press Secretary James C. Hagerty answered that the president was well aware of the plight of Native Americans: "You may be sure that the President, through the Bureau of Indian Affairs, will do all that it is possible to do to improve the status of the American Indian."[42] Expressed intent did not solve substandard living conditions soon enough on reservations where inadequate living conditions fostered diseases among communities.

Health remained a critical area for reform among Native Americans. To improve health treatment, the federal government sought to provide more able services. House Resolution 303, passed during the Eighty-third Congress, was the basis for P.L. 568, which authorized the transfer of Indian health facilities and services to the Public Health Service. BIA Commissioner Glenn Emmons, Minnesota Senator Hubert Humphrey, and other federal officials believed that the transfer would provide Native Americans with better health care.[43] However, the statistics for the next ten years did not substantiate this belief. Health records indicated that high disease and fatality rates persisted among Native Americans. Hepatitis cases were eight times greater among Indians than any other American ethnic group. Indians were three times as likely to die of pneumonia and influenza as non-Indians. Infant mortality, tuberculosis, and alcoholism rates among the Indian communities were higher than among all segments of the population. To compound this dismal situation, Native Americans had a life expectancy of forty-four years, compared with seventy years for white Americans.[44]

In a news conference held on 25 January 1956, President Eisenhower promised that the Public Health Service would construct and maintain urgently needed sanitation facilities to improve health conditions among the Indian population. As health services and other benefits became available to more Native Americans, a most startling question was raised concerning the administering of federal services: "Who is an Indian?" Eligibility to receive federal services and benefits was a question that concerned both the federal government and the tribes.

The desire to make tribes more independent and self-reliant upon their immediate resources captivated federal officials and inspired Senator Joseph C. O'Mahoney of Wyoming to sponsor House Resolution 5566, which would terminate the Indian

Claims Commission. Theoretically, tribes would then begin developing their resources rather than waiting in line for claim settlements. The bill proposed to abrogate the commission after five years, on 10 April 1957, or sooner if its final report was submitted before that date. Some speculation regarding the motive behind the O'Mahoney bill suggested that the Republican Congress wanted to avoid further expenditures on Indian settlements.[45] As more tribes won cases, the cost alone of the Indian Claims Commission began to spiral astronomically into millions of dollars.

The issue of termination became more complicated when individual tribal members sought an end to trust status, even though their tribal governments were not ready to assume full responsibility for all the tribe's members. In one instance, some members of the Oklahoma Peorias requested that individual legislative bills be introduced in Congress to terminate federal trust restrictions over their personal properties.[46] Ordinarily, a tribe's trust relationship with the federal government was initially terminated while most members remained inadequately prepared to supervise their own affairs.

Unyielding traditionalism among Indians impeded the implementation of the termination policy. Diverse tribal and cultural backgrounds affected how quickly Indian citizens became prepared for assuming full control over their assets. Meticulous evaluations of cultural influences were needed to determine each tribe's situation. Supposedly, federal officials paid particular attention to the tribe's human and natural resources, limitations, preparedness, and management abilities in determining the feasibility of tribal success after termination. The government slowly continued to dissolve trust relations. For those tribes who voluntarily wanted termination, the wheels of government moved slowly toward dissolving trust relations. Officially, the Bureau of Indian Affairs opposed "wholesale" termination of federal responsibility to Indians. The Bureau also objected adamantly to Senate Bill 401, a measure calling for the disposition of all tribal lands and the repeal of the Indian Reorganization Act. Commissioner Emmons stated: "I firmly believe that its enactment would be not only a tragic error but a flat repudiation of our basic principles of fair and honorable dealings. I am opposed to it completely and utterly."[47]

The federal termination policy led to considerable changes in government services to Native Americans. A letter, dated 1 August 1956, from the new Secretary of the Interior, Fred A. Seaton, to Editor Walter Christenson of the Omaha *World-Herald* explained the wide-reaching goals of the termination policy. Seaton stated that he had supported the termination legislation in 1954 regarding the withdrawal of trust status from six Indian groups. In addition, he thought that the transfer of the Indian Health program to Public Health, via P.L. 568, and the transfer of the Agricultural Extension program to states would help Native Americans become more independent. According to Secretary Seaton, these moves would make more services available to Indians.[48]

Like his predecessor, former Secretary Douglas McKay, Seaton believed that the solution for getting the government out of the Indian business was to improve the economy of Indian people, so that they would no longer require federal assistance. He stressed the development of mineral resources, such as oil and gas, and increased timber sales to attract industry to reservation areas. Secretary Seaton believed that too much federal involvement in Indian affairs existed; and this became apparent when he wrote that the number of Bureau employees had been reduced from thirteen thousand to ten thousand, a ratio of one official to every forty-three Indians, including Alaska Natives—and this, he exclaimed, was "still too damn many bureaucrats!"[49]

Opponents of termination accused congressional supporters, who promoted the legislation, of exploiting the issue for political gains, especially since the 1956 presidential election was fast approaching. The same critics also alleged that their colleagues exploited Indians for votes and political favors by making their lands and natural resources available to non-Indian constituents. Aside from the politicking, using Native Americans as pawns for political gain raised highbrow criticism from neutral congressional members. Idaho Senator Frank Church bombastically stated, "It is exceedingly disturbing that the exploitation policy is being carried forward in the name of our tradition of liberty and freedom."[50]

The early years of Eisenhower represented a period of loyal conformity to the norms established by post–World War II standards. The government emphasized national defense, social security, and public works to secure a middle class. Federal Indian policy, although not a major national concern, received serious attention. Dillon S. Myer was instrumental in "liberating" Indian Americans through the termination of federal supervision, and he reestablished a policy legacy that the next commissioner, Glenn Emmons, carried on to assimilate Indians into the mainstream society. Bureaucrats were prone to believe that H.C.R. 108 would serve as the official legislative blueprint for integrating Indian Americans, but they were blinded to the realism of the Indian's almost instinctive rejection of mainstream norms.

The height of termination occurred during the 1953–54 span of the Eighty-third Congress, a period of considerable controversy when charges were levied against those officials whom the Eisenhower administration depended upon as its Indian experts. Key figures in the Republican Congress who promoted termination were sharply criticized for exploiting the red man's already impoverished conditions. Despite all the controversies and the conflicting reports on Indian progress, the Congress rapidly passed legislation as the federal government continued its attempt "to get out of the Indian business."

6

Public Law 280 and State Interests Versus Indian Rights

Beginning with the passage of P.L. 280, Native Americans witnessed a trend of transferring federal responsibilities for Indian affairs to state governments. The law was a reform measure that called for liberating the tribes from federal trust dependence and placing them under state jurisdiction. Impetus for the act came from two sources. In the midst of decentralizing federal-Indian relations, the dispersal of power in the Bureau of Indian Affairs affected both Native Americans and the states. Termination of federal services meant that BIA responsibilities had to be assumed by the tribes or by the affected states. In addition, local problems on reservations, including criminal acts, created conflicts over jurisdiction, especially if both Indians and non-Indians were involved in a matter that mandated a quick solution.[1] The transfer of BIA responsibilities to states also created problems. Reservations containing rich timberlands, particularly those of the Menominee of Wisconsin and the Klamath of Oregon, became targets of local criticism and the victims of limited state budgets. Tribes without abundant natural resources, as well as smaller tribes, suffered both federal neglect and state domination. Native groups were finding themselves vulnerable to state supervision and local opportunists.

Persistent lobbying from the BIA and congressional members urged President Eisenhower to approve P.L. 280. Originally introduced in the House as H.R. 1063, the bill found support from the beginning. Minnesota Senator Edward J. Thye argued that approval of H.R. 1063 was vital if Indian people were to become full-fledged citizens.[2] Others concurred, like Senator Hugh Butler, who personally telegraphed the White House on 15 August 1953 to encourage the president to sign the bill into law. With reluctance, President Eisenhower signed the bill into law on 15

August 1953. Ike stated: "Although I have grave doubts as to the wisdom of certain provisions in H.R. 1063, I have today signed it because its basic purpose represents still another step in granting equality to all Indians in our nation."[3] In response to Butler's telegram, Eisenhower expressed hope that Congress would amend the new law during its next session to require consultation with the Indians prior to the application of state jurisdiction.[4] Seven bills were introduced in the Eighty-fourth and Eighty-fifth Congresses requesting such amendments, but all failed passage.

Public Law 280 authorized the states of California, Nebraska, Minnesota (except for Red Lake Reservation), Oregon (except for Warm Springs Reservation), and Wisconsin (except for Menominee Reservation) to exercise civil and criminal jurisdiction over all Indian lands within their boundaries. It was assumed that other states would receive the same authorization to regulate Indian affairs. The law was expected to contribute to the decentralization of the Bureau of Indian Affairs, but the tenacious legacy of federal-Indian relations seemed insurmountable. In addition to assuming civil and criminal jurisdiction over Indian country, the law authorized the states to supply government services to Native Americans. Frequently, state officials objected strongly to the increased burden of handling numerous responsibilities. States often lacked the expertise to deal with the complexities of Indian affairs, and they wished to avoid them. Moreover, tight budgets could not accommodate the additional costs of providing services to Indian citizens.

The enormity of the responsibilities that could be transferred to the states after dismantling the BIA overwhelmed state governments. In an attempt to resolve the pressing problems, Interior Secretary Douglas McKay announced the undertaking of a survey to study the organization of the BIA and its operations, and to recommend changes to ease the federal withdrawal from Indian services. Members of the survey team included Chairman Walter Bimson, chairman of the Valley National Bank of Phoenix, Arizona; Robert D. Lutton of the Santa Fe Railroad of Chicago; and J. R. Johns of Sears, Roebuck and Company of Dallas, Texas. George W. Abbott, counsel of the House Committee on Interior and Insular Affairs, served as the outside member of the group.[5]

The team recommended decentralization and consolidation of the Bureau of Indian Affairs in Washington through a reduction in its functions and its personnel. A significant portion of the Bureau's authority would be transferred to area offices for consolidation. Suggested plans included reorganizing the area offices in Window Rock, Arizona, and in Albuquerque, New Mexico, as one southwestern unit, and consolidating the two area offices in Oklahoma at Muskogee and Anadarko. Such moves entailed a reduction of staff technicians in area offices and a transfer of essential personnel to the newly reorganized offices.

The survey team submitted its report on 26 January 1954 to the Committee on Interior and Insular Affairs. The report advised the establishment of a legal definition of who was "Indian" so as to limit the number of applicants for services. But government officials were unable to come up with an acceptable definition. With a clarification of who was Indian, the government possibly could have shaped policy to suit the wishes of the Native American citizenry. Instead, the Indian Bureau opted to incorporate restrictive guidelines that disallowed so-called competent Indians from receiving special government services designated for disadvantaged Indians.[6]

Soon after the government took action to reduce the number of Native Americans eligible for services, a series of termination measures followed, seeking to implement the goals of H.C.R. 108. In April 1954, the Muskogee area office sent a memorandum to Indian leaders concerning an omnibus bill introduced in the U.S. Senate to promote a wide range of termination actions. Senate Bill 2515 proposed to eliminate the functions of the BIA by abolishing both guardianship over Indians and trusteeship over their lands and repealing the Indian Reorganization Act of 1934. Lastly, the measure called for the dissolution of the Bureau of Indian Affairs three years after the bill's enactment into law. If the bill had passed into law, approximately 73,400 Indians in eleven states would have been affected, involving 2,938,000 acres of land.[7]

In a letter to Alexander Lesser, executive director of the Association on American Indian Affairs, Oliver La Farge criticized the general direction of government actions on Indian affairs. He addressed the unpreparedness of California tribes and the effect that the government's reckless abandonment of Indian responsibilities would have on them. As case examples, the well-known Indian reformer pointed out that the Pitt River Tribe and the Yuma Indians opposed termination of their trust relations and noted that the Yuma were particularly unprepared for removal of trust restrictions. La Farge believed that mixed-bloods might withstand federal withdrawal, but that full-blood members would be unable to overcome the difficult adjustment period after having been so long under the government's paternalism. Indians who favored termination were likely to be enticed to sever ties with the federal government in order to receive sale proceeds from valuable timber or other property. The Palm Spring Indians owned similar valuable real estate in California, and La Farge alleged that they too were being manipulated for exploitation. The outspoken antiterminationist worried that removal of trust restrictions would create fraudulent opportunities for exploiting the red man, such as the travesties which had occurred during the allotment era of the late 1800s and early 1900s.[8] This possibility soon became a reality with the early termination of the Menominees.

In June 1954, President Eisenhower signed the Menominee Termination Bill, one of the first bills to deny a tribe its federal trust relationship. At this point, James Hagerty, presidential press secretary, issued a news release announcing Eisenhower's approval of the termination of federal supervision over the properties and affairs of the tribe, effective 31 December 1958. The president congratulated the Menominees for beginning a new era of freedom from governmental interference: "I extend my warmest commendations to the members of the tribe for the impressive progress they have achieved and for the cooperation they have given the Congress in the development of legislation." He added that the Menominees would have the assistance of the Department of the Interior and the state of Wisconsin in preparing for "full and final independence."[9]

Somewhat ironically, the Menominees opposed the termination move after earlier voting to accept it, but they found that it was too late to turn the tide of bureaucratic momentum. Setting precedent, the Menominees had taken the first plunge into the mainstream as a liberated group without federal tribal recognition. During the crucial moment of decision, the Bureau of Indian Affairs failed to provide requested assistance to the Menominees. The Shawano *Evening Leader* reported that the Bureau denied pertinent information to the Menominees, forcing them to appeal to Wisconsin state officials for advice. As a result, the Menominees had to accept a four-year period to establish their new government before the deadline for termination. Menominee leaders tried four times to consult with Bureau officials and were turned down each time.

While working to meet the deadlines, Menominees found it difficult and puzzling to adjust to Wisconsin state laws and to the pressure to make immediate decisions without the customary supervision from the federal government. The problems involved in setting up municipalities, especially at Keshena and Neopit, the main settlements on the reservation, increased their anxieties. They had to establish a tax system, provide law and order; decide whether to integrate the reservation with Shawano and Oconto counties, or become a separate county; and sell their vast timber and lumbering assets. They were unfamiliar with Wisconsin laws, and the state could be of only limited assistance since the tribe was still controlled by federal red tape until December 1958. For the present, their status and livelihood, which depended upon rich timberland, hung in abeyance. After having endured a century under the paternal wing of the federal government, unaccustomed liberation left the Menominees in a precarious, vulnerable position.[10]

Federal officials identified Menominee reluctance to embrace termination as procrastination, which unfortunately had to be tolerated. On 11 July 1957, in letters sent to Senator James Murray, chairman of the Senate Committee on Interior and Insular Affairs, and to Congressman Clair Engle, chairman of the House Committee of Interior and Insular Affairs, the Department of the Interior charged the Menominees with deliberately delaying action on termination. The Indians protested that they needed more time to prepare for the final liquidation of their trust relationship with the federal government and for what they considered to be a Pandoran future with no safety guarantees. Consequently, S. 2131 moved the termination date to 31 December 1959, which was extended again to 31 December 1960.[11]

Assistant Interior Secretary Roger D'Ewart argued that excessive time and money was being consumed. Furthermore, the Menominee adult educational program cost the federal government 250,000 dollars per year, and the final dollar figure was still not ascertained. To make matters worse, D'Ewart noted, the government had erred in assuming the total cost for Menominee termination, especially since the Indians had originally agreed to share in the expenditure. Naturally, the Wisconsin natives countered that their people required additional time to prepare for complete withdrawal from federal supervision. The tribespeople complained that they had been forcibly persuaded to accept termination, and now they could do little except delay its application. Hence, procrastination became their most effective strategy.

In December 1957, the Menominees and Wisconsin state officials requested deferment of Menominee termination to 30 June 1961. Additional time and money were needed specifically for tribal planning, for studying state legislation regarding county organization, and for finding ways to pay estimated taxes on the Menominee forest land.[12] Their request caused disagreement in the House and the Senate over the amount of reimbursement to the Menominees, with no immediate solution in sight. This further complicated the tribe's situation, and Senator William Proxmire, who became frustrated with the whole affair, sought a repeal of the entire Menominee Termination Act.

The Menominees' difficulties did not deter federal officials from undertaking termination procedures for the Klamaths, the second major target for ending trust responsibilities. Oliver La Farge alleged that the tactic of withholding money was also used to force the Klamaths to accept termination of trust relations.[13] On 10 August 1954, Assistant Interior Secretary Lewis officially recommended the liquidation of federal responsibility to the Klamath Tribe in Oregon. Lewis noted that the native group had attained sufficient skills and abilities to manage their own affairs without special federal assistance; this, he claimed, justified their termination.[14] On the same day, Deputy Attorney General William Rogers wrote to Rowland Hughes, director of the Bureau of the Budget, to declare that in addition to the Klamaths there were sixty small Indian bands, tribes, and groups in Western Oregon that could undergo federal withdrawal.[15] Economically, the government deemed that these groups and the Klamaths were self-sustaining, and especially the Klamaths since they were generating an annual gross income of about 2 million dollars from tribal timber. Only 10 percent of the Klamath families depended on welfare assistance. Such data was utilized to convince congressional members, and even the president, that the Klamaths no longer required federal assistance. Two days later, Roger Jones, assistant director for Legislative Reference of the Budget Bureau, informed President Eisenhower that his office supported Senate Bills 2745 and 2746 to terminate the Klamaths and other groups in Oregon.[16]

Forest conservationists argued that termination of federal-tribal trust would result in the transfer of Indian properties to white capitalists. The rich timberlands of the Menominees, as well as those of the Klamaths in Oregon, invited uncontrolled cutting that would damage the natural environments of the two states. For decades the BIA had maintained sustained yield cuttings, but after termination there would no longer be a need for such control. Harold B. Anthony, deputy director of the American Museum of Natural History, warned that the Klamath Reservation involved a considerable stake in wildlife conservation. The natural habitat for wildlife would be destroyed, and the birds and animals would have to seek other refuge. He warned that such potential dangers would arouse conservationists, who would threaten action.[17] Conservationist groups recommended that Indians be trained in sound forest management as a part of the preparation procedure for termination.[18]

The Klamaths, however, encountered difficulty with determining their tribal membership. Several times the tribal roll was closed and reopened after people had traveled long distances to plead their cases for enrollment. At one point, 80 names were stricken from the roll and 270 new enrollees were added before it was finally closed. Estimates of tribal assets ranged from 60 million dollars up to 100 million dollars, leading to speculation that each enrolled Klamath would receive from 25,000 to 45,000 dollars.[19] To help the Klamaths, the government placed the tribe under the supervision of three local private-management specialists—Thomas Watters, William Phillips, and Eugene Favell—who supervised property appraisals and managed the tribe's business affairs.[20]

Although the Bureau of Indian Affairs claimed that local public services would benefit Indians, their overall conditions did not improve. Religious organizations were quick to criticize the government for not doing enough. A June 1955 editorial in *The Christian Century* reported that Indian living conditions were little better than those of former Korean refugees and that only the president's personal attention would alleviate the miseries of American Indians. Because of its large bureaucracy, the federal government could not act quickly to provide simple justice to one of its minorities. The editorial charged that the United States Government "is either badly organized or badly served on its lower administration levels."[21] As a solution, the federal government tried to convince Native Americans to apply for state services.

Another biting article, in the July 1955 *Catholic World,* blamed the BIA's laxity for causing the Indians' impoverished conditions. The writer noted that Indians were at a disadvantage because of the Bureau's emphasis on "wardship" rather than "trusteeship."[22] As wards, the Indians had been taken care of, but as subjects of trusteeship they needed only government approval. An unhealthy spirit of paternalism had developed over the long years of federal-Indian relations, obstructing Indians from achieving financial independence and self-reliance. Now, in the 1950s, termination legislation was enacted to quickly dispel paternalism, subjecting Native Americans to potential harm. In the primary case of termination, the Menominees experienced confusion and uncertainty, especially among the traditional elders and veterans. Prior to their final termination date, the homes and buildings of the Menominees were still in great need of repairs. Enactment of Public Law 280, placing the Menominees under state jurisdiction, limited Bureau of Indian Affairs' assistance to Indians. While the Bureau refused to extend extra credit to the Menominees, it did set up a small agency staff to supervise the organization of an efficient and independent tribal body.[23]

La Farge wrote to the president on 10 November 1955 to criticize the government for its inadequate procedure in consulting with tribal leaders, particularly in reference to Public Law 280. The law authorized the placement of Indians under civil and criminal jurisdiction in five states: California, Minnesota, Nebraska, Oregon, and Wisconsin. Supposedly, Native Americans were allowed to consent to the law's implementation in those states.[24] Later, Congress authorized other states, especially Washington with its twenty-three Indian groups, to come under P.L. 280. This authorization considerably broadened the transfer of federal responsibilities to state governments. However, the statute remained unclear as to how the state governments could fund the extra burden of law enforcement in Indian communities.[25] Still, the objective of Public Law 280 was quite evident—it required Indians to come under state authority. Through the years, Native Americans had depended upon their relationship with the federal government. The parent-like attitude of the government frequently insulated the tribes from regional and local threatening interests, but now they had to contend with them. New, workable relationships had to be formed between Indians and state services.

In response to La Farge's letter regarding the special treatment of Indians, Secretary McKay claimed that they were no different from other American citizens. Nonetheless, he admitted that treaty obligations required that the United States honor such responsibilities, although these dealt primarily with land tenure. Therefore, land remained a key element in federal-Indian affairs, and also emerged as an important issue in state-Indian relations.

One of the problems related to the land issue surfaced when the BIA's report on the administration of Indian lands for the 1955 fiscal year disclosed difficulties in dealing with heirship lands. In such instances, when original allottees had died the land was divided among surviving family members. After several generations of such divisions, allotments were terribly fractionalized, and chaotic situations developed as the many owners attempted to determine whether to sell, lease, or develop the inherited land. The BIA's policy for dealing with heirship holdings mandated that a petition to sell inherited lands "be signed by all adult heirs on their behalf, by the guardian of a minor heir who has such guardian, and by the superintendent or another officer in charge of the agency or school on behalf of any orphan."[26] As a result, a sale of land was rarely approved by all of its owners, and fractionalization continued.

The report recommended that Congress should consider legislation to authorize the Secretary of the Interior to sell or partition such inherited lands held under trust patent, without requiring the consent of all competent owners. This proposed solution would expedite the paperwork and help all of the people involved. The report also suggested that fee patents be issued, thereby reducing the acreage of trust lands. The report acknowledged, however, that even competent Indians were reluctant to have the government terminate trust status of their lands. The federal government hoped that by resolving the heirship problem the release of restricted lands would enable Indian owners to utilize their properties more effectively and achieve greater economic self-sufficiency. Although termination of trust status meant freedom, it also thrust Indians into the complexities of property ownership and of adjustment to the ways of the mainstream society.

A heavy volume of protest letters to the Bureau of Indian Affairs indicated public concern for the welfare of Native Americans during this period. Such interest prompted the Bureau of Indian Affairs to issue a statement regarding its approach to termination and its special federal trustee relationship with Indians. The statement disclosed the government's awareness of the adjustment difficulties that many Indians experienced after the end of trust relations.[27] In spite of this knowledge, the government continued to abrogate trust relations with Indian groups.

The Bureau of Indian Affairs gingerly implemented termination procedures to prevent the possibility of endangering the tribes. In the Pacific Northwest, the BIA supervised all of the Klamath's business affairs, which elicited objections from some tribal members. Wade Crawford, a longtime Klamath leader and a member of the tribe's Investigating Coordinating Committee, testified before the Senate Appropriations Committee that the tribe wanted more participation in supervising the settlement of their business affairs in preparation for the termination deadline in 1958.[28] Federal officials acknowledged his point, and Klamath views were taken into consideration by BIA management specialists who supervised tribal leases, timber-cutting planning, sales, and other business matters. Overseeing the multiple business affairs of the tribe required time. In a hearing before the House Interior Subcommittee of Indian Affairs, Senator Richard Neuberger of Oregon requested that the Klamath Termination Act be amended to extend the 1958 deadline for implementation. More time was needed for the Klamaths to understand better the law's provisions and to settle their individual business affairs that derived from the tribe's timberland and other natural resources.[29]

Problems surrounding termination in the Pacific Northwest arose from conflicts over allotted and tribal timberlands. On the Quinault Reservation in Washington, individual Indian interests conflicted with the tribe's long-term contracts with the Indian Bureau. As a solution, the government set up a Joint Committee on Federal Timber to resolve the Indian Bureau contracts affecting both allotted and tribal timberlands.[30] The committee learned that individual Indians' socioeconomic progress toward assimilation presented various degrees of complexity. Frequently, officials had earlier been led to believe that Indian residents of the area were socially and economically ready for termination, when actually most were not. Moreover, confusion and opposition abounded among tribal members who were supported by critics of the BIA. The reluctance of the Indians to undergo termination made government attempts to assist Native Americans unpredictable, and poor results evoked a negative sentiment toward the Bureau.

In spite of the general apprehension, some tribes were not as reluctant as the Menominees and Klamaths in accepting termination. At the request of protermination Indian groups, Senator Joseph O'Mahoney introduced three bills in Congress for the withdrawal of federal supervision. Senate Bills 3968, 3969, and 3970 provided for the abolition of federal supervision over the properties of the Peorias, the Ottawas, and the Wyandots of Oklahoma, respectively.[31] All three groups were under the jurisdiction of the Quapaw Subagency, and their members were already assimilated within local communities. With small tribal populations and limited landholdings, these people found it necessary to integrate into local communities in order to find jobs for their subsistence.

Certainly the eight tribes of the Quapaw Subagency in Oklahoma—Wyandot, Ottawa, Eastern Shawnee, Quapaw, Seneca-Cayuga, Miami, Modoc, and Peoria—were among those Indians who desired control of their own destinies. A BIA field report, dated 30 September 1954, recorded that the subagency entertained about 4,700 Indians who held an estimated 33,000 acres of restricted lands.[32] Furthermore, in thirty-three meetings between BIA officials and 325 Indians from the eight tribes, approval on legislation to readjust trust relationships was obtained.[33]

On 9 December, Bureau official Homer Jenkins notified Oklahoma Congressman Ed Edmondson that the eight tribes of the Quapaw Subagency desired termination of trust relations with the government. During a ten-day period, from 23 November to 4 December, a series of meetings were held between each tribe and Bureau officials to discuss termination procedures.[34] On 9 January 1955, approximately two hundred Indians met with BIA officers from the Muskogee area office to discuss provisions of a termination bill that specifically addressed readjustment of the trust relationship with the federal government. The tribes varied in their decisions on termination. Walter King, Jr., chairman of the meeting, said that if necessary the readjustment bill would be redrafted and new criteria established for identifying those tribal members who were qualified for full trust-status removal. The tribes were concerned about a deluge of people who might claim membership if tribal assets were sold and the proceeds distributed.[35]

Another small tribal group faced termination when, on the first of July 1955, the Interior Department announced that federal supervision over the Alabama-Coushatta Indians of Texas would be terminated. Under the provisions of Public Law 280, the state of Texas would assume responsibility for all previous federal services. In this case, the law affected 426 Indians whose 4,181-acre reservation contained 3,071 acres of cutover timber.[36]

Other small tribal groups were visited by the Bureau during a tour of northeastern Oklahoma. After surveying their progress and small landholdings, BIA officials recommended termination. Almost a year later, Congress took action. Administrative Assistant Marie L. Hayes sent a memorandum to Paul L. Fickinger, area director at Muskogee, and C. C. Marrs, assistant area director, regarding congressional approval for terminating federal trust relations with the Ottawas, Peorias, and Wyandots. The memo included a notice of withdrawal of federal supervision and consent from the Eastern Shawnee, the Seneca-Cayuga, the Miamis, the Quapaws, and the Modocs. These tribes had carefully considered termination and agreed to limited withdrawal of trust status.[37]

For larger tribes with many full-bloods, like the Oregon Klamaths, termination caused internal strife and confusion. Younger Klamaths generally favored trust removal because it offered financial benefits and the freedom from federal restraints. Older Klamaths had mixed feelings since they did not fully comprehend it, and the thought of ending trust safeguards frightened them. The BIA reassured these elders of continued trust protection and government services, but they remained confused and resentful. Their frustration was substantiated in a Stanford University Research Institute report, which acknowledged that Klamath Indians were misinformed about the final termination set for 1958. Of one hundred Klamaths interviewed, only fourteen believed that the tribe had requested trust withdrawal. Only six Klamaths thought that they were more advanced than other tribes selected for termination. The report also disclosed that the tribal members did not understand the Klamath Termination Act. On behalf of the tribe, two management specialists, T. B. Watters and E. G. Favell, visited the Bureau of Indian Affairs in Washington to plead for protective amendments to the act. They requested more time for preparing the tribal members and some form of government protection guaranteed for the elderly.[38]

On 2 October 1956, a letter from Montana Senator James E. Murray, chairman of the committee on Interior and Insular Affairs, informed Colorado Senator Eugene D. Milkin that widespread concern existed among Oregon citizens about Klamath termination. Local whites feared that the Klamath Termination Act, P.L. 587, would jeopardize the Indians' future and the entire economy of the Klamath Basin. The removal of trust status over rich Klamath timberland might lead to a saturation of lumber on the open market, thus depressing prices. As the termination deadline of August 1958 approached, their fears mounted.

Senator Neuberger responded by introducing a bill in the Senate to defer the Klamath deadline for eighteen months; Representative Albert Ulman cosponsored the measure in the House. Neuberger prophesied that if the Klamaths' pine timber was sold recklessly the entire southeastern Oregon economy would suffer.[39] Hearings for the bill were being held when another bill, H.R. 2471, was introduced, calling for a deferment. The minutes of meetings between the BIA commissioner and the old and new members of the Klamath Executive Committee substantiated the senator's fears regarding loss of control over timber cuttings. These minutes also confirmed the Klamath's inadequate understanding of the termination law. In fact, only a few members realized that the Klamath Termination Act would end tribal benefits and that no more per capita payments would follow after final termination.[40] Several months later, the Indian Bureau asked Congress to amend the law to postpone the deadline to 31 August 1961, and the request was granted.[41]

Federal officials like Senator Neuberger and others who dealt with Klamath affairs were constantly blamed by the news media for the tribe's dilemma. Critics accused Neuberger of possessing ulterior motives in his attempt to assist the Oregon tribe by trying to defer their deadline. *The Oregonian,* a local newspaper, reported that the senator had denied a hearing for Klamath members who opposed a delay in termination, although one had actually been held at Klamath Falls on 18 October 1956.[42] In his own defense, Neuberger faulted other federal officials, claiming the Klamath problem was "a legacy from the Republican 83rd Congress which hatched the hasty and (I think) unwise termination bill, with McKay's consent."[43]

In spite of their criticism of the Klamaths and other tribes for hesitating to accept government policy, federal officials expressed the desire to assist and protect Indian Americans. At a conference with Cherokee delegates in December 1956, Emmons stated, "I want to see that every Indian is given an opportunity to select things in which he feels he will make good."[44] In the case of the Klamaths, the federal government questioned the possibility of the tribe selling their forest areas too quickly in order to obtain immediate cash. During the last few days in May, Secretary of the Interior Seaton warned presidential assistant Sherman Adams that termination endangered the Klamath's huge forest reserve. "This may well result in the destruction of one of the country's most valuable ponderosa pine forests," warned the secretary.[45] He added that the Klamath marsh, its water conservation, its wildlife population, and the economy of the Klamath Basin would be ecologically damaged. Simultaneously, acquiring a fair price for the tribe posed a problem for the Klamaths as well as for the Indian Bureau and local Oregonians.

Two days later, Adams wrote to Governor Elmo Smith of

Oregon about possible measures to amend existing legislation affecting the Klamaths. Members of the House of Representatives debated the extent to which the government should protect Klamath minors and others who might require future assistance to manage their assets. Both Congress and the Department of the Interior agreed to extend the deadline.[46]

Unfortunately, such a delay financially threatened those Klamaths who were making investments and were ready to assume responsibilities based on the provisions of the termination act. These people represented a bloc of tribal members who favored the termination policy, and they wanted the provisions to be carried out immediately. Factionalism developed among the Klamaths, causing complications and resentment. A small group of conservative full-bloods opposed the protermination bloc; but the majority of the members were mixed-bloods who moved easily within nearby white communities, and they supported the sale of tribal assets for per capita distribution.[47] Most Klamaths had been attending public schools since 1927, and apparently they were educated to handle their own affairs.

Other tribes who were assimilated, like the Klamaths, into local communities generally did not fare so well. Most had not attained a sufficient level of education to handle their own affairs. A special report entitled "Basic Needs of Indian People," released in June 1957, disclosed that most of the Indians were vastly undereducated. Bureau school administrators who prepared the report stressed that education was essential for Native Americans living away from their reservations. The government began to offer more vocational training and provided loans for college students in an effort to allow Indians to qualify for jobs outside economically depressed reservations. The suggestion that a scholarship program would provide Indian youths with the same educational opportunities as other students opened the door for federal assistance in higher education.[48] Although institutions of higher learning became more willing to admit minority members, Native Americans demonstrated limited interest in attending college. Whether or not this was due to Indians being content to learn about their old ways, a hesitancy to change was evident.

In December 1957, the Indian Education and Training Program released a report on "Termination of Federal Supervision over the Klamath Reservation." The authors noted that outwardly the Klamaths differed very little from their local non-Indian neighbors and they were apparently making excellent progress. They drove the same types of cars, lived in similar houses, dressed in modern-style clothes, and spoke English very well. The report emphasized, however, that they were experiencing social maladjustment problems. The transitional experience from a quiet and routine reservation life to a new urban life-style intrigued the people. Even the limited activities of local small towns excited Indian youth. The report noted an alarmingly high juvenile delinquency rate on the Klamath Reservation, and idleness and easy money were luring the youths away from attending school. The two management specialists hired to help the Klamaths prepare for termination developed a Tribal Management Plan that included steps for urbanizing younger Klamaths, particularly those from eighteen to thirty years old. Hopefully, the plan's implementation would alleviate the delinquency rate and assist the Klamaths in adjusting to white community life.[49]

Indian adjustment to a mainstream life-style resulted in alienation from traditionalism, creating a dichotomy between those members who wanted to remain in the tribe and those who wanted to withdraw from trust relations and obtain their share of tribal properties. Senator Neuberger proposed to solve the problem by introducing S. 2047, which authorized the appropriation of 100 million dollars or more to enable the federal government to purchase tribal holdings, which would be managed by an appropriate agency. The traditionalists' share of tribal property would be transferred into a tribal corporation or to a trustee for management as a tribal asset. The United States Forest Service would probably manage the timberlands, and the Wildlife Department would most likely supervise the marshlands. The Indians would get a fair price for their land, and the rich timberland would become a national resource safeguarded against exploitation.[50]

During October 1957, Neuberger sponsored a hearing in Oregon to help settle the issue of Klamath timberlands. During the three-day hearing, several witnesses protested against having federal agencies manage the land, declaring that they preferred to have it managed by a private company. Spokesmen for the

Western Forest Industries Association and the Weyerhaeuser Timber Company guaranteed the Klamaths a higher price for their land. As the discussion progressed, unexpected support for federal ownership came from civic groups of Klamath Falls and from chapters of the Izaak Walton League and the Audubon Society. The stakes involved were high: the tribe's property contained an estimated 800,000 acres of prime ponderosa pine, representing approximately 4 billion board feet, and 15,689 acres of marsh and grazing land.[51]

After the hearing, the government set 31 August 1960 as the final termination date for the Klamaths. This deadline meant that approximately 70 percent of the tribal forest would have to be sold within a two-year period. The Department of Interior proposed that the portion of the forest belonging to Klamaths who chose termination would be sold to private buyers on a competitive basis, with two restrictions. The purchasers had to agree to manage the forest land on a sustained-yield basis, and the price must not be less than its appraised fair-market value. If the land could not be sold under these conditions, the Secretary of Agriculture would make the land part of the National Forest program, and the Klamaths would be paid the government-appraised value of the property.[52]

Another difficulty with Klamath landholdings concerned the Confederated Tribes of the Warm Springs Reservation in Oregon. The tribal council of the Confederated Tribes wanted to maintain their reservation under trust status. However, almost three thousand acres of the reservation had passed into private ownership as a result of individuals selling fee patents. In addition, intertribal marriages with Klamaths placed parcels of the reservation under the Klamath Termination Act. By making fee patents available to Indian landowners, the government had to differentiate between lands belonging to the Warm Springs and the Klamath Indians.[53]

On 13 January 1958, federal officials made two concerted efforts to bring about a solution to the Klamath problem. Interior Secretary Seaton informed President Eisenhower about a proposed bill to amend the Klamath Termination Act, and the Department of the Interior requested Congress to consider legislative action to protect the Klamath forest. Seaton pointed to the threat of exploitation of rich timberland and emphasized the importance of the land serving as a nesting and feeding ground for migrating waterfowl, deer, and other wildlife. Three days later, Senator Neuberger officially introduced Senate Bill 2047. Since the government had not resolved the Klamath problem, Neuberger felt compelled to submit his bill to provide a solution in advance of the Klamaths' deadline.[54]

Undersecretary of the Interior Hatfield Chilson compared the two bills to determine which was more beneficial to the Klamaths. Neuberger's bill required the sale of all tribal land, whereas the government's bill authorized the marketing of about 70 percent of the land based on the percentage of withdrawing Klamaths. Furthermore, the government's bill allowed private buyers an option to purchase the Klamaths' land at the appraised value, while the Neuberger measure only allowed the federal government to acquire the land. Under the proposed provisions of the government's bill, the Department of the Interior would save a large sum of money, and the option of private buyers would enable the government to save even more. The ecological provisions satisfied the conservationists, since 15,689 acres of marshland would be purchased from the Klamaths and operated as a national wildlife refuge. This tract of land was known to be one of the most essential waterfowl breeding and feeding grounds outside the national wildlife refuge system. Large numbers of redhead, canvasback, and ruddy ducks visited the area during their migrations.[55]

Conversely, a possibility existed that no private buyer could afford to pay the retail price for timber to be managed on a sustained-yield basis. In addition, officials of the Klamath Federal Council and Klamath Executive Committee stated before the Senate Indian Subcommittee that the appraisals were underestimated. The general overall appraisal of the timber was 118 million dollars, but tribal officials estimated the actual value at 209 million dollars. They also claimed that not all Klamath property was appraised, including subsurface resources, pumice, titanium, and diatomaceous earth, water, and power resources.[56]

Senator Neuberger questioned whether Klamaths had been consulted in drafting the government's bill. He also claimed that the Department of the Interior had failed to consult the management specialists hired to supervise the tribe's business affairs. Moreover, section 5 of the bill eliminated the period for further study and planning, and substituted what Neuberger called a "crash program" for sale of tribal assets. He alleged that this had been done without the Klamaths' knowledge. And the senator asked why a per capita payment of 250 dollars had been suddenly inserted in the bill.[57]

The potential danger of the government's bill involved placing the tribe's prime ponderosa pine on the open market. An amendment to the bill proposed to negate the requirement that purchasers agree to sustained-yield cutting. Robert Homes, the newly elected governor of Oregon, vehemently protested the acceptance of the amendment, warning that the state's lumber market would be flooded with Klamath timber and the Indians robbed of a fair price.[58] In its final form, the government's bill retained the sustained yield provision and also increased the amount that the Klamaths would receive for their timberlands. Satisfied, Neuberger allowed his own bill to expire.

Interestingly, a meeting on 6 February 1958, between the Modocs of Oklahoma, Donald Foster, area director of the Portland area office, and local BIA officials in Miami, Oklahoma, addressed the sale of Klamath assets in Oregon. The Modocs received the welcome news that they would share in the disbursement of land sale proceedings. Originally, they had been included in the Klamath Reservation, according to a treaty negotiated with the United States in 1864.[59] Hence, they were entitled to share in the proceeds.

During mid-February 1958, Bureau officials called a special meeting with another Oklahoma group, the Seneca-Cayuga. The two sides discussed the dissolution of federal supervision over the trust property of the Seneca-Cayuga. Although the Indians originally had agreed to trust withdrawal, they were now reconsidering. One person asked if his people would continue to have access to boarding schools and hospitals. Former Chief David Charloe expressed concern for tribal elders and inquired if they would have to pay taxes on their property after the withdrawal of federal trust. Paul L. Fickinger, area director of Muskogee, assured Charloe that the law exempted original allottees from paying taxes for the rest of their lives. At the end of the discussion, Chief Peter J. Buck asked for a standing vote of all tribal members in favor of the proposed termination legislation. Not one person stood. When those opposed to termination were asked to stand, a majority of the Seneca-Cayuga rose to their feet.[60] The frustrated area director related to Commissioner Emmons the difficulty in obtaining the group's consent: "We have over a period of the last two or three years held at least five meetings with them on this subject. We cannot go on indefinitely this way."[61] No doubt, Fickinger supported immediate termination legislation, pointing out that the small tribe appeared assimilated within the local community and held only 1,052.89 acres in trust. In his eyes, the small groups posed no effective opposition to termination, and their successful integration with other citizens mandated federal withdrawal for them.

While termination activities were temporarily diverted to the Oklahoma tribes, the Department of the Interior finally announced in January 1959 that Klamath lands had been appraised at 90,791,123 dollars. After selling tribal assets, it was estimated that 1,659 terminating Klamaths would each receive 44,000 dollars. Furthermore, the Interior Department announced that a revolving fund would make loans available to Klamaths, possessing at least one-quarter Indian blood, who agreed to withdraw from the tribe.[62] This undoubtedly persuaded many Klamaths to support the abolition of trust relations with the federal government.

To protect the business interests of the Klamaths, the Department of the Interior announced on 4 March that the National Bank of Portland, Oregon, would take over the trusteeship of Klamath property. The bank replaced the Bureau of Indian Affairs as trustee of business matters for the 473 members remaining on the tribal roll. Deeds for approximately 140,000 acres of land, and $737,608.61 in cash, were turned over to the bank; but problems ensued.[63] L. B. Staver, vice-president of the National Bank and executive trust officer, explained that the bank had experienced difficulty in supervising Klamath affairs because of the complex details of tribal members' business and tribal contracts with the government and outside interests.[64] This series of problems soon jeopardized the entire economy of the Klamath Basin. Simultaneously, termination procedures delayed carrying out Klamath timber sales to mills in the area.[65] As more delays occurred, local mill owners worried that Klamath problems would not be resolved soon enough to prevent them from going bankrupt.

A few weeks later, Interior Department officials announced that Klamath lands could not be sold until after the termination deadline of 1 April 1959. Necessary postponement of the sale prompted the Interior Department to propose legislation that would permit the BIA to make interest-free loans to the terminating Klamaths. Departmental officials estimated that from 250 to 275 Klamath families would need financial assistance. Tribal members of less than one-fourth Klamath blood, approximately 253 members or 15 percent of the tribe, would be allowed to file for these loans.[66] Congress finally set Klamath termination for 1961, when each withdrawing member would receive 43,000 dollars in per capita payments. When the termination deadline arrived, 78 percent of the Klamaths voted for cash settlements, and the government distributed roughly 68 million dollars to the tribe.

The inefficient slowness of the government in handling Klamath termination, and the last-minute steps taken to expand federal trust withdrawal plans to other tribes, provoked criticism and reevaluation of federal Indian policy. One irate citizen who wrote to California Senator Clair Engle typified the public reaction: "I protest with real indignation the virtual seizure of Indian lands by our Government to be used by non-Indians for grazing and development."[67]

In the north central United States, a similar charge was made about the termination of the Menominees. A law firm alleged that the government had acted immorally in pressuring the tribe to accept termination as the price for a per capita distribution.[68] The Menominees' situation resulted in numerous requests from people living in all parts of the country who wanted to know more about them. Public curiosity and concern for the Wisconsin Indians prompted Melvin Robertson, superintendent for the Menominees at the Keshena Agency, to issue a report on the tribe's history and affairs, and the federal legislation affecting the Menominee people. Unfortunately, while attempting to clarify the tribe's socioeconomic status, the superintendent recited numerous misconceptions about the Menominees. He noted that about 75 percent of the households owned televisions, and that nearly every home possessed a radio and a car. In addition, he said that they were predominantly Catholic and appeared devoted to the Christian religion. He gave the public a false impression by saying that the Menominees had largely adopted white American ways and had retained little of their native culture.[69] To the outsider, the tribe seemed well adjusted to the mainstream life-style, but Menominees remained psychologically more traditional than perhaps even they realized.

During the planning and preparation stage, dubious Menominees asked what would happen until final termination in 1961. The tendency of the BIA to delay final action, combined with bureaucratic slowness, led skeptical tribal members to believe that termination would not actually happen. In April, the Menominee Indian Study Committee met with tribal members to obtain opinions on the tribal plan for preparing for termination. Menominees like Agnes Dick believed that the tribe's fullbloods were not ready. She asserted that if the government terminated the reservation it would have to take care of a significant portion of its tribal members. "I want to remain the way we are for another fifteen or twenty years," she said. "Then maybe most people will be ready."[70] Many Menominees had harbored a weak hope that termination might not occur.

On 26 January, the Menominee Coordinating and Negotiation Committee recommended to Secretary Seaton the formation of a tribal corporation for their tribe. Their plan called for a business corporation with a voting trust that possessed the flexibility and stability required for post-termination operation of Menominee properties.[71] A board of trustees would oversee the corporation's voting stock and supervise business for a maximum of thirty years. The Menominee corporation would invest in various business enterprises without any assistance or control from the government. In essence, the tribe would become a private business corporation after termination—a promising precedent for other tribes to follow. In December 1961, the Menominees were officially terminated, and the people had accepted suggestions that the tribe become a business corporation and that the reservation become a separate county in Wisconsin.

During the fifteen years of termination struggles, the responsibility of the federal government was to help Native Americans prepare for termination. The government, however, lacked an adequate program for successfully assisting Indian people through the troublesome process. Meanwhile, haphazard efforts contributed to the socioeconomic plight of the red man. Only in a few cases did Indians seem to fare well in adapting to the white man's society. Although Indians mingled with local white communities, the majority of rural towns demonstrated prejudice toward them.

Additional legislation and inadequate BIA efforts to help Indian people fostered a growing criticism of the federal termination policy at the state level as well. Undoubtedly, federal officials wanted what was best for Indians, but they lacked the ability to perceive the social and psychological consequences that termination created for Native Americans. The federal government's efforts to pass the buck to state governments, under P.L. 280, forced American Indians to form new relationships with state agencies. Learning the system of applying for state services while trying to assimilate into the mainstream society, especially when conflicts existed between local and tribal interests, was too much to ask of a people who had learned to become dependent upon the federal government for over a century. Legislation put forth to help the assimilation effort often became a hindrance. In the years that followed, most members of terminated tribes would not become middle-class citizens and would have to settle for lower-class status in American society.

7

The Relocation Program and Urbanization

The experiences of Native Americans during the war years had a two-fold effect on federal-Indian relations in the postwar period. The courageous performance of Native American men abroad and native women in the war industries at home impressed federal officials, convincing them that Indians possessed an aptitude for working side by side with other Americans. Barton Greenwood, acting commissioner of Indian affairs, estimated that 50 percent of the returning veterans had sufficient experience in working with other Americans away from the reservations to compete with them for jobs.[1]

Unfortunately, returning Indian veterans increased the burden on the reservations' already limited economic resources. High unemployment and widespread poverty pervaded Indian country. In response, the government proposed relocating unemployed Indians or those who returned from the war to urban areas where they could find jobs. Greenwood advised that these people be moved as far as possible from their original communities to prevent them from returning easily to their homelands. Theoretically, this strategy would be conducive to successful Indian adaptation to urban living. Federal officials believed that once the new urban migrants had adjusted to living in the cities there would be no need for reservations.[2] Until then, Indians continued to live on reservations under submarginal conditions.

The severe blizzard of 1947–48 worsened the already poor economy for Indian communities, especially for the populous Navajos in Arizona and New Mexico, who suffered extreme destitution. To help alleviate their suffering, the government supplied emergency aid, but the deplorable conditions on the reservation continued. This impelled the federal government to take one more step in establishing a job placement program, which laid the foundation for the relocation program. The Bureau of Indian Affairs began to resettle employable Indians from the Navajo Reservation in urban areas.[3] The Interior Department soon established additional placement offices in Denver, Salt Lake City, and Los Angeles.

Relocation took its place beside termination as the second goal of federal Indian policy in the 1950s. After the withdrawal of trust restrictions from the lands, Native Americans were encouraged to pursue a livelihood in the cities. Although the program began with the Navajos, the government soon began to extend relocation services to all tribes.

In a conference with area directors in January 1951, Commissioner of Indian Affairs Dillon S. Myer had urged funding for the relocation program to begin the recruitment of Indians for urban placement. He had hoped to be able to expand the program quickly by intensifying and broadening recruitment efforts. Critics alleged that relocation had swept Indians off the reservations, scattered them throughout cities, and then they were abandoned by the Bureau.[4] The commissioner denied that the Bureau of Indian Affairs had forced Native Americans to relocate. Myer insistently advocated relocation as a policy congruent with his philosophy of termination—the view that Native Americans should be encouraged to live without federal supervision like other Americans. Moving Indians to urban areas to work and to live would, he believed, escalate their standard of living. Although Myer enthusiastically supported relocation during his three years at the helm of the Bureau, the program failed to gain momentum during his administration.[5]

Even though the application procedure for relocation was amazingly simple and open to young and old alike, Native Americans initially hesitated to volunteer for the new program. However, curiosity about city life eventually induced many people to apply for relocation. Native Americans of all types would frequently arrive at an agency office to inquire, "What is this relocation that I've been hearing about?"[6] A survey of the Klamaths who were known to relocate to Chiloquin and Klamath Falls, two small urban centers near the reservation in Oregon, revealed that they were attracted to stores, schools, and movie theaters.[7] In addition, veterans, relatives, and friends who were among the first to relocate made people on the reservation envious when they talked about their adventures and good times in the cities.

After an initial request for relocation had been filed with a BIA official at an agency or an area office, the paperwork began. After completing a review of the applicant's job skills and employment records, the official usually contacted the relocation office in the city of the applicant's choice. With clothes and personal items packed, the applicant customarily boarded a bus or train to the designated city, where he or she would be met by a relocation worker. Upon arrival, the newcomer received a check to be spent under the supervision of the relocation officer. Next, the officer usually accompanied the new urbanite to a nearby store to purchase toiletries, cookware, groceries, bedding, clothes, and an alarm clock to insure punctual arrival at work. In the city, the poorest of America's poor began a new day in what they hoped was a promising future.

Living by a strict timetable was a new experience for almost all relocated Indians. Often, instructions had to be given to show how a clock worked and the relocatee taught how to tell time. One young Crow Creek Sioux, who began to take college courses to improve his job qualifications, expressed exasperation in adjusting to an hour-by-hour schedule of classes. His traditional conviction that people should live in harmony with nature during a continuum of time conflicted with the concept of regulating one's life according to the minutes of a clock. "I nearly went crazy during the first two weeks of college," he said. "No matter where I was, I always had to be somewhere else at a certain time. There was no rest."[8]

Relocation officers assisted the new migrants in locating places to shop for groceries, and informed them about nearby churches of their denominations. After the relocatee and his or her family were settled, the relocation worker and neighborhood clergyman visited on a regular basis. Normally, the BIA paid the relocatee's first month's rent, including clothing and groceries, and the expenses incurred while traveling to and from work. After the first month the relocatees were on their own, although Bureau workers remained available for counseling and assistance in job placement; BIA officials would keep tabs on the progress of relocatees for the next nine years.[9]

Young adults, especially men, were the most common applicants for relocation. Frequently, they left families behind until they found jobs and housing, and then sent for their families. The most ambitious relocatees were young Indians who possessed some college education. They chose to move to large cities, far from their homelands, to escape their past poverty, and perhaps to forget their traditional heritage. Undoubtedly, they succeeded much better in the transition from native life to urbanization than less-educated relocatees. They successfully competed for jobs, and found adequate housing.[10]

During midsummer 1951, the Bureau of Indian Affairs assigned workers to extend the relocation services in Oklahoma, New Mexico, California, Arizona, Utah, and Colorado. In November, a field office was opened in Chicago to place Navajos in jobs, but shortly afterwards, the BIA incorporated the office as a part of the relocation program to serve all Native Americans.[11] The first relocatees arrived in Chicago in early February 1952.[12] In all, relocation workers processed 442 Native Americans for employment in Los Angeles, Denver, and Chicago during that year. With the Bureau expanding the Navajo placement offices in Salt Lake City, Denver, and Los Angeles to service all Native Americans, a new generation of urban Indians came into being.[13]

Commissioner Dillon Myer strove to expand the services of the relocation program. For fiscal year 1952 Congress appropriated slightly more than half a million dollars for the first year's operation and authorized the opening of additional offices. In his budget request for the following year, Commissioner Dillon Myer requested 8.5 million dollars for vocational training and relocation. He recommended to Congress that the Bureau of Indian Affairs should negotiate contracts with state and private vocational schools in areas throughout the nation where employment opportunities were most available. "Unfortunately we did not get approval of this full program," said the commissioner, "although we did secure enough funds to establish a pilot relocation program throughout the country."[14]

By the end of 1953, BIA relocation offices had placed 2,600 Indians in permanent jobs. Financial assistance during that year enabled 650 workers to move their families to the nearby communities where they worked, but Bureau officers experienced problems in locating enough jobs for relocatees. They relied primarily on public employment agencies, which too often placed relocatees in seasonal railroad and agricultural work, the lowest paying and least secure type of employment. Because of this, the program received criticism, and suggestions were made to try to find more meaningful jobs.[15]

The Bureau of Indian Affairs' fiscal report for 1954 indicated that the relocation program had assisted 2,163 applicants. Some 1,649 persons, comprising over 400 family units and 514 single men and women, had relocated to metropolitan areas. Approximately 54 percent of the relocatees came from the three northern areas serviced by the Aberdeen, Billings, and Minneapolis offices. Forty-six percent were processed through the southern offices of Anadarko, Gallup, Muskogee, and Phoenix. Relocatees were placed in twenty different states, with Los Angeles and Chicago the leading cities in welcoming most of the new urbanites.[16]

To help process the increasing number of relocatees, the Bureau opened an office in Oakland in 1954; another office opened in San Francisco a year later, and in 1956 offices were established in San Jose and St. Louis.[17] Soon, additional offices were operating in Dallas, Cleveland, Oklahoma City, and Tulsa. The rising number of applicants prompted the government to quickly expand the relocation program. By late 1954 approximately 6,200 Native Americans of an estimated 245,000 reservation population had resettled in large cities.[18] From 1952 to 1955, in Chicago alone some 3,000 reservation Indians, mainly from the Southwest, had relocated.[19] In fiscal year 1955, the Indian Bureau placed 3,461 Indians, including 2,656 persons from 708 family groups, and 805 single men and women. They were enrolled in thirty-three different courses of the vocational training program.[20]

During the first week in January 1955, Commissioner Glenn Emmons addressed the Muskogee, Oklahoma, Chamber of Commerce, reaffirming the need for the relocation program. Poor land quality and the increasing Indian population required such a program in order to alleviate crowding and poverty.[21] In a memo to the Secretary of the Interior, dated 20 May 1955, he outlined how the relocation program helped Native Americans escape poverty on the reservations: "We furnish transportation both for the worker and his family to the community he has selected. We help in finding a job, in locating a suitable home, and in getting generally adjusted in the new surroundings."[22]

The commissioner foresaw improvement for American Indians through combining relocation and education. On 25 October, Department of the Interior officials announced the creation of a new adult education program to serve five particular tribal groups: the Seminole of Florida; the Papago of Arizona; the Rosebud Sioux of South Dakota; the Turtle Mountain Chippewa of North Dakota; and the Shoshone-Bannock of Fort Hall in Idaho, who were among the neediest of the Indian population.

Emmons recognized that a lack of educational opportunities impeded the overall advancement of Indian people. He began to stress the need to make schooling available to all Indian youngsters of normal school age, and he envisioned elementary schooling for adults who had never received any formal education. In essence, education was believed to be an important key to Indian urbanization. And educational reform soon became an integral part of the relocation program to assist Native Americans in better adjusting to and assimilating into the mainstream society.[23]

BIA publicity portrayed relocation as a "New Deal" for Native Americans, one that offered them a chance to improve their economic status. Indian Bureau officials encouraged Indians to relocate, although ostensibly on a voluntary basis. Throughout the reservations, BIA workers circulated brochures and pamphlets suggesting that a better life awaited Indians in urban areas. Pictures of executives dressed in white shirts, wearing ties, and sitting behind business desks insinuated that similar occupational positions could be obtained by Indians. Photos of a white frame house with shutters enticed the women. The scene suggested that Indians could provide their families with similar homes in suburban America.

Unfortunately, the hard realities of urban life soon destroyed Indian hopes for a successful livelihood and dashed their many dreams. For those who left the reservation and traveled a long distance for the first time, the relocation experience was a threatening cultural shock. Once off a bus and alone in a strange, large city, relocatees encountered a foreign and threatening new world that often proved to be traumatic. Relocatees knew little about such modern gadgets as stoplights, clocks, elevators, telephones, and other everyday objects that Americans took for granted. To avoid a frightening elevator, they would climb the stairs in apartment buildings. Newly relocated Indians who had not yet mastered the English language experienced even more difficulty, and many were embarrassed to ask for assistance. A magazine article described one incident: "In situations of distress, the Indian often remains proudly silent. One relocatee was 'lost' in his room for 24 hours. He had lost the BIA address. And although he had the phone number he was 'ashamed' to ask how to dial."[24] Perhaps the most important complaints from Indians dealt with the noise, tension, and hectic pace of the city life. Some Native American women found the outside bustle of the city too difficult to face and locked themselves in their apartments, afraid to even go to the supermarket.

Toward the end of 1955, the Muskogee area office in Oklahoma reported a decline in people volunteering for relocation from its area.[25] Fear of big-city life inhibited many Native Americans, making them feel lost, insecure, and inferior to the majority population of urban white Americans. Compared to other, more aggressive urban minorities—blacks, Mexicans, and Puerto Ricans—the uneducated, traditional Indians were isolated and at the bottom of the social order.[26]

Relocation officers attempted to prepare Indians for the drastic changes that lay ahead of them and to ease their adjustment to city life. They informed the relocatees of the conditions they would face in industrial areas—working according to a regular schedule, moving through city traffic, paying high rent, encountering hospital expenses, learning to budget money, purchasing suitable clothing for themselves and their children, and living in a generally non-Indian neighborhood.[27] Despite these efforts, Indians going on relocation experienced considerable difficulty in adjusting to urban areas. An article in the *Christian Science Monitor* described the reality of an Indian couple relocating to a city. The story itself depicts a true picture of what relocation was probably like for a family.

Tony and Martha Big Bear and their family had just arrived in Los Angeles from the reservation. Everything was new to Martha and she never said a word and scarcely raised her eyes while holding the children during the bus ride to the relocation office. The first thing the relocation officer did was to advise Tony about spending money wisely. A $50 check was drawn up for Tony and he was told how to open a bank account. The Big Bears were then temporarily lodged in a nearby hotel.

Although Tony wanted to be a commercial artist, he settled for a job in an aircraft plant. The Indian Bureau placement officer persuaded Tony to accept this job first and then he could check into the art field later after he became familiar with Los Angeles and when his family had a more permanent place to live. Everything was moving too fast for the Big Bears. The field office helped Tony find an apartment—a 'slum,' according to most people, but it was better than anything Martha was accustomed to.[28]

The experience of the Big Bears could easily have been more difficult. Sometimes factories closed down and welfare agencies had to assist relocated families. Out of necessity, Indian centers soon sprang up in almost every large city to help deprived Native American people by temporarily furnishing groceries and clothes. Nearly all relocatees experienced difficulties of one kind or another. A writer for the *Atlantic Monthly* published a true account involving Little Light, her husband Leonard Bear, and their five children, a family originally from a Creek Indian community in Oklahoma. "Today they are slum dwellers in Los Angeles, without land or home or culture or peace."

The author described meeting Little Light and her children "in the chairless kitchen-dining-living room of a small shanty on the outskirts of Los Angeles. Five children, black eyes round with wonder in their apricot faces, sheltered against her skirt. The walls were unpainted, the floor a patchwork of linoleum. Through an archway, another room was visible where three beds crowded together. A two-burner stove stood on a box, and on the only other piece of furniture in the room—a battered table—rested the remains of a dinner; some white, grease-soaked bags which had contained hamburgers and fried potatoes prepared by the restaurant a few blocks away."

In response to the interviewer's questions, Little Light spoke of how her husband went out drinking every night, of people in stores laughing at her, and about the need for a doctor for her sick child. She wanted to return to Oklahoma, but there was not enough money to go back. The woman stared solemnly, and her face became distorted as she lamented, "They did not tell us it would be like this."[29]

Similar descriptions of unfortunate incidents were published in current magazines and newspapers, thereby reinforcing the negative public image of the BIA that the termination program had first created. Federal officials countered with defensive news releases: "As some of you know—if you have been reading your magazines lately—that word 'relocation' seems to upset certain people—apparently because it suggests uprooting the Indians from their serene pastoral environment and plunging them down in some kind of a nerve-wracking asphalt jungle. For at least a generation, and probably longer, Indian families have been moving away from the impoverished environment of reservations and seeking better opportunities."[30]

Despite the radical socioeconomic problems facing them, the number of applicants for relocation began increasing on the whole. In the 1956 fiscal year, BIA workers processed 5,316 relocatees through four offices—Chicago, Denver, Los Angeles, and San Francisco. Of this number, 732 were single men, 373 were single women, and 424 had families. Relocation officers noted a growing interest in relocation among Indians, and a backlog of applications existed at almost all Indian agencies.[31]

Some 12,625 reservation Indians had relocated to urban areas by 12 July 1956, and the Bureau expected another 10,000 to apply before 1 July 1957.[32] The proliferating number of applicants prompted the BIA to enlarge the relocation program. To meet the costs of a growing program, Congress authorized generous appropriations for relocation. Commissioner Emmons announced in 1956 that relocation funding had more than tripled, from a level of 1,016,400 dollars in 1955 to a current sum of 3,472,000 dollars. Increased funding enabled the Bureau to broaden its scope of relocation services. Two new offices were planned, and steps were taken to enlarge relocation guidance staffs.[33]

The growing relocation program received encouragement from tribal councils. From 19 to 21 July Indian leaders held a conference in Omaha, Nebraska, to discuss ways to improve relocation services among their people. One participant suggested that tribal meetings be held once or twice a week to instruct members in budgeting and to explain how to use modern household facilities. "Many of our people do not know what these things are," he said, "and have never had running water in their house and other modern conveniences."[34] A training program for Indians became pertinent to solving the existing relocation problems as well as in preventing future problems. Mishandling money was one such problem. Superintendent Ben Reifel, a mixed-blood Sioux, noted a tendency by relocatees to overspend their income, thereby convincing other individuals that Indians received checks from the government on a regular basis. "Some people think that the Indian gets a regular check from the Federal Government. The salesman thinks an Indian is a good subject for the installment plan."[35]

Congress passed Public Law 959 during the first week in August 1956, providing improved vocational training for adult Indians. Shortly afterward, vocational training became a part of the relocation program and offered three types of general services. First, on-the-job training provided a twenty-four month, apprentice-type training for Indian employees. Work in factories on or near reservations trained individuals for jobs and gave them valuable vocational experience. Young Indians, especially, obtained such experience and were trained in rudimentary skills that would increase their chances for employment in urban areas.

Second, the adult vocational training program, designed for Indian adults who usually had families, provided training in specific occupational areas—carpentry, plumbing, and other related manual job skills. Program officers based enrollment selection on the past employment and school records of applicants. The program specified that applicants be between eighteen and thirty-five years of age, but older applicants were accepted if they took full advantage of the training and had a reasonable prospect of being employed in their specialty.

The third branch of the relocation program provided employment only. The direct employment subprogram provided job information and employment for Native Americans near reservations. Hence, industries were urged to locate nearby. Otherwise, program workers negotiated with employers in urban areas to hire relocatees, and the unemployed were placed where jobs were available.

The initial meeting between a potential employer and a relocatee was a crucial step. The Indian who had recently left the reservation sometimes did not make a good first impression. Tattered and threadbare clothes caused employers to pause and study Indian applicants with apprehension. The area director at Gallup, New Mexico, mentioned this point to the commissioner of Indian affairs in his report on Navajo placement activities. The director reported that the Navajos dressed in worn and torn clothes; some dressed in traditional garb; and men wore their hair long, arousing stares from people who were unaccustomed to Indians. Naturally, unconventional dress and sometimes shabby appearance hindered Indians who were looking for jobs and housing, or provoked derogatory comments while they shopped in stores.[36]

The physical appearance of relocatees was less of a problem at factories located near reservations. To encourage Native Americans to seek vocational training and employment, the Bureau of Indian Affairs negotiated contracts with business firms to build plants near reservations. Bulova Watch Company built a jewel-bearing plant near the Turtle Mountain Reservation at Rolla, North Dakota, the first company to locate near a reservation and to hire exclusively Indian employees. On the last day in December 1956, the company threatened to close the installation, provoking sharp reactions. Native American leaders, as well as public officials and Indian interest organizations, urged congressmen and the BIA to retain the plant. Closing the facility would threaten the progress of the Turtle Mountain Indians and the relocation program. Bureau officials believed if all 150 Indian employees at Bulova lost their jobs other Native Americans would question the practicality and advisability of urban relocation or of receiving employment or vocational training through the relocation program. The BIA was also concerned that other industries would be reluctant to accept government subsidies for locating near reservations.[37]

The Department of the Interior especially encouraged industrial development on and near the Navajo Reservation in the Southwest. In December 1956 the Interior Department announced that 300,000 dollars of the Navajo tribal fund was marked for creating an industrial development program. The program would induce industrial plants to locate near the Navajo Reservation, and provide payrolls and job opportunities for tribal members. Two manufacturing companies, Navajo Furniture, Incorporated, and Lear, Incorporated, constructed factories near the reservation. Navajo Furniture, a subsidiary of Baby Line Furniture of Los Angeles, and Lear, a manufacturer of electronic equipment of Santa Monica, California, were each expected to employ an estimated one hundred Navajos.[38]

The need for on-the-job experience among the Navajos was especially important because of the limited supply of jobs near reservations and the threat of layoffs to those who had jobs. Unskilled Indians had to compete with other workers in urban areas for jobs requiring specific skills. Vocational training would prepare relocating Indians for earning their livelihoods in the cities. The Indian Vocational Training Act of 1957 authorized the establishment of job training centers near reservations and in cities to teach trades to relocating Indians. The variety of training increased for several years; eventually, vocational training centers offered training in 125 occupations, and accredited schools existed in twenty-six states.[39]

Vocational training and employment assistance for Native Americans were two primary objectives of the relocation program. The availability of employment in cities naturally led to relocation in urban areas. Hence, the need for employment became the basis for relocation. Relocation did not merely mean removing Indians from reservations to cities, but involved preparing them for placement through vocational training and moving them to areas with high employment opportunities. Public Law 959 emphasized employment for Indians, which became the main service provided by the relocation program and led to changing the name of the "relocation program" to "employment assistance."[40] More importantly, "relocation" had become associated with the negative image of dragging Indians from reservations and abandoning them in cities. The BIA hoped the name change would improve the program's image.

The vocational training program aroused considerable interest among Indian people. The offer of free training, without necessarily having to move to some city, attracted applications. In addition, Bureau officials visited numerous council meetings to promote the advantages of vocational training opportunities. Their efforts increased Indian interest, which also meant increasing the annual cost of the entire relocation program. Congress appropriated $1,016,400.00 for the 1956 fiscal year. The expense per person amounted to $196.00. In fiscal year 1957, the total budget climbed to $3,472,000.00, at a cost of $347.20 per relocatee.[41]

The Department of the Interior sensed a growing Native American voluntarism for relocation services, and announced on 24 July 1957 that seven hundred positions were available for on-the-job training opportunities. Federal efforts to entice industrial expansion, which would produce jobs, were successful when the BIA negotiated contracts with eight companies, including Whitetree's Workshop, an Indian-owned firm that manufactured souvenirs on the Cherokee Reservation in North Carolina. Saddlecraft, Incorporated, of Knoxville, Tennessee, intended to operate a leather-goods plant at Cherokee, North Carolina; and Lear, Incorporated, of Santa Monica, California, had already developed an electronics plant at Flagstaff, Arizona. The others included Casa Grande Mills, a garment factory in Arizona; New Moon Homes, Incorporated, of Rapid City, South Dakota, which made trailer homes near the Standing Rock Reservation; Navajo Furniture Industries, Incorporated, with a company at Gallup, New Mexico; and Bably Manufacturing Company, a denim garments factory located near the Yakima Reservation. Unfortunately these companies could hire only a small percentage of the growing number of applicants for vocational training.[42]

Federal funding increased in correlation with the rising number of applicants until the high cost caused disagreement among federal officials. Some congressmen supported the relocation program, while others advocated the development of tribal economic resources, a less expensive route. In a confidential letter to Commissioner Emmons, dated 9 October 1957, Congressman E. Y. Berry of South Dakota complained of federal spending on Indian relocation. "I think the time has come to stop this useless waste of the taxpayers' money in hiring an army of bureaucrats to do something that does not in any way benefit the Indian people," Berry wrote.[43]

Skeptical congressmen questioned the high overhead costs. People, especially those unfamiliar with Indian affairs, wanted clarification of the goals and objectives of the relocation program, fearing that the program was getting out of control. Terminationists who wanted to get the government out of the "Indian business" complained about the expanding and ever-increasing cost of the Bureau of Indian Affairs.

A report entitled "The Program of Relocation Services," dated 28 October 1957, reiterated the purpose of relocation. The prime directive was to assist Native Americans who wanted independence from the federal government and were eager to find their place in the free-enterprise system. The Indian citizenry, the report claimed, would eventually become a component of the urban community scene.[44]

The relocation program reinforced the termination policy in decentralizing the federal authority in Washington. With the dispersal of federal responsibilities according to Public Law 280, the states assumed many services to Native Americans. States supplied relocation assistance that Native Americans needed. Homer B. Jenkins, assistant commissioner of Indian affairs, informed the area directors of Portland, Phoenix, Minneapolis, and Muskogee, as well as field relocation officers at St. Louis, Oakland, and Chicago, that applicants who desired vocational training should be referred to state agencies.[45] Jenkins's order was congruent with the termination directive calling for federal withdrawal of government intervention in Indian affairs.

Indian veterans of World War II and the Korean War had a much better chance of succeeding in relocation than reservation Indians who had never left their rural communities.[46] Previous experience with the outside world, plus the possession of knowledge of white American norms and values, accounted for this advantage. For the majority of relocatees, however, urbanization presented a difficult social and psychological adjustment to an alien environment. In early December 1957, a relocation specialist emphasized such problems in a memo to the area director of the Phoenix area office: "Relocation is not easy. It calls for real stamina and vigor—adaptability and strength of character."[47] He added that the Papago Indians possessed these characteristics, for since 1952, 566 Papagos had successfully relocated to urban areas. Among the Navajos, Tribal Chairman Paul Jones admitted that the relocation program was helpful in removing the surplus population on the reservation that the land could not support.[48] Frequently, tribes worked to rid their reservations of undesirable members through relocation. Shiftless, unmotivated members burdened families, friends, and reservation resources, and relocation offered them an opportunity to leave.

In summarizing Indian affairs for 1957, the Department of the Interior reported that nearly seven thousand Native Americans had received relocation assistance in finding jobs and establishing homes in urban areas. Expenditures for the relocation program in 1957 totaled 3.5 million dollars, more than twice the sum appropriated for the previous year. From the close of World War II to the end of 1957, approximately one hundred thousand Indians had left reservations. Interestingly, three-fourths of this number had relocated without federal assistance.[49] Although reservation revenues and economic development were on the rise, with royalties from oil, gas, and other mineral leases doubling over the previous year to total more than 75 million dollars for 1957, the growing Indian population from the war boom was severely straining tribal efforts to provide for all the people.[50]

Relocation climaxed between 1952 and 1957, when over 17,000 persons received services. About 12,625 people were resettled in cities, many of whom were living there with their families. The average cost per relocatee amounted to $403.00. The Chicago field relocation office reported for February and March 1957 that the average male relocatee earned $1.60 an hour, or about $66.00 for a forty-hour week. To maintain services for Native Americans, a total of twelve relocation offices were in operation across the country.[51]

The rising demand for relocation was temporarily jeopardized during the economic recession of 1956–57, when jobs became scarce and cutbacks in production occurred. Employers usually laid off relocatees first, due to their lack of job experience or seniority.[52] As a result, for fiscal year 1958 the number of relocatees decreased by 1,236, or about 18 percent, from the previous year.[53] To survive their economic ills, many Indians of terminated trust status sold their lands at depressed prices. The drop in applications was brief; interest returned the following year, and on 1 April, the BIA reported a surplus of 3,000 applicants.[54] And so the deluge of Indians moving to the cities continued.

Unfortunately, many potential relocatees did not anticipate the difficulties that they might encounter in the cities. Louis Cioffi, a missionary, wrote to President Eisenhower: "Under this program, as you know, Indians are urged away from their reservations, given jobs, which soon come to an end. As you may not know, many have returned to the reservation, discouraged 'and worse off than before.' Successful relocation achieved by the government has been very small indeed."[55] One Indian in Southern California called relocation an "extermination program," and said that Eisenhower believed "the Indians would be integrated by taking all the youngsters off the reservation, the old would die off, the young would be integrated, and the land would become free for public domain, and all the people could grab it."[56]

Conversely, the government reported optimistically that the majority of Indian relocatees were acclimating to urban conditions successfully, and the number returning to reservations was actually miniscule. The Bureau of Indian Affairs maintained that between 1953 and 1957 only three out of ten relocatees returned to their home communities. The BIA claimed that one-half of those 30 percent who returned home did so within the first three months, and that 71.4 percent remained in their urban environment. Critics charged that the percentage of returnees was 75 percent.[57] Such differences in statistics helped to fuel the controversy over the relocation program. In fact, both sides probably manipulated figures to favor or disfavor the "return rate."

Another problem area arose when vocational training programs encountered a significant dropout rate in various occupational areas. In the nurse's aide program the rate was 21 percent; for sawmill workers 50 percent; for manufacturers of Indian artifacts 54 percent; and for furniture workers about 62 percent. Specialized occupations, such as diamond processing, wig-making, and the production of women's fashion items, had the highest dropout rates, due to the monotony of the work.[58] Most likely, a disinterest in the work and its long-range impracticality accounted for the high dropout rate in wig-making and the production of women's fashion items. Often, the relocatees were persuaded to enroll in a number of widely ranging courses, merely to prove that Indians were being trained in diverse occupations.

Monotony and disinterest were not the only reasons why Indians dropped out of vocational training programs. Frequently, relocatees placed in seasonal jobs, like agricultural work, and in other jobs that lacked employee security. For these reasons, relocatees became suspicious of government officials who ostensibly would find jobs for them. Unfortunately, low wages accompanied these insecure jobs, forcing Indians to gravitate toward poor housing areas in the cities. In Los Angeles, Indian families were placed in slum dwellings and in rundown motor courts.[59] As more families moved to these areas, Indian ghettos developed. Frustration and discouragement compounded homesickness, prompting many to leave the cities.

Other relocatees chose to return because they missed the "openness" of their reservations. Some left well-paying jobs just to return home. In a few cases, however, if a family member died in an apartment the other members of the family did not want to stay because it was taboo to continue living there. One relocatee had a bad dream and decided to go back to the reservation. Relocation officers thought that these reasons were only excuses to leave. What they failed to understand was that bad omens and taboos were a part of the Indian reality and affected behavior accordingly. Other Indian urbanites found modern institutions too overwhelming; in buying on credit, for example, their inability to make installment payments created indebtedness, possibly even bankruptcy.[60]

Racism was another serious problem confronting relocatees in some areas, although Indian–white relations had improved in general. A 1958 "Report of the Labor Force and the Employment Conditions of the Oneida Indians" revealed that discrimination against the Oneidas in northern Wisconsin had declined. Urban communities surrounding the Oneida Reservation, like Green Bay, Appleton, and Neenah, hired Indians on a regular basis; but employers were now selective in their hiring practices because of the Indians' high rates of absenteeism from previous jobs.[61]

A social services director of the Minneapolis Native American Center depicted the Native American hopes and disillusionment with the relocation experience: "I think everybody who comes to the city has a dream—a dream of making it, a dream about improving their lives. But then prejudice slaps them right in the face and they're worse off. Call it culture shock. When your bubble is burst, there's nothing left but to go back home and start dreaming again."[62]

After failing to adjust to urban life and returning to the reservation, the relocatees at least had some job experience for a potentially better livelihood. Many chose to attempt relocation a second or a third time, selecting a different city for each move. Periodically, such opportunistic Indians took advantage of the relocation program and went to different cities for a couple of months on adventurous vacations. Upon returning, they boasted to friends about their good times in Los Angeles, Chicago, or whatever city they had visited.

Although relocation officers were flexible in accepting applicants, not all were easily approved. Reasons for rejection included records of drunkenness, arrests, marital problems, and poor health. Upon resolving these problems, however, Native Americans could have their applications reconsidered. In some instances, relocation officers were criticized and charged with racism for disqualifying certain applicants. But the prejudice was not always directed against Indians. John Dressler, a wise and elderly Washo, stated: "I think the Indian people also is prejudice against the white people because of the mistreatment that they've had. I don't know who's right, whether the Indian's right or the white man's right." Dressler advised that Native Americans should try to prove themselves to be as "hearty, diligent people as they used to be" in order to eliminate poor opinions of other races. In fact, the Washo elder believed that prejudice was mutually practiced. "But in order to eliminate any kind of prejudice, I think two people have to understand each other to eliminate it," Dressler concluded.[63] Cooperation between the two races was essential, both for improving relations between the two peoples and for the successful placement of Indian Americans in urban areas.

Relocation centers varied in their success in carrying out their difficult tasks. Several factors caused the ineffective administration of the relocation program. Most relocation officers were non-Indians who lacked a sound understanding of Native American cultures, thus preventing them from comprehending traditional behavior patterns. Some had worked previously with the War Relocation Authority, which had displaced Japanese Americans during World War II, and they proved to be insensitive to Indian needs and problems. In addition, some offices lacked staffs sufficient to handle the large number of relocatees. Shortages in adequate housing added to the problems, and efforts to stretch funds forced officials to place Indian families in slums and in downtrodden neighborhoods that were mostly populated by other racial groups.[64]

Poor living conditions in relocation areas increased public criticism of the government. "We are going to pay the debt owed to the Indian, a debt born of broken treaties, harsh treatment, and 'Indian business' such as the morale-breaking relocation program," wrote Louis Cioffi, in a second irate letter to President Eisenhower.[65] Another angry citizen attacked the commissioner of Indian affairs: "Mr. Emmons is optimistic about the success of his Indian Voluntary Relocation Service. I have known many Indians who have been sold this bill of goods, only to write home begging for their families who were 'provided housing' that consisted of condemned quarters where Negroes were moved out and where the mothers had to stay awake nights and fight off the rats to keep them from biting their children."[66]

Some problems of ineffective relocation were attributed to the Native Americans' lack of marketable job skills. In November 1959, the superintendent at the Fort Apache Indian Agency in Arizona reported that the low education level of White Mountain Apache applicants disqualified them for relocation. Lacking any usable skill was another reason for dismissing applicants. The superintendent said that "we feel that it would be a disservice to the applicant if he were sent to a metropolitan area on relocation when we feel sure they could not succeed."[67] He recommended vocational training in the unskilled and semiskilled trades for the White Mountain Apaches. However, their lack of education, would hinder their potential success in adjusting to urban life. Fortunately, a vocational training agreement was negotiated with Southwest Lumber Mills to assist the Indians, and a local radio station agreed to publicize relocation opportunities and adult vocational training programs.

In another report during mid-November of the same year, John C. Dibbern, superintendent of the Colorado River Agency evaluated the relocation program for tribes under his jurisdiction. The Native American's individual concept of an acceptable standard of living, he commented, was dependent on government services, and those represented a federal security blanket. A living standard acceptable to traditional Indians did not satisfy the expectations of relocation officers and the mainstream society. Citing relocation records, Dibbern noted that nontraditional Indians seeking an improved standard of living had a better education and some experience in living off the reservation; and they possessed individual qualities to ameliorate their socioeconomic status.[68]

Dibbern listed several problems that hindered the traditional Indians under his jurisdiction. Drinking was common among unemployed and idle persons. But numerous individuals, who took advantage of relocation services and became gainfully employed, discontinued drinking. "Illegitimate children and unmarried mothers" presented another problem, as job placement for these women was difficult, if not impossible. An additional problem involved locating nursery care for their children. "Large families" proved to be troublesome: it was difficult to find employment for a father that paid him enough to support his entire family as well as to locate housing for families of six or more people. "Obesity" was also a problem, for employers tended to refuse to hire overweight relocatees—the case for many Indians of the Colorado River Indian Agency.[69]

On 25 November 1959, Dr. Sophie Aberle, former general superintendent of the United Pueblos Agency, sent a memorandum to Commissioner Emmons about the "weak or wrong policies held by the B. I. A," in an effort to provide possible solutions for a more effective supervision of Indian affairs. Aberle attributed policy breakdowns to the difficulties experienced in the relocation program. She recommended better screening and more training of applicants to reduce the large number of returnees. She noted that relocation workers processed relocatees too hastily in an effort to meet quotas and to prove the program successful. Therefore, the program seemed to be self-defeating. In brief, relocation did not offer a workable "solution" to the "Indian problem," according to Aberle, because of the high expense involved in placing people and the large number who returned to the reservations.[70]

Dr. Aberle expressed sympathy for Native Americans as victims of federal policy, but her views and recommendations received scant attention from federal officials. The processing of relocatees was aided by Indian eagerness to apply for relocation, thereby fueling official efforts to meet quotas regardless of whether it was right or wrong to place Native Americans in urban areas. Hence, officials made every effort to place the program in a positive light. In fact, articles in Phoenix newspapers on 28 and 29 February 1960, reported that Commissioner Emmons had pronounced the relocation program successful. "About 70 per cent of the 31,259 Indians who left their reservations for Western and Midwestern cities since 1952 have become self-supporting," stated the Commissioner.[71] The highest reported rate of successful relocations was 76 percent in 1955, and the lowest was 61 percent in 1958.

In an effort to find out for themselves, the Navajo Tribal Council established a four-member committee to survey Navajos to determine the success of the program. The committee suspected individuals of fraudulent practices and organizations of taking advantage of relocatees' difficulties; but it could not find supportive evidence. According to the Navajos, individuals and self-interest groups allegedly used the problems of relocation to denounce the BIA and the whole relocation program for their own purposes and for publicity.[72]

Increasing criticism of the BIA forced officials to respond regularly to allegations of wrongdoing in relocation and termination. Assistant Indian Commissioner Thomas Reid attempted to enlighten the delegates of the Province of the Midwest of the Episcopal Church at Cincinnati, who inquired about the negative spiritual impact of relocation on Indians. Reid mentioned that it was well known that the majority of reservation tribes were becoming poorer each year, while their increasing populations depleted reservation resources. "In order to help the Indians in breaking out of this vicious cycle of poverty, paternalism, and despair, we in the Bureau of Indian Affairs are taking a number of constructive steps," Reid added.[73]

The relocation program maintained a staff at forty-five agencies; nine area offices, including Alaska; and nine field offices. The adult vocational training program offered the most assistance to Indians in obtaining jobs skills. Comprehensive training opportunities had been developed, and 346 courses were approved at 130 different institutions. The courses that interested Indians included auto mechanics, welding, cosmetology, and radio and television repair, as well as stenography and typing.

In Oklahoma, relocation officers worked with a dedicated

enthusiasm to place Native Americans in urban areas. They ignored assigned quotas from the Washington office, working solely from the standpoint of human welfare. In general, the Oklahoma Indians reciprocated the officials' enthusiasm, and they perceived relocation as an opportunity to improve their personal economic status. However, some full-blood Cherokees, who recalled the "Trail of Tears," and some elderly Kiowas and Comanches resented relocation as another government scheme to get rid of them.[74]

As Americans were undergoing an overall economic adjustment to urbanization, dependency on land for a livelihood became less important. The nation's economy now rested on mechanization, which began to replace labor and enabled industrialization in urban areas to develop at a rapid pace. While industries thrived, increasing technology demanded more qualified workers. Schools, colleges, and universities supplied the training for a work force that became increasingly specialized. The relocation program offered Native Americans the opportunity to share in this development.[75]

One of the chief objectives of the relocation program was the desegregation of the reservation Indian population. Federal officials hoped that relocation would assimilate Indians into urban neighborhoods of the dominant society. Instead, Indian ghettos soon resulted. Chicago's Uptown neighborhood is indicative of the Indians' substandard economic living conditions.[76] Bell and Bell Gardens in Los Angeles are other examples. Such areas fostered feelings of isolation, loneliness, and estrangement for Native Americans. Many resorted to alcohol to escape the competitive and social coldness of highly individualized urbanization. Marital and delinquency problems became acute; broken marriages, school dropouts, and increases in crime were so rampant that discouraged relocatees became severely depressed and sometimes committed suicide. Tragically, a people who traditionally cherished life were now broken in spirit. Many would not return home to reservations because of self-pride: they did not want to admit failure, even though relatives beckoned them to return.

As relocation continued, some program officers became sensitive to the new problems that urban Indians faced. One such official recalled her own personal experience of being alone in a large city: "Some of my first friends were the Indian people that I worked with, being alone when I first came. My children were in New York City at the time, so I came out and stayed here alone; it was school time then. They came out to join me when I found a house. But, I realized what they [the relocatees] were faced with—the big city, the traffic, the noise, the many, many people, just the strangeness of it, and how alone you could be in the midst of so many people."[77]

A remedy for Indian estrangement in the cities was the establishment of Indian centers. For instance, St. Augustine's Indian Center and the American Indian Center, both in Chicago's Uptown neighborhood, continue to provide counseling, temporary shelter, and other assistance to urban Indians. Similar centers in other cities offer the same services as well as opportunities for socialization among traditional Native Americans, who are a communal people. Interestingly, mutual tribal concerns and interaction dissolved many barriers between tribal groups who had never before associated with each other. Increasingly, Indian Americans in urban areas have identified themselves as Indians rather than by tribal designation.

Such socialization saved the relocated Indians. In essence, the communal tradition of Indians on reservations was imitated in urban areas. Powwows, dances, Indian bowling teams, Indian softball teams, and other related activities have intensified the survival of Indians as an identifiable ethnic group in the large cities.

Those people who remained on reservations during the relocation years of the 1950s experienced considerable economic difficulty. Even though their living conditions have improved since 1945, they often paid a high price for staying in their reservation homelands. In particular, relocation perhaps resulted in less efficient leadership among reservation tribes during the 1950s.[78] Unfortunately, those tribal members possessing the best qualifications, and who could probably have provided a more effective leadership, were apt to relocate; and after relocating, they rarely returned to the reservation to help their tribes.

Ironically, at the same time, the majority of Indians who moved to urban areas suffered socially, economically, and psychologically. In many cases, urban Indians have traded rural poverty on reservations for urban slums. Their survival in urban areas, however, yielded hope and a brighter future for their offspring. Indian youths growing up in an urban environment often become teachers, lawyers, doctors, and other professionals. It is an unfortunate fact that success in the white world is costing them the heritage of their native culture. Today, Indians continue to experience difficulties in substituting traditional values for those of a modern world—materialism and competition.

One Indian living in California summarized the Native American reaction to relocation best:

> At the very outset, we thought it would be a good thing. It would give Indians an opportunity to spread their wings and gain education and employment and generally become equal to all other men. But after about a year or two years, at the outside, we discovered that there was an ulterior motive behind the earlier relocation program. It was designed, in fact, to get all Indians off all reservations within X number of years. I think at that time, it said twenty years; since then it has been erased, however. So, then we started digging in our heels to prevent total assimilation; assimilation to the degree that we would lose our identity as Indian people, lose our culture and our [way] of living.[79]

8

Commissioner Glenn L. Emmons and Economic Assistance

Federal Indian policy continued to flounder during the years of the second Eisenhower administration. The lack of a consistent policy for termination, along with a rash of withdrawal legislation, caused confusion and mixed feelings among Indian people. Many believed that all services to the tribes would be cut, and some Native Americans actually feared that termination meant their tribe might be stripped of everything. The BIA became their common enemy; and Commissioner Glenn L. Emmons became the focal point of tribal criticism, as federal-Indian rapport suffered. Ironically, Emmons tried to serve Indian interests, but the termination policy overshadowed the commissioner's endeavors to improve ties between the government and tribal groups. To avoid negative reactions while speaking with Native Americans, federal officials often justified policy with euphemisms like *withdrawal, readjustment, assimilation, liberation,* and *desegregation.* However, already poor relations continued to deteriorate, and even successfully assimilated Indians, who favored their own termination, frequently refused to endorse the policy for all Indian people.[1]

Native American affairs under the direction of Commissioner Emmons moved toward the implementation of economic recovery plans for post-termination Indian communities. Various programs were begun for improving the welfare of Indian people and tribes, while attempting to convince them to accept a steady withdrawal of federal trust. On 21 February 1957, the Department of the Interior announced new loan regulations to aid tribes in attracting industry to their reservations. Tribal groups could borrow money from their trust accounts; the Navajo Tribe, for example, received a loan of 300,000 dollars to pursue industrial development in their area.[2] Several months later, the

Interior Department announced the appointment of Noel Sargent as a consultant to develop industrial programs for the Indian Bureau; Sargent's role would lead to the creation of a new department in the Washington office to supply business advice to tribal groups.[3]

One of the tribes with promising potential for business development was the Menominee. In March, Commissioner Emmons met with the Menominee Indian Study Council to discuss post-termination plans and to urge the development of free-enterprise business. Committee member Professor Ray A. Brown, a lawyer who was placed on the committee to answer legal questions, commented on the many changes facing the Menominee, saying that "termination seems to be the beginning of the end—the beginning of a new era for the Indian people."[4] He felt that P.L. 399 would work, but to succeed, the Menominees would have to deal with many hazards and changes. Brown referred to the Menominees' sawmill, which quickly became central to the tribe's economic hopes. Although the sawmill earned an estimated profit of half a million dollars from the tribe's vast timber forest, Brown pointed out that there were taxes to be considered. After termination, about half of that profit would go to state taxes, and land taxes would amount to roughly ten cents per acre. In order for the tribe to sustain financial growth over a long period, considerable care would need to be taken to make certain that the forest was not logged out. Consultants estimated real estate taxes and state taxes to be about one-quarter of a million dollars annually. Such threats to financial survival worried both the study committee and the Menominee Tribal Council as they worked to create a profitable plan before the deadline for termination arrived.

Two main objectives of the BIA under Emmons involved making the tribes economically independent and providing them with sound planning assistance. Additional funds were designated for the credit extension program to enable tribes to obtain loans, which could then be loaned to individual members or to tribal enterprises. Under the loan program the BIA acted as a business consultant, teaching tribal officers how to review loan applications and make disbursements.

By coming to the financial aid of tribal groups, Emmons enhanced his efforts to improve the reputation of the Bureau of

Indian Affairs. In 1957, the Washington *Post* reported that the Department of the Interior would commend him with its highest honor for outstanding achievement, the Distinguished Service Award. The Interior Department recognized Commissioner Emmons for advancing the health protection, educational facilities, and economic potential of Indian people. He was especially cited for his reform efforts among the Navajos since 1953. Many citizens who were impressed with his work wrote to express gratitude for his aid to Native Americans.[5] The Bureau's public relations had indeed somewhat improved due to the emphasis on economic assistance in place of the Myer policy for immediate termination of trust.

Although the federal termination policy continued, Emmons eased the transition confronting tribes by stressing economic preparation for federal withdrawal. He clarified policy aims by explaining that through research, evaluation, education, and protection of Indian rights appropriate aid could be supplied to Indian communities to help them achieve self-sufficiency. In a proposal presented to the Secretary of the Interior in 1958, Emmons focused on economic optimism, writing that "termination of trusteeship means no loss, only gain, to the Indian." He noted that the "policy of the Bureau of Indian Affairs was to encourage the tribe to incorporate so that every enrolled member of the tribe will be a stockholder in the corporation."[6] Otherwise, the members could select a private trustee who would be responsible for holding the tribal properties and for assuming the functions previously exercised by the Secretary of the Interior as the trustee for individuals. The BIA aimed to give all American Indians full rights and guaranteed privileges of citizenship, as well as freedom from discriminatory federal restrictions, by 4 July 1976, the celebration of America's bicentennial.

With Emmons's focus on the economy of tribes, additional legislation was necessary to protect Native American rights after the termination of trust status. In 1957, Senator James Murray and Representative Lee Metcalf introduced Senate Resolution 3 and House Concurrent 155, calling for continuous development of Indian human and economic resources based upon the principles of consent of Indian groups, self-determination, and self-government. It is important to note that the bills deviated from the absolute termination of federal supervision ordained in H.C.R. 108.[7] Giving tribal groups "consent" rights would prolong the withdrawal process, and would likely increase federal appropriations for services. Interestingly, Indian participation had now become a factor in the policy activities of the government.

While the nation slipped into an economic slump during the fall of 1957 and the first half of 1958, Indian opposition and spiraling Bureau expenditures rekindled public scrutiny and criticism. With their comments directed to the president and other federal officials, concerned citizens publicly denounced the government's termination policy and its lasting effects on Indians. In response to one person's complaints involving the Navajos, President Eisenhower stated that he had the utmost concern for Indian problems and that he had urged the Department of the Interior to give high priority in fulfilling government obligations to the tribe.[8] The president explained to another person that the central guideline of federal policy was to work constructively and cooperatively with Indians toward the development of programs that would prepare them for full independence. In fact, the government's position on termination had shifted to an emphasis on economic development. Defenders of the new policy assured the public that both the Secretary of the Interior and the commissioner of Indian affairs explicitly and vigorously opposed "wholesale" or "overnight" termination of federal trust responsibilities in Indian affairs.[9] In spite of the government's revised policy, public opinion became an effective watchdog for scrutinizing the federal supervision of Indian policy.

Even with assurance from the president of his positive intentions in federal-Indian relations, a barrage of criticism pelted the Bureau of Indian Affairs and Congress. During early November 1957, an article in *The Christian Century* magazine charged that the two federal bodies were mishandling Indian affairs and ignoring Indian interest groups who wanted to assist. Federal policy based on H.C.R. 108 was bluntly condemned as ineffective and as floundering under a clumsy bureaucracy. Such vigorous attacks probably spawned the introduction of two new bills, S. 3 and H.R. 2787, which gained support in Congress. Both measures contained provisions to reform federal Indian policy by allowing Indians to participate in decisions affecting their affairs.[10] Although neither bill supplied specifics, S. 3 called for the principles of consent, and H.R. 2787 would allow tribes to develop programs best suited for their needs.

The need for change in federal Indian policy, and perhaps in the organization of the BIA, was further exemplified by the misfortunes of the Northern Cheyennes of Montana. The tribe attempted to purchase sixty tracts of land within their reservation from the BIA, which had advertised the land for sale. The availability of a sufficient water supply made the land especially desirable. Months before the sale, the tribe sold some of its cattle to raise money for the land purchase, accumulating forty thousand dollars in tribal funds. Tribal officials tried to withdraw their money for the purchase, but the BIA held up the funds for an audit, thus causing the Indians to miss the sale. The frustrated Cheyennes lost almost one thousand acres of land due to the red tape of the Bureau of Indian Affairs.[11]

The case of the Northern Cheyennes, combined with general BIA ineffectiveness, caused Oliver La Farge to fire criticism at the Bureau. He pointed out that during the past three years the BIA had authorized the sale of more than 927,926 acres of Indian land, of which more than 292,488 acres was fee-patented and open for non-Indian purchase.[12] The Bureau professed that it was acting in the best interests of the tribes, when in reality it was hindering the Indian groups in their business ventures. In brief, there were no simple solutions to the multiple problems in Indian affairs, especially when tribal affairs, like the Klamath's, often involved highly complicated situations that sometimes overwhelmed the Bureau.[13] Furthermore, each tribal group represented a unique and individual case, and the government's federal policy was not always applicable. The size of the tribal population, the amount of assets, and the types of holding properties affected decisions, often creating complications. One axiom existed; larger tribes with vast holdings presented the most problems.

In spite of numerous complications with tribes, federal termination proceeded smoothly for some Indian groups, usually the smaller ones. On 17 December 1957, the chief of the branch of tribal programs began termination programs for the seven small tribes in northeastern Oklahoma. Bureau field-workers kept tribal members updated, and the tribes and the BIA frequently conferred on withdrawal procedures. The small amount of tribal property involved helped to expedite the termination proceedings. The Eastern Shawnees possessed 58.19 acres, the Seneca-Cayuga 1,052.89 acres, and the Modocs owned two individual allotments and a four-acre cemetery. The landholdings of the Peorias, Wyandots, and Quapaws were also small.[14]

In summarizing federal-Indian affairs at the end of 1957, one change in the termination policy was especially noteworthy. The termination policy became an expensive operation that was incongruent with the retrenchment guidelines of the Republican Congress of Eisenhower's early administration. Congress appropriated a record 109,410,000 dollars for Indian programs and the operations of the Bureau of Indian Affairs in 1957, amounting to 25 percent, or 21 million dollars, more than had been appropriated for the previous year. Efforts to improve the economy of Native American groups mainly accounted for the increased expenditures on Indian affairs. Furthermore, dealing with the problems of the Klamath and the Menominee, who captured more public attention than any other Indian group, aroused the utmost concern among federal officials.

Due to the national attention given to the Menominees, the first major tribe to be terminated, what happened to them could be expected to influence the other tribal groups' responses to termination. Their troubled experiences led to a growing Indian reluctance to accept termination, which hindered the government's efforts to bring about the end of federal supervision over Indian affairs. By the end of March 1958 termination programs existed only for the Klamaths and Uintah-Ouray; although other programs were still being developed for six groups, including three small Oklahoma tribes.[15]

Ineffective communication resulted in frequent misunderstandings between the government and the tribes, which affected even the smaller Indian groups. A few of the smaller tribes lacked an official body to represent their interests to Bureau officials. In an effort to solve the communication problem, Muskogee Area Director Fickinger informed other area directors to follow the procedures used to terminate the Quapaws. The Quapaw plan created a tribal council and a business committee to represent them in negotiations with the federal government.[16] Initially, Bureau officials had met with all of the tribal members, and the lack of an organized tribal body resulted in confusion. By adopting this plan, federal officials would not need all tribal members present at meetings, and a better working relation between the government and the tribes could be achieved.

One of the small tribes, the Catawbas of South Carolina, had no difficulty in conveying their wishes for federal withdrawal. In April 1958, Congressman Robert W. Hemphill of South Carolina proposed termination legislation for the tribe. The Catawbas, a proud people, had long ago adapted to white ways. Unfortunately, their numbers had declined over the years from 6,000 people, owning 144,000 acres of land, to 614 members. Hemphill contended that holding the Catawba land in trust prevented the people from improving their economy. The Indians appeared comfortable with the ways of their white neighbors, but trust status prevented them from obtaining loans for homes or for conducting business affairs. As a solution, the Catawbas adopted a tribal resolution authorizing Hemphill to introduce a termination bill in Congress.[17] Almost a year later, the Catawbas met at the request of Congressman Hemphill to discuss the proposed bill. In a vote taken on the withdrawal of federal supervision, forty out of fifty-seven members favored ending trust relations, while seventeen were opposed.[18]

During the meeting concerning Hemphill's bill, one Catawba, Gladys Thomas, described the conditions that her people faced: "We live out in the country and use old country roads. When I went to school we were not even permitted to ride the school bus. I had to quit school in the ninth grade because they didn't allow our people on the reservations to hold public jobs which amounted to anything more than cutting sorghum."[19] Mrs. Thomas stated that the Catawba Indians were refused government services many times on the pretext that they were not taxpayers. She responded that she paid taxes on her income and sales tax on all purchases. Her only exemption was freedom from property taxes. She agreed that trust status hindered the Catawbas from earning better livelihoods, but she pointed out that termination was not for all Indians. Just like any group of people, there would be a few who would not try. After discussion of the Hemphill bill, Congress approved the legislation to dissolve trust relations with the Catawbas.

Unlike the Catawbas, who wanted termination, other small tribes, like the Fort Sill Apaches, were reportedly forced into accepting termination although they were not ready for it. Such alleged mishandling of Indian affairs rallied immediate public support to the Indians' side. America's capitalistic society was blamed for pressuring even the larger tribes, like the Klamaths and Menominees, into accepting termination. In both cases, Emmons tried to convince the tribes to become competitive in order to survive in the business world. Economic pressures compelled the tribal members to favor the abrogation of trust restrictions over their properties, but some federal supervision was still needed to assist the tribes in their self-determined efforts to prepare for termination deadlines. In a letter to California Senator Clair Engle, one citizen wrote that all Native Americans deserved the right to government assistance in the management of their own affairs and reservations until they became self-supporting.[20]

While the government continued its policy of federal withdrawal of supervision over tribal affairs, the BIA promised to assist Indians in the areas of health and education. During the first week in July, Commissioner Emmons addressed the Triennial Conference of the National Fellowship of Indian Workers at Estes Park, Colorado. His address highlighted the progress in Indian health under the Eisenhower administration, especially in the late 1950s. Emmons stated that twice as many physicians now served in Indian health programs; the number of public health nurses had tripled; and health education and sanitation staffs had been enlarged. Broader and more adequate educational opportunities were noted. In reference to the Navajos, 90 percent of Navajo children now attended school, as compared to 50 percent in 1953. Emmons asserted that Indian success depended upon individual effort, whereas a communal life-style undermined morale. Furthermore, he said, individuals and groups who convinced Indians that they should be allowed to maintain tribal status only jeopardized their possibilities for successful livelihoods. As a result, the traditional Native Americans became demoralized when they attempted to intermingle with people in the dominant society. This common experience baffled federal officials who believed that Indians possessed the inherent capability to succeed.[21] It was imperative that Indians realize that their values had to adjust to those of white Americans before they could achieve the mainstream's level of success.

At the end of August 1958, a surge of optimism enveloped officials of the Department of Interior who reported on the progress of Indian education. Some tribes, like the Wind River Shoshones of Wyoming, had created college scholarship programs with assistance from the federal government and philanthropic organizations. The number of Indians studying beyond the high school level had risen noticeably from approximately 2,300, in the 1954–55 academic year, to more than 3,800, in 1957–58, an increase of about 65 percent in three years. In fact, twenty-four tribes had scholarship programs to encourage higher education among their members. The realization of the importance of education among Native Americans was quite apparent in the late 1950s.[22]

The overall improvement in Indian education convinced federal officials that certain Indian groups had progressed enough to have little need of future government supervision. In the case of California Indians, the Eighty-fifth Congress passed Public Law 671, with Eisenhower's support, authorizing the distribution of lands and assets of forty-one Indian *rancherías* and reservations to their members.[23] The measure accounted for one of the largest number of Indian communities to be terminated with one sweep. California Indians included under P.L. 671 were believed to be among the most advanced because they seemed to possess the qualities and values of their white neighbors. After the passage of P.L. 671, Emmons urged Area Director Leonard Hill of the Sacramento Agency to encourage BIA field-workers to persuade Indians under his jurisdiction to develop their own programs toward economic independence.[24] Unfortunately, the Bureau's assumption that federal withdrawal would not harm the California Indians drew further criticism of the termination policy.

On 18 September, Interior Secretary Seaton spoke on radio station KCLA in Flagstaff, Arizona, to clarify the relationship of current federal Indian policy to the 1953 H.C.R. 108. Seaton acknowledged that the media had recently given considerable attention to the pros and cons of public opinion about Indian policy, and he complained that the views against termination policy were heavily prejudiced. He said some people believed that Congress and the Department of the Interior intended to "abandon Indian groups regardless of their ability to fend for themselves."[25] The Interior Secretary assured the radio audience that this was not the case, and that the government was assisting Indian groups until aid was no longer needed.

While Emmons's office emphasized the positive aspects of termination policy, individual citizens and organizations questioned the motives of the government. Montana Congressman Lee Metcalf claimed that the BIA had occasionally pressured Indians into accepting termination. He asserted that the federal government had failed to protect Indian rights and land titles. As evidence, Metcalf pointed out that funds for the Menominees were withheld until the Indians agreed to termination.[26] At the 1958 annual NCAI conference, President Joseph Garry of the National Congress of American Indians told an audience of tribal delegates that the present federal policy was the worst one since the beginning of the twentieth century. He alluded to the number of real-estate offices that had mushroomed across Indian country, charging that the Bureau's position on individually owned Indian land encouraged a greedy surge in acquiring Indian properties. The administration's policies, in short, resulted in impoverishment for Indians.[27]

Accusations of unjust treatment of Native Americans and mishandling of Indian affairs constantly forced federal officials to clarify the objectives of federal Indian policy. A television special on the program *Kaleidoscope* reported on the plight of Indians and reinforced viewers' beliefs that the Bureau of Indian Affairs mishandled Indian affairs. The program prompted one viewer to write to his congressman: "In all my life I've never heard a good word for this Bureau. Couldn't this Bureau be transferred to the Department of Health, Education, and Welfare where it might get more human and Christian leadership than it apparently receives from the Interior?"[28]

In response to the wave of criticism generated by the program, the Department of the Interior released a statement explaining its position and emphasizing its generous services to Indian people. The Interior Department stated that more sources of financing were now available to Indians to fund their activities than ever before. In 1958 the total financing exceeded 90 million dollars, or more than double the amount in 1953. Tribal funds and loans through the Bureau totaled 30,557,000 dollars, about 33 percent of the total financing. The remainder was furnished by customary financial institutions.[29]

As a part of its defense, the Interior Department press release asked the question: "Why, then do we still have a so-called 'Indian problem' in the United States today?" In answering its own question, the press release stated that, basically, the government had been too paternalistic with Indian people throughout the history of federal-Indian relations. In addition, the government had given the Indians every reason to believe that it would always furnish them with free food, lodging and other services. Its fatherly image undermined Indian initiative and encouraged an attitude of drifting. Obviously, Indians could not always expect the government to provide for them as it had done in the past. Successful Indian livelihood depended upon adjusting to the life-style of a modernized American society, which meant Indians should stop being dependent and learn to stand on their own feet.

A November 1958 report to Congress from the Comptroller General reviewed the current programming, budgeting, accounting, and activities of the Bureau of Indian Affairs. The report disputed the Bureau's optimistic claim to effective administration of Indian Affairs. It disclosed weaknesses in federal supervision over the termination program, and cited area offices in Gallup, New Mexico, and Aberdeen, South Dakota, with a failure to employ the BIA's policy of long-range planning for tribes slated to be terminated. Evidence indicated that too much effort was placed on dealing with old business rather than on making recommendations for the financial future of the tribal members. The report also criticized the Bureau in Washington for delays in programming for construction and maintenance of buildings and utilities throughout the reservations. When top officials of other departments had requested immediate action, the Bureau of Indian Affairs was slow to process the paperwork necessary to facilitate projects. In essence, the report disclosed that the BIA had become such a cumbersome bureaucracy that it could not keep up with its obligations to Indians.[30]

Despite the delays in administering federal services to Native Americans, appropriations for all BIA programs for 1955–58 increased. The Indian Bureau had now expanded its emphasis to include funding health programs, resource management, and educational assistance. Such generous services were noted in the commissioner's 1958 annual report to the Secretary of Interior, which also emphasized that tribes undergoing termination received special treatment.

Although federal funding for Indian programs in educational, health, and economic matters had increased, the actual progress in these areas remained questionable. For example, a determination of the percentage of Indian children who attended public schools in the late 1950s was difficult. In the extreme South, whites discriminated against Indians as well as blacks—despite the *Brown v. Board of Education of Topeka, Kansas* decision in 1954, and the Little Rock Arkansas, incident in 1957, which supposedly assured equal and desegregated educational opportunities. In Mississippi less than twenty-five Indian children went to public schools in the state's large areas, and none attended in the rural districts where most Indians lived. The Indian children were denied enrollment in rural white schools, and their parents refused to send them to schools populated by blacks. Similarly, in North Carolina only limited progress had been made in enrolling Indian children in public schools. In Louisiana the Bureau of Indian Affairs had operated a school for Indian students only since 1940. And in Florida, two-thirds of the Seminole children in the state lacked the same educational opportunities of white youths.[31]

In the area of Indian health the government reported considerable improvement. Conflicting reports indicated that more needed to be done. Secretary Arthur S. Flemming of Health, Education, and Welfare reported significant improvements in Indian health, while other reports disclosed startling cases of Indian suffering throughout the 1950s. Flemming reported that tuberculosis, once the leading cause of death among Indians, had dropped 40 percent for all Indians from 1954 to 1957, and for Alaska Natives it had decreased 63 percent. A 12-percent reduction in infant deaths was cited as well as a 26-percent drop in the death rate for diseases of the stomach and intestines.[32]

Flemming noted the importance of educational deficiencies among Indians. Many Indians possessed a limited understanding of health and diseases, which impeded health improvement. Furthermore, the geographic isolation of some 250 federal Indian reservations and hundreds of Alaska Natives' villages handicapped the government in providing health services in the field. Poor economic conditions among Native Americans also hindered the improvement of their health because many simply could not afford to travel to treatment facilities.[33]

Continued efforts by Commissioner Emmons and other Bureau workers to aid Native Americans did not produce praise from Congress. In fact, Senator Mike Mansfield of Montana lashed out at the BIA's general supervision of Native American affairs and urged his colleagues to support Senate Concurrent Resolution 12, calling for a restatement of federal Indian policy. In Mansfield's words, the BIA was "trying to move too fast and many of its policies on welfare, land sales, and relocation tend to thrust responsibilities on many Indians before they are ready, and to dissolve traditional Indian relationships."[34] Senators James E. Murray and Richard Neuberger, who introduced S.C.R. 12, stressed that rapid liquidation of tribal-federal ties should be halted.

In response to general Indian fears of premature termination and their difficulties in comprehending H.C.R. 108, Murray and Neuberger introduced another resolution in the Senate, proposing that Indian groups should not be terminated unless they understood fully the withdrawal procedure and agreed to end trust relations. Congressman Lee Metcalf sponsored a similar bill, H.C.R. 93, in the House, but neither measure passed into law.

Unlike some tribes who had difficulty in comprehending the political implications of H.C.R. 108, the Oklahoma Choctaws seized the initiative in abrogating their trust relationship with the government. In April 1959, the Choctaws requested the introduction of legislation that would call for limiting government restrictions over tribal properties. The Choctaws supported House Resolution 2722, a measure which proposed the sale of tribal lands but did not affect individual allotted lands. More than seventeen thousand acres were to be sold and the proceeds deposited to the credit of the tribe in the United States Treasury. The Choctaws already had 433,000 dollars in the tribal fund for distribution to its 19,139 enrolled members.[35] Like many Oklahoma Indians, they appeared successfully integrated with local whites and were considered to be one of the more advanced Native American groups, which assured federal officials that they were correct in extinguishing trust relations with the Choctaws.

The integration of Choctaws in non-Indian communities, as well as the willingness of tribes like the Catawbas to become independent, encouraged BIA officials to promote industrial development on or near reservations. Other factors included the rapid increase in tribal populations, which made farming and stock-raising impractical as rising demands on the land exhausted the soil and depleted grazing areas. To seek possible solutions, Commissioner Emmons met with the Navajo-sponsored Conference of Industrial Development at Gallup, New Mexico, on 21 May 1959, to discuss the prospects and possibilities for industrial development, at least in the Southwest where Indians were in greater need of economic relief. The commissioner recommended attracting more industries near the reservations to supply more jobs for local Indians and to improve tribal economies.[36]

Commissioner Emmons then turned his efforts toward other parts of the country. In Florida, his efforts to help Indians impressed the Seminoles so much that they passed a tribal resolution to honor the commissioner. The ceremonial presentation was held in Washington, D. C., on 26 May 1959. In addition, the Seminoles recommended that Emmons should again be awarded the Distinguished Service Award of the Interior.[37] His rapport with Native Americans had gained for him the respect of a large number of other tribes. The commissioner continually sought cooperation with Native Americans, which made him quite popular, although Indian Americans generally remained skeptical of the federal government.

In June 1959, H.R. 7701 was introduced during the Eighty-sixth Congress, calling for improvement in the general welfare of all Indian people. The resolution proposed a program of economic uplift, entitled "Operation Bootstrap," which was patterned after a similar undertaking in Puerto Rico. House Resolution 7701 was liberally constructed to include tribal self-determination, and it reemphasized the goal of industrial development rather than concentrating on farming and ranching.[38]

In hopes of advancing tribal efforts for economic independence, the federal government endorsed a policy of donating land to selected tribes suffering from a shortage of natural resources. In June 1959, Assistant Secretary Roger Ernst presented a draft of a bill to the president of the Senate, Richard Nixon, proposing the donation to Indian communities of approximately 346,370 acres of federally owned submarginal lands, located next to tribal lands, to help Indians obtain maximum benefits from their land.[39] In the mid-1930s, the United States government had purchased the lands under the National Industrial Recovery Act, intending to protect the lands from exploitation by private interests and to maintain them for possible use by local tribes. Conservation considerations required federal supervision to prevent damage to the lands, thereby raising the question of whether the tribes should have actual or trust ownership of the lands. Ernst believed that either choice would be acceptable. Senator Murray followed up on Ernst's draft by introducing S.B. 2345, which was approved. The donated lands increased both the size of reservations and the amount of natural resources available for tribal advancement.[40]

The ultimate objective of federal policy continued to be the withdrawal of government supervision over tribal affairs. Emmons viewed economic development as the final phase of preparation for termination, and he pushed to assist and advise tribes in that area. At this time, Senator James Murray criticized the Bureau and Commissioner Emmons for their inept handling of Indian affairs. The senator alleged financial mismanagement of Indian affairs since the beginning of Emmons's tenure. He particularly referred to the revolving loan fund, an Indian New Deal reform that John Collier had established under the Indian Reorganization Act in 1934. According to Murray, the BIA did not have adequate guidelines for evaluating requests for loans from tribes that wanted to develop lands. Moreover, the development of some reservations was not practical because of the poor quality of the soil, lack of sufficient water, and overgrazed land.[41] When tribes were able to produce revenue from their lands, their delinquency in paying back loans often jeopardized their financial status, thereby increasing their dependency on the government.

Murray also faulted the Eisenhower administration's attitude in the mismanagement of Indian affairs. He claimed that the administration expounded dogmatic ideas about assimilation and failed to inform Indians about the reality of living in cities. Expounding the principles of the American way of life, Murray noted, did not alleviate either the Indian's deplorable health conditions or their substandard economy. He further contended that the government should first consider the social and economic welfare of Native Americans. After improving the Indians' livelihoods, the government could then work toward convincing Indians that they no longer required federal assistance. The senator made a valid point. The Eisenhower administration's concern with assimilating Indians to help realize the government's goal of a middle-class society did not consider the Indians' retention of their own traditional values. Cultural differences among Native Americans also hindered the effectiveness of federal supervision of Indian affairs. Murray made an important point in stating that the objectives of federal Indian policy should consider their effect on human beings. Until the government showed more concern for the social and economic problems involved in any federal policy, that policy would fail.

Emmons was well aware of the differences between traditional Indians and whites, although he adhered to the general Indian policy established under the Eisenhower administration. After the Bureau was accused again of terminating tribes for the purpose of selling their lands, Emmons attempted to explain the government's Indian policy for what seemed the one-hundredth time. He pointed out the Bureau's efforts in developing long-range tribal programs for improving the Indians' social, economic, and political welfare. The government's goal, he said, was to help tribes achieve self-sufficiency to the point where they no longer needed special government services; then, the Bureau's involvement in Indian affairs could be terminated. Hence, Emmons advocated gradual termination to liberate the tribes and their members from federal trust restrictions. But he wanted restrictions to be withdrawn only after tribal members were capable of handling their own affairs. On this principle, Emmons's policy resembled John Collier's advocacy of his plan to restore tribal governments until Native Americans were confident of their abilities to supervise their own affairs and chose to dissolve their relationship with the federal government. Although termination continued as a policy, not enough credit has been attributed to Emmons for helping Native Americans through one of the most crucial periods of federal-Indian relations. To the misfortune of the federal government, the plight of American Indians during the termination years subjected the

Eisenhower administration to constant criticism.[42] The legacy of the termination policy inherited from the Eighty-third Congress—and from Dillon S. Myer, Arthur Watkins, and other staunch terminationists—plagued later humanitarians like Emmons who tried to assist Indian people.

Federally supervised programs that were ineffective in preparing terminated tribes were continued, along with the persistence of substandard living conditions on reservations, as Native Americans entered the 1960s. In brief, the termination program of the previous decade had not remedied the economic malaise on reservations, in spite of Emmons's efforts in pushing for economic recovery. In 1960, the Denver *Post* reported that Indian communities at Rosebud and Pine Ridge, South Dakota, were experiencing severe economic hardships. The Oglala at Pine Ridge, who numbered 12,300, averaged a monthly income of less than 100 dollars per family, and most of that amount came from public assistance. To alleviate financial ills, the tribal leaders considered the development of a business enterprise to attract tourists. The plan included construction of a trading post; a teepee village, to entertain visitors with ceremonial dances; restaurants and motels; and possibly a museum.[43] The success of the business would rest on seasonal tourist interests, but the venture was considered too risky; therefore, it did not go much beyond the planning stage. Thus, the Sioux's despondent outlook continued.

The economic and social malaise at Rosebud and Pine Ridge typified the conditions on many reservations in 1960. Graham Holmes, superintendent of the Rosebud Reservation, noted a pervasive attitude of resignation among the Sioux. To provide hope, the Uwipi medicine men told their people that white men, who were aggressors, would ultimately destroy themselves by some act of folly.[44] By outwaiting the suffering, the Sioux would be relieved of the demoralization that tormented them. But many Sioux did not wait. They searched for relief by participating in the peyote rites of the Native American Church. Other tribespeople turned to alcohol to escape the social and economic pressures of the outside world, which they felt closing in on them.[45] Many reservation Indians realized that the government could offer only limited assistance, and they looked to the old ways to see them through their socioeconomic crisis.

The Sioux and other Indians who relocated to cities faced the problems of urbanization and living in poverty. Rows of slum dwellings evolved, and Indians were looked down on by other Americans. Young and unmarried Indian mothers sometimes turned to prostitution in order to support their children and themselves. Resorting to social vices, even out of a need for survival, contradicted traditional values and created additional stress and guilt. Feeling degraded and inferior, many Native Americans turned to alcohol. In Rapid City, South Dakota, Sioux migrants constituted an Indian population of nearly six thousand. About 75 percent of those people arrested and jailed in the city for alcohol-related charges were Indians.[46]

The windfalls received from the sale of lands, once trust restrictions had been removed, did little to help relocatees. Too often, individuals lacked the experience or knowledge to be able to handle large sums of money. In one instance, a Montana Blackfeet Indian squandered forty thousand dollars in a few months after selling his land and moving to a city. He returned with his family to the reservation, begging for tribal assistance. Another Blackfeet quickly spent eighty thousand dollars. Similar incidents occurred frequently between 1948 and 1957, when the government removed 3,307,217 acres from individual Indian trust status.

From the government's viewpoint, the termination of trust status on Indian properties, together with relocation, compounded the "Indian problem." One frustrated BIA official stated: "We haven't been able to resolve the Indian problem in nearly 100 years of stewardship. So let the Indian take care of himself."[47] Increasing demands on the Indian Bureau to provide needed services enormously complicated the supervision of tribal affairs. Instead of working itself out of a job, as federal officials had predicted in the early 1950s, the BIA increased the number of personnel and escalated the costs of administering federal-Indian affairs. Each year, during the late 1950s, government appropriations for Indian programs rose, particularly those that were related to relocation. In Oklahoma, the increasing number of applicants at the Anadarko area office required increased personnel and funding to process the relocatees.[48] Overall, in 1959 the Bureau of Indian Affairs employed 11,477 workers, including 4,520 in the Indian Health Division, a total rise during the decade of almost 1,600, or 20 percent. In fact, on the last day of July 1959, President Eisenhower signed Senate Bill 56, authorizing the Public Health Service to provide essential facilities to Indian communities. For the Indian Health Service alone, 50,287 dollars was appropriated, in addition to the BIA's mushrooming budget of 115,467,000 dollars for the 1960 fiscal year.[49]

Increased appropriations and services marked a tremendous effort to make the Indians permanently self-supporting. Unlike the early 1950s, when the Republican Congress had sought to cut funding and terminate services to Native Americans, federal officials increased funding for social programs for Indians during the latter part of the fifties and early sixties. Slowly, Native Americans were beginning to adopt white American values as federal officials expanded programs for Indians. However, the American institutions of individualism and materialism acutely contradicted traditional ways. For instance, in the old days, the Sioux believed that one who acted ideally by sharing with the unfortunate and practicing communal life was "Wakan"—touched by the influence of the Great Spirit.[50] Most whites did not understand the religious significance of this belief, nor was it congruent with their social norms. It is important to note that such devotion to tradition prevented Native Americans from completely adopting the independent and assertive attitudes of other Americans in the early 1960s—a factor that remains significant even today.

To add to the woes of federal officials, the media reported that Native Americans did not have to accept termination and relocation, and it charged the government with infringing on Indians' rights. Newspaper and magazine articles reported that termination had confused the Menominees, the first tribe to be terminated, and had diminished the effectiveness of the tribal advisory council's leadership in guiding the people through the transition. James C. Frechette, chairman of the council, expressed concern when a newspaper article quoted Wisconsin Congressman Melvin Laird as saying, "It is my firm opinion that chaotic conditions would arise if termination takes place as now contemplated."[51] Frechette felt that Laird's statement indicated a lack of confidence in the Menominee leaders' abilities and undermined the tribe's decision to accept termination. Such confusion caused the council itself to question the manner in which the original decision had been made.

In contrast, certain tribes, like the Sac and Fox of Tama, Iowa, steadfastly maintained their opposition to termination. On 2 May 1960, Sac and Fox leaders wrote to Superintendent E. J. Riley of the Bureau of Indian Affairs to state that they were against termination but still wanted the right to manage their own affairs. Tribal officials wanted the benefits of both trust status and termination. They declared that they did not want "to see the extermination of our tribe which would follow from the so-called 'termination' policy of the Federal Government, and yet we do not want a return to the complete Federal paternalism of the past."[52] The response of the Sac and Fox typified the attitude of those tribal groups who opposed termination. Out of frustration in having to deal with a federal effort to abrogate trust and to dissolve services, the tribes fought for their survival.

As the 1960 presidential election year progressed, Native Americans found themselves caught up in the campaign struggle. Residents of the Red Lake Reservation in Minnesota requested a new superintendent from the Department of the Interior, but they were refused. The Red Lake Indians needed a superintendent whose first-hand knowledge of the tribe's needs would influence government action for assistance. Ed Vieham, state chairman of the Minnesota Republican Central Committee, informed Secretary Seaton that the president of the Red Lake Tribal Council was a Republican, and he added that helping the Indians could gain votes for the party.[53] However, general Indian support for the Republicans hardly seemed likely since party leaders had originally created the termination policy. Furthermore, federal terminationists—including Dillon Myer and Arthur Watkins, whom many Indians disliked—were Republicans.

On 27 May, Frank George, a Nez Percé, advocated support for the needs of Native Americans before the Democratic Platform Committee in Denver, Colorado. He denounced the termination policy of the Eisenhower Administration: "THE FACT REMAINS that the Indian Bureau field personnel and the Washington staff devote considerable time in planting ideas in the minds of the general public and even of tribal governing bodies that the solution to the problems of the American Indians is the termination of Federal trusteeship."[54] He suggested several reforms. One called for each Indian group to maximize utilization of assets to assist its members. Other reforms would request the government to advise the tribes during post-termination and to extend loans to individuals for developing their properties. George added that the tribes and the government should agree on disposition of property and on actions affecting treaty rights. He emphasized that a major effort should be made to retain tribal properties, and as soon as possible, eligibility guidelines for hospital and medical care to Native Americans needed to be reformed. Lastly, George requested that a progressive education program be implemented, particularly in the area of adult vocational training.

In Montana, Burton J. Goodyear, investigator of the United States Civil Rights Commission, reported that living conditions were deplorable at Hill 57 of the Indian community. About one hundred people received water from one well with a two-inch pipe and a defective hand pump. The county hospital of the Public Health Service refused to treat or hospitalize the Indians, and the BIA refused to give or pay for any services unless the Indians returned to the reservation. Goodyear recommended that the state fulfill its responsibilities of providing services to Indians such as these, who lived off the reservation.[55]

In the Southwest, Indians were excluded from voting because Arizona and New Mexico considered them to be wards. In Gallup, New Mexico, Indians were frequently refused services at public places. Discriminatory practices and prejudice toward Indians had been present for years in the Southwest, especially in rural areas where large populations of Indians resided.[56] Prevailing discriminatory actions undoubtedly undermined the objectives of termination and relocation programs, which sought to assimilate Native Americans into the mainstream communities.

Such conditions throughout Indian country made the 1960 presidential election year an ideal opportunity for protest. The Miccosukee Seminoles of Florida made one of the strongest demands. Under the guidance of their attorney, the Miccosukees requested that the United States recognize them as a sovereign nation because they were claiming the entire state of Florida![57]

The government viewed such a claim as totally unrealistic, and waited for time to quiet the Seminole demand. However, such tactics did not always work when Indian rights were in question.

During August, La Verne Madigan of the Association on American Indian Affairs, supported the effort of Indian Americans in claiming their rights. She stated that "an honorable Federal Indian Policy must recognize the right of the conquered American Indians to choose without coercion between assimilation and life in cultural communities of their own people." Madigan advocated the government adoption of "An American Indian Point 4 Program," which provided loans to help the tribes preserve their land-base. The program provided for technical assistance to Indians in the areas of economic development and social welfare programs.[58]

One of the most vocal Indian complaints came from Robert Yellowtail, a Republican and the former superintendent of the Crow Reservation. He denounced the Democrats and criticized their twenty years of administration under Presidents Franklin Roosevelt and Harry Truman. In referring to Indian affairs under Secretary Oscar Chapman and Commissioner Dillon Myer, Yellowtail said that "the Indians were very lucky to come out with their shirts under their policy of liquidation."[59] After berating the Democrats, Yellowtail stated that neither political party proposed an adequate stand on Indian affairs. He favored the Republicans and hinted that the political winds were blowing in favor of Richard Nixon for the presidency; if Nixon won, Yellowtail said, Emmons would be replaced as commissioner of Indian Affairs. Most American Indians did not agree with Yellowtail. They were antagonized by the previous eight years of the Republican administration's Indian policy, and most tended to support John Kennedy for the presidency.[60]

Another Indian supporter of Nixon, Omaha Tribal Chairman Alfred W. Gilpin, voiced negative views of the past Republican Indian policy. He maintained that from 1952 to 1958 the intent of the BIA's policy had been to break up tribes against their will. However, the tribal chairman praised Secretary of Interior Fred Seaton. Seaton had declared that no Indian tribe would be terminated without its consent, and that the Bureau of Indian Affairs would help Indian communities to survive and develop.[61]

As the decade was ending, one of the last important tribal

actions involved the Menominees. In December, the Menominee council passed a resolution to amend Public Law 399 again, to defer the date of their final termination to 30 April 1961. In their fight against termination, the Menominees received support from the National Congress of American Indians. Irene Mack, a spokesperson for the Menominees, criticized the government's termination policy, asserting that the Menominees, one of the initial tribes scheduled for termination, were "guinea pigs" and that irreparable harm could be done. Mrs. Mack also described the mood of members at the annual meeting as they discussed termination. In observing the delegates, she surmised that the tribes feared termination because its disastrous consequences affected all Indian people. The Indians charged that termination policy was a federal effort to undermine tribal governments, and in reality, it failed to assist Indians in assimilation.[62]

Commissioner Emmons had an opportunity to defend the termination policy before an Indian law committee of the Federal Bar Association panel discussion held in Chicago on 17 September 1960. He stressed that House Concurrent Resolution 108, the legal basis for termination, had been approved only ten days before he took office as commissioner of Indian Affairs. The commissioner pointed out the distinct differences that existed among various tribes, which made it difficult to supervise federal policy in carrying out the H.R.C. 108 mandate. Emmons opposed the idea of having the government sell all tribal lands and distribute the proceeds among enrolled members. His main concern was to protect Native Americans who might be exploited and to prevent them from squandering their money. The commissioner believed that members of each tribe should have the opportunity to retain their lands in group ownership, even after the end of federal trusteeship.[63]

On December 22, the Department of the Interior announced an extension of trust restrictions on all allotted Indian lands for an additional five years. Originally, the restrictions had been scheduled to expire in 1961.[64] Such action contradicted the termination policy of the early 1950s, when the government had mandated prompt abrogation of trust status on individual Indian lands. From 1954 through 1960, a total of sixty-one tribes, Indian groups, communities, *rancherías,* and allotments were terminated by congressional legislation.[65]

The end of 1960 also concluded the administration of Glenn Emmons as commissioner of Indian affairs. He submitted a letter of resignation to President Eisenhower on 23 December, but he felt obligated to stay in office until 1961, when the next commissioner would be appointed. Emmons had served for nearly eight years, under Eisenhower's two administrations. With the aid of his colleagues, Secretary Douglas McKay and Secretary Fred Seaton, Emmons believed that much had been accomplished since 1953 to help the long-neglected Indian citizenry along the road toward a better way of life.[66] As a final matter remaining from the 1950s, thirty-five California *rancherías,* the Oklahoma Choctaws, the Oregon Klamaths, the Wisconsin Menominees, and the mixed-bloods of the Uintah-Ouray of Utah were listed for final termination in 1961. Throughout the entire termination period, which lasted into the 1960s, 109 cases of termination were initiated, affecting a minimum of 1,362,155 acres and 11,466 individuals.[67]

The development of tribal economies became a distinguishing characteristic of federal Indian policy in the late 1950s under Glenn Emmons, whose leadership exemplified a more patient and humanitarian attitude toward Indian affairs than that of his predecessors. In contrast to the tough, "get-out-of-the-Indian-business" approach of the Eighty-third Congress, later Congresses exhibited a concerned, "prepare-the-Indians" approach. Much of this change in federal attitude can be attributed to Emmons, for this was the dominant approach during the remaining years of the second Eisenhower administration, when the government listed fewer new tribes for termination and the essence of federal-Indian relations focused on seeking resolutions for federal withdrawal problems of terminated groups.

In spite of all this, the federal termination policy of the second Eisenhower administration can be considered a failure since tribes continued to exist under federal supervision and relocated Indian citizens were only partially assimilated into the mainstream society. Some of the fault lay with Eisenhower's subordinate officials in charge of Indian affairs, who, except for Emmons, failed to understand the enormity of social and economic transitions confronting Indians when the government's policy of federal withdrawal was enacted. When they attempted to adjust to such changes, Indians encountered serious social and economic traumas. Furthermore, the Indian experts had overlooked the Indians' reluctance to become subjects of the social experiment of assimilation, and they had misjudged the attitude of the dominant society. Americans were not yet ready to receive Indians as neighbors coexisting within their communities. This was undoubtedly a great irony of legal denial that has continued to plague Indian Americans and the federal government.

9

Termination and Relocation in Retrospect

The years from 1945 to 1960 constituted one of the most crucial periods in the history of federal-Indian relations. Since 1960 Indians, bureaucrats, and the public have had ample time to digest the effects of termination and relocation policies on Native Americans and to formulate opinions about the intent of these policies. In everything that it represented, termination threatened the very core of American Indian existence—its culture. The federal government sought to de-Indianize Native Americans. The government hoped to ultimately negate Indian identity through assimilation into the mainstream society. First, however, government obligations to tribes had to be dissolved. Relocating Native Americans would help to achieve the goal of termination by removing them from the source of their cultural existence. Once Indians had given up their cultures for life in mainstream America, the government could abrogate special services to them. A former relocation officer recalled that "in the 50s Relocation was the instrument of termination," and "this was the policy of the Bureau."[1]

Between 1945 and 1960 the government processed 109 cases of termination affecting 1,369,000 acres of Indian land and an estimated 12,000 Indians. The end result of relocation is that over one-half of today's Indian population now resides in urban areas. So many changes within such a short time has had a tremendous effect on Native Americans; yet a high degree of tribal traditionalism has been retained.

Termination and relocation have often been mistakenly attributed to the nationalistic movement of the Eisenhower administration. Actually, the germs of both policies originated during the Truman administration. In fact, the results of two studies, the Hoover Task Force Commission Report and the

Zimmerman Plan, laid the foundations for termination and relocation. The Hoover Task Force Commission reported that Indians were ready to become "just" Americans and that they should begin to assume their roles as full citizens of the United States. The commission's report advised the dissolution of the federal government's involvement in Indian affairs and recommended that Native Americans utilize state services like other citizens. The Zimmerman Plan went farther by categorizing tribes into three groups based on criteria that supposedly measured readiness for withdrawal of federal trust.

It is unusual that the policy of termination and relocation began under Harry Truman, a president whose Democratic party traditionally advocated social justice for minorities and freedom of choice. However, Indian policy under the Truman administration disregarded Native American cultural integrity by reinstating the philosophy that Indians should be assimilated into the mainstream society. This irony is partially explained by the effects of World War II. Truman did not have the time to oversee Indian affairs, and the ensuing budget restrictions encouraged the move to reduce the costs of providing special services to Indians. Also, Truman's Fair Deal ideals, aimed at fitting everyone to a middle-class America, included Indians.

Today, many Indians and non-Indians alike remember well the negative repercussions of termination and relocation. They recall the fear and the threat that termination brought to Indian people. Relocation, also remembered for its negative impact, was overshadowed by the enormity of the fears surrounding the termination program. Termination was seen as an all-inclusive destroyer of Indian life-styles. George Pierre, former chief of the Colville Confederated Tribes of Washington, vividly described the fears that termination evoked in Native Americans:

> House Concurrent Resolution 108 adopted in 1953, sent the word termination spreading like a prairie fire of a pestilence through the Indian country. It stirred conflicting reactions among my people; to some it meant the severing of ties already loose and ineffective; others welcomed it as a promise of early sharing in tribal patrimony. Many outsiders realized that it provided a first step towards acquiring Indian resources. The great majority of my people, however, feared the consequences. The action of Congress, accompanied by the phrase "as rapidly as possible," sounded to them like the stroke of doom.[2]

Many people remember termination as just another land grab for Indian properties. This seems to have been the case in many situations. In Nevada, Senator Pat McCarran repeatedly attempted to pass legislation to fee-patent certain lands for squatters living on the Paiute Reservation. In another case, one former relocation worker estimated that the Fort Peck tribes lost approximately a quarter of a million acres in land sales to non-Indians in Montana.[3] In the Klamath Basin, the lumber companies clearly became the actual beneficiaries of Klamath termination in 1961. Although federal officials expressed concern in preventing exploitation of the Klamaths, the lumber interests in southwestern Oregon dominated their actions. Lumber companies, banks, and numerous merchants depended on the Klamath timber cuttings. Although conservationists fought to prevent the lifting of restrictions on Klamath lands, they too were more concerned with the land. They argued that removal of trust restrictions would open up wilderness areas to lumber companies, and wildlife breeding and feeding grounds would be destroyed.[4]

Another dimension of Klamath termination concerns the monetary windfalls from timber sales that were distributed to members and the repercussions that followed. Each Klamath receiving the per capita payment of 43,000 dollars became game for local merchants, who aggressively sold them automobiles, televisions, and other goods at inflated prices. Many Klamath people were inexperienced in dealing with unscrupulous merchants and opportunists. There are numerous accounts of debauchery and schemes that tricked the Klamaths out of their properties. The same scene was repeated after the Menominee and other tribes received per capita payments. The government's plan for reducing the number of Indian people eligible for special services backfired when the suddenly rich Indians lost the monies and properties they had received after termination. They soon found themselves in need of assistance, and many tribes have since applied for restoration of recognition. The Menominee have regained recognition and are again eligible to receive special services, and the Klamath now possess federal recognition.

The government was convinced that monetary settlements authorized by the Indian Claims Commission would improve tribal economies and benefit their livelihoods generally. By the end of the 1950s an estimated 42 million dollars was awarded to the tribes, while the total number of filed claims rose during the following years. In 1960 a claims attorney predicted that 25 million dollars would be spent on Indian claims, but by 1966 the figure had quintupled.[5] The Indian Claims Commission eventually awarded a total amount of 669 million dollars. In September 1978, Congress finally dissolved the Indian Claims Commission, and 133 unresolved dockets out of the original 617 were transferred to the U.S. Court of Claims.

Robert Bennett, formerly commissioner of Indian affairs, from 1966 to 1969, recalled that in the 1950s congressional reasoning for supporting the Indian Claims Commission was that a final dissolution of government obligations to Native Americans would result. Bennett stated that "the feeling grew up in Congress that if the people were to be paid for all their claims and unjustified acts on the part of the federal government, . . . this would mark the end of any kind of relationship with the federal government."[6] Finally, the government would pay its debts to the tribes once and for all. Such compensation would redeem the American government of its guilty history of mistreating American Indians.

Land has always been a common factor in federal-Indian relations. Since the early years of Indian–white contact, government officials have been convinced that division of tribal lands was the key to liberating Native Americans from impoverished communal life-styles and making them a part of mainstream America. In the 1950s, a deluge of legislation and federal actions poured forth efforts aimed at relocating Indians to urban areas. These efforts were motivated by the attempt to terminate costly government services to Indian people and to make lands available to interested whites.

Vast differences existed between the Indian policies of the 1950s and the early 1960s. Commissioner Dillon S. Myer and officials like H. Rex Lee, assistant commissioner during the early 1950s, took a direct approach in supporting termination legislation without regard to the possible harmful repercussions to Indian Americans. Although officials in the 1960s were also interested in eventually reducing government services to Indians, their actions were offered as reforms.

There were two types of individuals in government who were responsible for termination policy. Commissioner Dillon Myer, Senator Arthur Watkins of Utah, and Senator Pat McCarran typified the group identified as proassimilationists and Eisenhower men (although Myer was a Truman appointee). They were convinced that all Americans should conform to one society while participating in a personal struggle for achieving success. These men came from rural backgrounds that stressed hard-work ethics, and they admired individual accomplishments. Most had succeeded through their own efforts, and they believed strongly in laissez faire. Their approach to Indian affairs was often influenced by personal or political gains.

The second category included humanitarians like Senator Reva Beck Bosone of Utah, Senator Richard Neuberger of Oregon, and Senator James Murray of Montana. They worked in the best interests of the Indians and only introduced termination legislation when the tribal groups requested such bills. Some individuals, like Florida Senator George Smathers, originally favored assimilation, but after becoming familiar with the conditions of Native Americans and understanding their problems, they joined the ranks of the humanitarians to prevent the exploitation of Native American people. Certainly, numerous other federal officials played a part in the policies affecting Indians, but the ones mentioned above dominated federal-Indian affairs.

Without doubt, the Eisenhower administration encouraged the movement to abrogate government relations with Indians. Interestingly, Dwight D. Eisenhower symbolized the 1950s and the motives behind termination. His image as a World War II hero manifested another image that reflected a new Americanism. American citizens would have likely elected Ike as president of the United States in 1948 if he had chosen to be a candidate. Four years later, his popularity was still at its zenith, although no one really knew whether he was a Democrat or a Republican until he publicly declared the latter. The presidential election of 1952 held little doubt that Ike would win. His campaign platform called for a modernized middle-class society, encouraging citizens to redefine the American dream and to pursue it. At the time, most of the nation's citizenry were conservative, hard-working, and Republican. The mood of the country and the ideology and doctrines of the Eisenhower era amplified intense termination policy. The grand plan was for all Americans, including minorities, to conform to a middle-class society.

The architects of federal Indian policy failed to realize that assimilating Native Americans into middle-class America would take more time and effort than they wanted to provide. A large portion of the Indian population continually preferred to maintain distinct cultural communities within the larger urban communities. Furthermore, the existence of minority enclaves in large cities today is evidence that Indians and other ethnic groups were not ready to assimilate. Doubtlessly, urban Indians chose not to assimilate and white society did not encourage acceptance of Indians. One Apache suggested that whites maintained contradictory attitudes toward Indians. He asserted that white society deemed "everyone had a right to be himself, to be an individual. But on the other hand as soon as one person is different or tries to remain different, everybody asks, 'why can't he be like the rest of us?' "[7]

Several factors were at work in creating the appearance that the mainstream society was receptive to Indians. The Eisenhower administration attempted to unify all sectors of society into one culture. Ike envisioned a crusade to advance the American civilization into a position of world leadership, with the democratic principles of the United States serving as the cause. This ideology required all citizens to integrate into a middle-class society. If necessary, existing minority cultures would be forfeited in order to reach this grand ideal. As Americans enthusiastically embraced Eisenhower's grand plan, it appeared that assimilation of Indians into mainstream society would become a reality.

A grave error was made in assuming that Indians were ready for assimilation into urban life. Federal officials failed to comprehend the existing strength of Native American cultures and the tenacity with which Indians would try to preserve their heritage. The unfamiliarity of federal officials with the dynamics of traditional tribalism resulted in frustration for both them and the Indians. The officials became discouraged especially with apprehensive tribal governments that took lengthy periods of time to decide on termination questions. From the viewpoint of federal officials, the tribal leaders appeared unable or unwilling to deal with termination, and prodding was necessary to convince them to accept termination.

Traditionally, most tribes took whatever length of time was necessary to settle an issue by general consensus. Naturally, the more important the issue, the more time they required. In deciding on termination, or any significant issue, tribal officials continued to hold meetings for discussion until a nearly unanimous decision was reached. Sometimes this approach delayed action past the termination deadline set by Congress, as seen in the Klamaths' case; frequently, the magnitude of the issue caused strife within the tribal community.

Indians who successfully survived the withdrawal of trust status from their properties and assimilated readily into the mainstream were exceptions to the norm. Most Indians simply were not prepared socially, psychologically, or economically for the sudden removal of federal trust status. One individual said that recollections of the termination years of the 1950s brought back harsh memories, and she did not think Indians were ready for termination "because they couldn't take care of themselves even with help" from the government.[8] "We're not ready for termination right now," another elder Brule Sioux exclaimed. "I said at least twenty-five years is a short time. But I think the next generation through education will stand to compete in this world with the non-Indians."[9]

The intense social and psychological adjustments that confronted Indians has been best described in novels like N. Scott Momaday's *House Made of Dawn* and Leslie Silko's *Ceremony.* Both books portray Indian veterans who are adjusting to a new way of life after World War II, while coming into contact with the American mainstream society. These two works are invaluably perceptive and vividly convey, from an Indian point of view, the intense human trauma of adjusting to a different culture.

In reality, relocation was difficult for Indians whose cultural integrity was challenged by urbanization. After finding the street life of the cities unbearable, many resorted to alcohol to escape the social and economic pressures of assimilation. Economic survival in the city forced many single Indian women into prostitution in order to provide for themselves and their children. "I have seen divorces, I have seen the kids, I have seen so many women that go to prostitute, you know they have to have money," lamented one Kiowa woman.[10]

From 1952, when the relocation program began, until the end of the 1967 fiscal year, 61,500 Indians received vocational training. Nonetheless, the unemployment rate for Native Americans during the 1960s averaged 40 percent. On reservations the unemployment rate was much higher. At Pine Ridge the rate was 75 percent for most of the year, and rose as high as 95 percent during the winter. Average Indian family incomes were horribly substandard in comparison with average American earnings. In 1964, for example, Native American family incomes averaged less than one-third of the national figure. In 1968 the net income for Indian families was about 1,500 dollars, while more than one-half of all white families earned at least 5,893 dollars. High unemployment and underemployment were partly attributable to the lack of education among young adults. The high school dropout rate for Indians averaged 60 percent in 1964.[11] Indian housing remained substandard both on reservations and in cities. On reservations 63,000 families lived in dilapidated houses without plumbing. Statistics indicated that Indians suffered far more health problems than other Americans. Whereas the average life span for white Americans was seventy years, an Indian could expect to live only forty-four years.[12]

Life in slum areas demoralized Native Americans, especially after relocation officers had led them to believe that their livelihoods would be vastly upgraded after moving to urban areas. For the small number who had received vocational training or attended college, improvement was possible. Many men worried about their families and their personal lives; and when they could no longer cope with their problems, they turned to alcohol and/or abandoned their families to escape the tortuous reality of relocation.

The social and psychological problems of relocatees mounted as maladjustment to city life fostered an identity crisis that tormented many relocatees. After leaving their traditional social structures on reservations and in rural communities, which served as the basis for their psychological balance with kin and nature, they had nothing. Isolation and loneliness in the big cities confronted them. The city's alien environment was unlike anything they had experienced. Their perceptions of space, time, matter, energy, and causality differed vastly from that of the urban scene.[13] Their concepts of values, norms, and behavior, different in comparison with those of white society, bred cultural conflicts with other urban Americans. As members of a small minority attempting to adjust to the urban scene, Indian Americans felt inferior. Loss of morale and pride threatened their personal identity, causing many relocatees to wander and drift within the cities, searching for fundamental elements as they knew them traditionally in an attempt to reestablish some sense of their mental equilibrium. In seeking comfort through socialization, the relocatees tried to locate other Indians, especially those from their own tribe and reservation. Interactions with other Indians did not erase the loneliness or the coldness of an insensitive urban society. Some Indians contemplated self-destruction; the more depressed individuals committed suicide.

Difficulties with relocation to American cities were not unique to Indians. Other ethnic groups had migrated to metropolitan areas throughout the United States, and they shared many of the experiences that urban Indians encountered. But the dynamics involved in relocation from reservations to cities differed from that of migration from foreign countries. Groups from different nations have a better chance than Indians in adapting to urban areas for two major reasons. First, they elected to migrate to American cities and often desired to become quickly Americanized. Foreign immigrants left their motherlands for political, economic, and/or religious reasons, electing to come to America, where they could exercise their beliefs and strive to live their dreams. They shared a belief in many American ideals—individualism, attainment of wealth, and advancement. In contrast, many Indian relocatees did not leave their country but, rather, left the center of their culture and beliefs. In the cities, their beliefs in communal life-styles and their intolerance of close encounters with other people were misunderstood by the mainstream society.

Secondly, relocation and termination programs were aimed at destroying Indian cultures to speed up the process of assimilation. Immigrants, on the other hand, could move into cultural enclaves that already existed within the cities. No one expected them to give up the elements of their cultures since they shared the same basic ideas as other Americans.

Obviously, centuries-old Indian cultures could not be undone by the mere enactment of termination and relocation policies. Federal officials of the early Eisenhower years were interested in abolishing federal obligations and saw little importance in preserving Indian traditions. Stewart Udall, Secretary of the Interior during the Kennedy administration, recalled that the basic attitude of the Eisenhower administration was "a general demoralization and a feeling on everyone's part that there ought to be some simple solution" to the Indian problem. "Their so-called termination policy," he added, "is that what we ought to do is put them on their own and let them sink or swim."[14]

There were no "simple" solutions for reforming Indian conditions. Further reform measures actually compounded the problems for Indians who were attempting to assimilate into the American mainstream. Public Law 280 was enacted as an effort to convince Indian people to utilize state services, but provisions within the law also established state jurisdiction over reservations within certain states—a move which was received negatively by Native Americans. Former Indian Commissioner Robert Bennett recalled that "the Indian tribes have never been in favor of the extension of civil and criminal jurisdiction of states over Indian reservations, and they fought constantly since the enactment of this legislation to have it amended." The effort to alter the act focused on allowing Indian consent to its application, so that states unilaterally could not extend civil or criminal jurisdiction over Indians. Bennett recalled that "this policy placed great fear in the hearts and minds of Indian people because the Indian identity rests with the individual tribes and the tribal identity."[15] Nothing stopped state governments from extending their control over Indian communities until 1968, when the Indian Civil Rights Act amended the law to require referendums among the tribes affected.

Assimilation of Indians into the American mainstream at all costs was the objective of the early Eisenhower administration. Years later, in an interview, Senator Arthur Watkins of Utah described his efforts in Indian affairs to help Native Americans assimilate. "I was chairman of the Indian subcommittee of the

Interior Committee of the Senate. For a number of years, at least while the Republicans were in power, I put over a lot of projects for the Indians, along with my western associates."[16] The Senator believed in immediate reform for Indians, and he dismissed the idea that Indians were *not* ready economically and socially for termination. Watkins and his associates pushed termination to its apex during the Eighty-third Congress, thus leading to a movement in Congress that continued through the early 1960s.

During the Kennedy years, some newspapers also supported the termination philosophy that Indians were ready for assimilation. Blind to the social and economic maladjustment that Indians encountered, an editorial in the Washington *Star*, on 27 August 1962, maintained that Indians should "join the rest of the Country and stop stagnating as museum pieces." The same piece stated its biased view that the "average Indian was not stupid" and did not require special treatment from the federal government."[17] Such commentary supported the belief that Indians could easily assimilate; and white conservatives could not understand why Native Americans did not easily adjust to the norms of the mainstream.

Congress continued to pass trust removal legislation through the mid-1960s. The following statement of the Senate Committee on Interior and Insular Affairs in 1964 indicates the members' support for termination.

> The Committee is deeply concerned about the failure of the Bureau of Indian Affairs to carry out the intent of House Concurrent Resolution 108, 83rd Congress, relating to termination programs for tribes, many of whom were reported by the Bureau itself as being ready for termination legislation more then ten years ago. As the Indian Claims Commission continues to make awards to tribes and substantial sums become available to the Indians, it becomes imperative that legislation be recommended to permit withdrawal of Federal Services where the Indians are able to conduct their affairs without supervision by the Bureau. At the beginning of the 89th Congress the committee plans to hold hearings on this subject, and the manner in which the Bureau has performed its responsibilities pursuant to the 1953 concurrent resolution.[18]

In April 1964, the House of Representatives passed H.R. 7883 to terminate federal control over one particular California Indian *ranchería,* but only with the permission of its residents. In 1958, Congress had authorized the eventual termination of trust for forty-one *rancherías.* Shortly thereafter, the government terminated fourteen more *rancherías,* and the other jurisdictions remained in various stages of trust withdrawal.[19] In 1966 the Department of the Interior announced the end of trust relations for four *rancherías:* Scotts Valley, Robinson, Guidiville, and Greenville; and in February of the following year, five more *rancherías*—North Fork, Picayune, Graton, Pinoville, and Quartz Valley—were also freed of trust restrictions.[20] In 1964 this number was amended to include more than one hundred *rancherías.*[21]

Since 1960 Native Americans from California *rancherías* and the Pacific Northwest have mingled with white neighbors in nearby communities and appear adjusted to white American norms. One Colville tribesperson wrote to President Johnson to report: "Our tribe is ready for Termination and Liquidation. Of the 45 Indians in our tribe only a few live on the reservation." Her tribe was one of many Colville tribes; she estimated that most of her people were fairly well educated, and she asserted that they had been fighting several years for their equal rights as citizens.[22] A majority of California Indians expressed similar sentiments about termination and claimed that they were ready to supervise their own affairs.[23]

Although many Indians of California and the Pacific Northwest requested termination of federal supervision, they frequently experienced social and psychological problems while adjusting to their new status. Relocation to urban areas was eased by socialization with other urban Indians. Father Wilfred Schoenberg, a Jesuit priest at the Pacific Northwest Indian Center, wrote to President Lyndon Johnson about urban Indian adjustment and the need for assistance in the cities. Schoenberg stressed that Indian centers were essential to the survival of Indian people in metropolitan areas because they provided a tangible cohesiveness for relocatees, something to cling to during the painful period of urban adjustment. He maintained that federal officials had neglected Indian problems, and he hoped a new era in federal-Indian affairs would bring relief to the Indian people.[24]

President Johnson depended on his Secretary of the Interior,

Stewart Udall, to fulfill federal obligations to Native Americans and to oversee Indian affairs. He reported to the president when inquiries were made, but the Interior Secretary actually drew his information from the commissioner of Indian affairs, whose office was in daily contact with the tribes. Thus, it was important for the secretary and the commissioner to be in close communication.

Secretary Udall asserted that the Bureau of Indian Affairs could do more to help Indians in the relocation process. He suggested a change in its leadership, proposing that the BIA needed a dynamic commissioner to replace Philleo Nash and to formalize a new policy to help Indians.[25] Increased dissatisfaction with Nash paved the way for the appointment of Robert Bennett, a Wisconsin Oneida, as the new commissioner of Indian affairs in 1966.

The reforms of the Johnson Administration in its "War on Poverty" caused problems for Commissioner Bennett. Dissatisfied Indians who suffered economically sharply criticized the federal government.[26] Years later, in an interview Bennett recalled that the whole political climate in Washington had changed dramatically since the 1950s. He particularly believed that Congress would not consider approving a piece of legislation like the infamous termination measure H.C.R. 108 during the mid-1960s. In fact, President Johnson expressed opposition to unilateral termination in a message before a national meeting in Kansas City in February 1967. Afterward, federal Indian policy moved in a different direction, dedicated to the development of human and natural resources on reservations with federal assistance.[27]

Even during the 1970s, Native Americans remained angry about termination during the 1950s. A Northern Cheyenne stated during an interview in 1971: "I'm . . . 100 percent against this termination, [in] any shape or form, and I've been this way for as far back as i [*sic*] can remember."[28] Even when tribespeople did not fully understand the termination policy, they denounced it as part of a protest against past injustices. Their complaints consisted of objections against numerous legislative measures, trust status removal by the Interior Department, BIA control, and the failure of the government to achieve liberation for Indians from second-class citizenship. Naturally, the BIA was the target for some very harsh criticism. One Indian spokesman stated on television in 1970: "The only thing to do with the B.I.A. is to abolish it. I want to make something right now certain, that I am not for termination, I am for the abolishment of the Bureau of Indian Affairs."[29]

On Indian-white relations, John Dressler, a wise and elderly Washo, clearly expressed the differences between the two peoples:

> Today, what plays an important part within our Indian nation communities—our Indian people and their culture—is the introduction of the white man's culture, and we became bicultural. And it's difficult at times to define the white man's culture and use it as our culture also because of the educational processes that exist. There is no other means. We cannot accept it any other way because I feel its necessary that we adopt some areas of the white culture with ours, we being the minority in this case. This is what makes it difficult for a lot of our people to understand. At times, with some of the people, it gets to the point where they become frustrated because they see no sense in participating in the white man's culture and entirely forgetting their own.[30]

Fortunately for Indian Americans, the termination and relocation policies during the 1960s and 1970s were not as harmful as those applied in the 1950s. Today, Indians are better adjusted to the norms of the dominant society, whereas previously termination and relocation had thrust Native Americans into an alien culture without regard to the possible social and economic upheavals facing them. Federal officials in the Bureau of Indian Affairs and Congress were at fault for professing that the time had arrived for the red man to live as a white man in the city. To some extent, the Indians' voluntary attitude in leaving their homelands after World War II enhanced the government's conviction that they were ready for termination and relocation. The conditions on reservations also convinced federal officials that they were right in assuming that Native Americans were ready to assimilate into urban society. In effect, termination was thought to be the answer to the Indian problem. For the most part, termination frightened American Indians, while bureaucrats envisioned it as the panacea for all of their own problems in working with Indians.

As an attempt to Americanize Indians, the federal Indian policy of termination and relocation failed. Ironically, the federal government did not learn from its history of relations with Native American peoples that no single policy can be devised that will successfully serve all Indians, who represent many different tribes, languages, and cultures. Even within the tribes, there are differences represented by various kinship systems, social roles, and political status; and yet, the federal government's attempt to design a termination program to suit individual tribes drew criticism for not establishing one definite policy. Such a paradox has continually plagued the federal government, and Indians have suffered the consequences.

Epilog

The early 1960s witnessed an upswing in the nation's mood as the Kennedy administration professed a "New Frontier" program for reforming society. The government began to take action to aid those people who needed it—the poor, the unemployed, the sick, and the elderly. Advanced technology, new ideas, and effective leadership were valued by the nation. A "New Trail" policy attempted to assist Indian Americans through special federal programs and by removing the threat of termination.

Dr. Philleo Nash, commissioner of Indian affairs from 1961 to 1966, became the primary proponent of John Kennedy's Indian policy and assumed the lead in federal-Indian affairs during the early years of the Johnson administration. Under Nash's administration, termination came to a halt, with the new policy focusing on maximizing Indian economic self-sufficiency, encouraging Indian participation in American life, and assuring equal citizenship privileges and responsibilities to Indian citizens.[1] Previous commissioners had professed rhetoric in stating similar aims, but Nash heavily stressed the preservation of American Indian cultures. An emphasis on retaining tribal identities and tribal cultures, while working toward a greater Native American adjustment to society, reflected the post-termination attitude prevalent in the 1960s. Nash and other Bureau officials hoped to encourage Indians to improve their standard of living with increased governmental assistance. This plan was obviously not a new idea, for Nash drew heavily on the ideas of Commissioner Glenn Emmons, who had believed that while Indian conditions should be improved federal assistance should not be abandoned.

As termination came to an end during the Johnson years, federal policy became more favorable to Indian interests. Native

Americans were still wary of termination, and they took advantage of the climate of the civil rights era to voice their concerns. The timing proved advantageous to Indians who had protested the federal government's handling of Indian affairs throughout the history of Indian–white relations. The Inter-Tribal Council of Nevada expressed the popular feeling in Indian country that House Concurrent Resolution 108 had followed an incorrect approach in attempting to assimilate Indian Americans into the dominant society, and that "Congress should seriously reconsider this 'termination' policy."[2] Indians began to demand the right to have a voice in decisions concerning them that included federal policy.

The Native Americans' attack on termination distinguishes the Indian movement of the 1960s from the other civil rights movements. Civil rights activities jolted the nation in regard to the legal and social oppression suffered by minority groups. Their highly visible efforts moved the American public, and concerned whites joined in minority protest marches and rallies for alleviating social suppression of ethnic groups. Their protests pressured Congress into enacting civil rights legislation, but the statutes did not specifically outline Indian rights, abolish termination policy, or address the relocation program. One Indian organization objected that the law excluded Native Americans. I. J. Spencer, executive secretary of the Indian Claims Association, informed President Johnson that the legislative measures pertained to deprived whites and blacks only. He proclaimed that Indians wanted equal protection under the law as American citizens.[3]

In support of the Indian cause, President Johnson included Native Americans in his reform campaign to construct the "Great Society." His special message to Congress on 6 March 1968, entitled "The Forgotten American," called specifically for the end of tribal termination and proposed a new goal for the government's Indian policy based on "self-determination." Johnson's reform in federal Indian policy actually developed from the Kennedy administration's concern for improving Indian livelihoods and preserving Native American cultures. Furthermore, the Johnson administration continued relocation assistance while attempting to fulfill many of the Democratic campaign promises of 1960 to assist disadvantaged people. Even more,

President Johnson began to put forth his own reform plan of self-determination for Native Americans.

President Johnson did more than sympathize with Indian needs; he took action to support the Indians' right to freedom of choice in controlling their own destinies. His crowning achievement in Indian affairs was the Indian Civil Rights Act of 1968. Title II and Title VII of the legislation specifically addressed Indian concerns—tribal governments, rights for tribal courts, and the requirement of Indian consent before states could extend their jurisdiction over Indian country. The act prompted optimism that Indians had finally won limited civil rights.

In spite of these limitations, Native Americans felt the threat of termination was over. However, more substantial action was needed. Wendell Chino, tribal chairperson of the Apaches and president of the National Congress of American Indians, stated that the Civil Rights Act eased the apprehensions of Indian people. Next, Congress needed to repudiate the termination policy once and for all, and then declare a new Indian policy. "A new policy statement will remove all psychological impediments that stifle development of Indian tribes," said Chino.[4] The Association on American Indian Affairs concurred with the Apache leader in urging President Johnson personally to inspect impoverished Indian reservations. In short, Native Americans wanted relief from the impoverished conditions in their communities. Paul Harvey, the well-known news commentator, amplified the Indian view in commenting during one of his radio broadcasts: "Our much-vaunted comparison for the rights of minorities is nine parts hypocrisy as long as we continue to exclude this minority from our Great Society. Five hundred years is patience enough. Now you know why the Indian says 'ugh.' "[5]

The late 1960s were an exceptional period in the history of federal-Indian relations, for various factors coalesced to form a new policy to replace termination. The president supported the BIA's efforts for reform, which were influenced catalytically by the civil rights movement. Red Power activism drew public attention to needed social reforms for Native Americans. Young Indian activists of various tribes proclaimed themselves as leaders of the Indian people, while voicing charges against the government. Hank Adams, an Assiniboine; Clyde Warrior, a Ponca; Dennis Banks, a Chippewa; Russell Means, a Sioux; and the Bellecourt brothers of the Chippewas angrily demanded Indian rights. After the founding of the American Indian Movement (AIM) in 1968, Indian activism developed into militancy. Indian protests during the 1970s attacked a series of Indian problems. In 1971, a group of young Indians seized Alcatraz Island, marking the beginning of an embroiled decade of Indian militancy. A year later, the Trail of Broken Treaties march on the nation's capitol resulted in the occupation of the BIA building. In 1973, the small town of Wounded Knee, South Dakota, was seized by disgruntled Indians, who called for a federal review of the treaties and the removal of Chairperson Richard Wilson from the Sioux tribal government. Then, in 1978, the Longest Walk, from the West Coast to Washington, D.C., depicted a nationwide Native American protest of past wrongs inflicted upon the tribes by the United States.

Interestingly, the federal government responded favorably to Indian demands for further reform measures in the 1970s. President Richard Nixon's administration made an unusual special effort to assist Indian people. In brief, Nixon opposed termination and supported Indian self-determination. During early July 1970, he renounced termination in a special message to Congress on Indian affairs, asserting that the government was wrong to assume that it could abolish its responsibilities to Indians without consulting them. Removal of federal trusteeship caused disorientation among Indians, leaving them unable to relate to other federal, state, and local agencies. In summary, he stated that any threat of termination created apprehension among Indian people, and that applications of such policies had often caused excessive dependence on the federal government.[6]

During the early 1970s, several reform measures included an unprecedented return of land to Native Americans, with the Taos Pueblo Blue Lake settlement occurring in 1970 and the Alaska Native Claims Settlement Act in 1971. Three years later, the Nixon administration supported the restoration of the Menominees to federal recognition as a tribe. In 1975, the American Indian Policy Review Commission (with its 206 recommendations for changes in Indian policy) and the Self-Determination and Education Assistance Act marked the end of the Nixon reform period affecting Indian Americans.[7] Nixon had done much to ameliorate Native Americans' problems.

Unfortunately for Indian Americans, the above reform measures of the early and middle years of the 1970s were soon followed by a brief period of white backlash, a temporary phase of quasi-termination. Other Americans had grown tired of Indian preference, which allowed Native Americans, by law, to be given priority in government job hirings related to Indian affairs. Such favoritism upset many people as continued special treatment for minorities in general became intolerable to them. As a part of the backlash sentiment during the late 1970s, Congressmen Lloyd Meeds and Jack Cunningham introduced bills which were analogous to termination actions in the 1950s to cut Indian services. These two politicians, as well as other assimilationists, deemed that Indians were competent and self-sufficient enough to supervise their own affairs, and that they were abusing government services. Unfortunately, the renewed termination backlash in Congress misconstrued the objectives of the government's Indian policy of self-determination, giving it negative implications.

Self-determination has since acquired an ambiguous meaning. The extent of its repercussions will be unknown until an evaluation of Indian affairs can be made over a longer period of time. But at least some parallels can be cited between self-determination and federal termination policy during the 1950s. Both have been aimed at ultimately abrogating federal responsibilities to Indian Americans. The termination policy was undoubtedly implemented to dissolve the federal-Indian relationship as soon as possible, while self-determination enables Indians to decide when they are able to sever this relationship. When Native Americans are able to supervise totally their own affairs, the government believes that Indians will see no need for special federal services.

The Republican administrations of Gerald Ford and Ronald Reagan have demonstrated that the federal government will continue to assist Indians in self-determination, but with limited funding and reduced services. To make his position clear, during July 1976 President Ford met with several Indian leaders to make public his views on self-determination and termination.

"I am committed to furthering the self-determination of Indian communities," said the president, "but without terminating the special relationship between the federal government and the Indian people. I am strongly opposed to termination."[8] In addition, Democratic President Jimmy Carter took a similar position during his administration's handling of Indian affairs in trying to convince Indians to apply for other government services.

Reaganomics has severely affected federal funding of Indian programs, a mainstay of the Native American economy. During 1981 the Reagan administration cut back one-half of the health services for urban Indians, and it plans to eventually dissolve these services. Furthermore, federal funding for Indian higher education in the same year was initially cut from 282 million dollars to 200 million dollars, and later trimmed to 169 million dollars. The Bureau of Indian Affairs' budget was cut back by 76.9 million dollars, and other Indian-related programs funded by the federal government encountered drastic budget reductions.[9] In essence, the cutbacks reflected the termination policy of the 1950s and were disguised as self-determination in President Reagan's program of "New Federalism."

As Indians progress, the government sees them as taking upon themselves the termination of their dependency on federal services. Simply put, self-determination implies termination, and relocation means urbanization. Well over one-half of the total Indian population, an estimated 1.5 million people, resides in urban areas; and this was the goal of the relocation program of the 1950s—to urbanize Indians. Yet the federal government remains incapable of fully comprehending the extent of social adjustment confronting Indians in the mainstream society.

Appendix 1

Indian Claims Settlements during 1950s

Awards by Fiscal Years

Fiscal Year	Number of Judgments		Net Final Judgments	Administration
1950–51	2		$ 3,489,843.58	H. Truman
1951–52	0		0	
1952–53	1		600,000.00	D. Eisenhower
1953–54	1		927,668.04	
1954–55	3		3,262,327.57	
1955–56	2		1,515,495.06	
1956–57	1		433,013.60	
1957–58	2		4,759,081.88	
1958–59	1		2,067,166.00	
1959–60	14		20,263,568.40	
		Total	$37,316,164.13	

Awards by Calendar Years

Calendar Year	Number of Judgments		Net Final Judgments	Administration
1950	2		$ 3,489,843.53	H. Truman
1951	1		600,000.00	
1952	0		0	D. Eisenhower
1953	0		0	
1954	1		927,668.00	
1955	6		4,777,822.63	
1956	0		0	
1957	1		433,013.60	
1958	2		4,759,018.88	
1959	5		5,957,194.56	
1960	10		16,373,539.84	
		Total	$37,328,101.03	

Appendix 2

Report on Tribes Ready for Termination of Federal Supervision

Local officials of the Bureau of Indian Affairs reported "Yes" for those tribes believed ready to handle their own affairs and "No" for those not qualified. This report appeared in House Report Number 2680, 83d Congress, second session, 1954.

1. Blackfeet: Yes (except for a minority)
2. California (115 groups listed Yes in H. Rept. 2503, 82d Cong., 2d sess.)
3. North Carolina Cherokee: No
4. South Carolina Catawba: Yes
5. Cheyenne River: No
6. Mississippi Choctaw: No
7. Hualapai: No
8. Yavapai: Yes (conditionally)
9. Havasupai: No
10. Campe Verde: No
11. Fort Mohave: No
12. Cocopah: Yes
13. Colorado River: No
14. Colville: Yes (conditionally)
15. Spokane: Yes
16. Chippewa Fond du Lac: Yes
17. Chippewa Grand Portage: Yes (conditionally)
18. Chippewa Leech Lake: Yes (conditionally)
19. Chippewa White Earth: Yes (conditionally)
20. Chippewa Nett Lake: Yes (conditionally)
21. Chippewa Mille Lac: Yes
22. Southern Ute: No
23. Ute Mountain: No
24. Crow: No
25. Crow Creek: No
26. Lower Brule: No
27. Five Civilized Tribes: No
28. Eastern Shawnee: Yes (conditionally)
29. Ottawa: Yes
30. Quapaw: Yes (except for minority)
31. Seneca-Cayuga: Yes (conditionally)
32. Wyandot: Yes (conditionally)
33. Flathead: Yes
34. Fort Apache: No
35. Fort Belknap: Yes
36. Rocky Boy's: No
37. Fort Berthold: Yes
38. Fort Hall: Yes (if gradually)
39. Fort Peck: Yes (except for minority)
40. Great Lakes Bad River: No
41. Great Lakes Bay Mills: Yes
42. Forest County Potawatomi: No
43. Great Lakes Hannaville: Yes
44. Great Lakes Keweenaw Bay: Yes
45. Lac Courte Oreilles: No
46. Lac du Flambeau: Yes (conditionally)

47. Oneida: Yes
48. Red Cliff: Yes
49. Sac and Fox of the Mississippi in Iowa: No
50. Saginaw Chippewa or Isabella: Yes
51. St. Croix: Yes
52. Sokaognon or Mole Lake: Yes (conditionally)
53. Stockbridge-Munsee: Yes
54. Winnebago of Wisconsin: Yes (conditionally)
55. Hopi: No
56. Jicarilla: No
57. Klamath: [?]
58. Menominee: Yes
59. Mescalero Apache: No
60. Navajo: No
61. Battle Mountain Colony: Yes
62. Nevada Carson County: Yes
63. Nevada Duck Valley: Yes
64. Nevada Elko: Yes
65. Nevada Ely: Yes
66. Nevada Fallon Colony: No
67. Nevada Fallon: Yes
68. Nevada Fort McDermitt: Yes
69. Nevada Goshute: No
70. Nevada Las Vegas: Yes
71. Nevada Lovelock Colony: No
72. Moapa: Yes
73. Pyramid Lake: Yes
74. Reno-Sparks: Yes
75. Ruby Valley: Yes
76. Skull Valley: Yes
77. South Fork: Yes
78. Summit Lake, Yes
79. Walker River: Yes
80. Washoe: No
81. Winnemucca Colony: Yes
82. Yerington Colony: No
83. Yomba: Yes
84. Northern Cheyenne: No
85. Kalispel: No
86. Kootenai: No
87. Nez Percé: Yes
88. Coeur d'Alene: Yes
89. Osage: [?]
90. Papago: No
91. Fort McDowell: No
92. Salt River: Yes (conditionally)
93. Gila River: No
94. Maricopa or Ak Chin: No
95. Pine Ridge: No
96. Pipestone: [?]
97. Red Lake: No
98. Rosebud: No
99. Yankton: Yes (conditionally)
100. San Carlos: No
101. Florida Seminole: No
102. Sisseton-Wahpeton Sioux: Yes
103. Absentee Shawnee: No
104. Alabama-Coushatta: Yes (except for minority)
105. Caddo: Yes
106. Cheyenne-Arapaho: No
107. Citizen Potawatomi: Yes
108. Fort Sill Apache: Yes
109. Iowa of Kansas and Nebraska: Yes
110. Kaw: Yes
111. Kansas Kickapoo: Yes
112. Oklahoma Kickapoo: No
113. Kiowa-Comanche-Apache: No
114. Otoe-Missouria: No
115. Pawnee: Yes (except for minority)
116. Oklahoma Ponca: No
117. Kansas Prairie Potawatomi: No
118. Sac and Fox of Kansas and Nebraska: Yes
119. Oklahoma Sac and Fox: Yes (except for minority)
120. Tonkawa: Yes
121. Wichita: Yes (except for minority)
122. Standing Rock: No
123. Turtle Mountain: Yes
124. Fort Totten: Yes (conditionally)
125. Uintah and Ouray: No
126. Shivwits: No
127. Koosharem: No
128. Indian Peaks: Yes (conditionally)

129. Kaibab: No
130. Kanosh: No
131. Umatilla: Yes (conditionally)
132. Acoma: No
133. Cochita: No
134. Isleta: No
135. Jemez: No
136. Laguna: No
137. Nambe: No
138. Picuris: No
139. Pojaque: No
140. Sandia: No
141. San Felipe: No
142. San Idlefonso: No
143. San Juan: No
144. Santa Ana: No
145. Santa Clara: No
146. Santa Domingo: No
147. Taos: No
148. Tesuque: No
149. Zia: No
150. Zuni: No
151. Cañoncito: No
152. Alamo: No
153. Ramah: No
154. Warm Springs: No
155. Chehalis: Yes
156. Hoh: Yes
157. Lower Elwaha: Yes
158. Lummi: Yes (conditionally)
159. Makah: Yes
160. Muckleshoot: Yes
161. Nisqually: Yes
162. Ozette: Yes
163. Port Gamble: Yes
164. Port Madison: Yes
165. Public Domain: Yes
166. Puyallup: Yes
167. Quileute: Yes
168. Quinault: Yes
169. Shoalwater: Yes
170. Skokomish: Yes
171. Squaxon Island: Yes
172. Swinomish: Yes (conditionally)
173. Tulalip: Yes
174. Wind River: Yes
175. Omaha: Yes
176. Ponca: Yes
177. Santee Sioux: Yes
178. Winnebago: Yes
179. Yakima: No

Source: Memorandum no. 55, A Work Paper on Termination, Box 69, William A. Brophy Papers, Harry S. Truman Presidential Library, Independence, Missouri.

Appendix 3

Branch of Relocation Organization Chart—1957

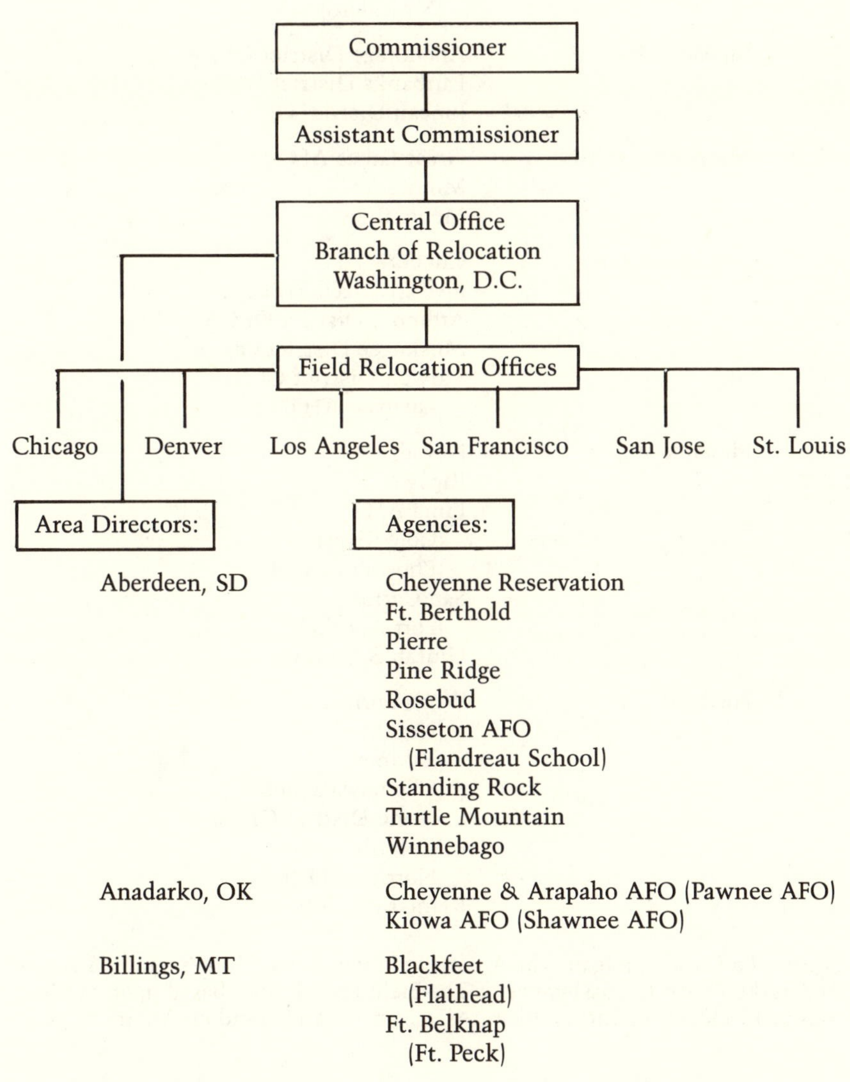

	Northern Cheyenne
	(Crow)
Gallup, NM	Navajo
	Chinle SA
	Crown Point SA (Zuni AFO)
	Fort Defiance SA
	Shiprock SA
	Tuba City SA
	United Pueblos
	(Jicarilla)
	(Mescalero)
Juneau, AK	Anchorage District Office
	Fairbanks District Office
	Juneau District Office
Minneapolis, MN	Great Lakes AFO
	Minnesota
	Menominee
Muskogee, OK	Choctaw AFO
	Five Civilized Tribes
	Ardmore District Office
	Muskogee District Office
	Stilwell District Office
	(Quapaw AFO)
Phoenix, AZ	Nevada
	Papago
	Pima AFO
	(Cole River)
	(Phoenix School)
	San Carlos
	(Fort Apache)
	Uintah & Ouray
Portland, OR	Warm Springs
	(Umatilla)
	(Yakima)
	(Chemawa School)
	Spokane District Office
	(Colville)
	(Northern Idaho)
	Klamath

Source: La Verne Madigan, The American Indian Relocation Program, A Report undertaken with the assistance of The Field Foundation, based upon the findings of a Relocation Survey Team, Assoc. on American Indian Affairs, 1956.

Notes

Chapter 1

1. *Indians in the War, 1945* (Chicago: Department of the Interior–Bureau of Indian Affairs, 1945), p. 1.

2. U.S. Congress, House, George H. Dunne, "The Indian's Dilemma," 85th Cong., 1st sess., 1957, *Congressional Record,* 103:6459. Other literature, including information on Ira Hayes, is in Dorothy Van de Mark, "The Raid on Reservations," *Harper's Magazine* 212 (March 1956), pp. 48–53; and in Tom Holm, "Fighting A White Man's War: The Extent and Legacy of American Indian Participation in World War II," *Journal of Ethnic Studies* 9 (Summer 1981), p. 72.

3. *Indians at War, 1945,* p. 1; Helen Peterson, "American Indian Political Participation," *The Annals of the American Academy of Political and Social Science* 311 (May 1957), p. 123; and William T. Hagan, *American Indians* (Chicago and London: University of Chicago Press, 1961), p. 158.

4. Ruth Underhill, *The Navajos* (Norman: University of Oklahoma Press, 1956), p. 242. A volume of essays on Navajos in the war is Broderick H. Johnson, ed., Navajos and World War II (Tsaile: Navajo Community College Press, 1977). Cultural differences between Indian soldiers and other American soldiers are covered in John Adair and Evon Vogt, "Navajo and Zuni Veterans: A Study of Contrasting Modes of Culture Change," *American Anthropologist* 51, no. 4 (1949), pp. 547–61.

5. *Indians in the War,* pp. 1 and 49.

6. Stan Steiner, *The New Indians* (New York: Dell Publishing Company, 1968), p. 20.

7. Underhill, *Navajos,* p. 241.

8. Chaske F. Wicks, interview by Bea Medicine, 15 February 1969, Little Rock, California, microfiche, tape 356, pt. 2, American Indian Research Project–Doris Duke Indian Oral History Collection, University of South Dakota, Vermillion.

9. *Indians in the War,* pp. 1 and 9–11. Both accounts of Childers's and Montgomery's deeds are in William Coffer, *Phoenix: The Decline and Rebirth of the Indian People* (New York and London: Van Nostrand Reinholdt Company, 1979). Childers's feat is also reported in the John Collier Papers, microfilm, reel 31, Newberry Library, Chicago.

10. "First Americans are last; Pro and Con Discussion," *Senior Scholastic* 62 (4 March 1953), pp. 5–6.

11. *Indians in the War,* p. 25.

12. Oliver La Farge, "They Were Good Enough for the Army," *Reader's Digest* 52 (February 1948), pp. 115–18.

13. Ibid.

14. Berlin B. Chapman, *The Otoes and Missourias: A Study of Indian Removal and the Legal Aftermath* (Oklahoma City: Times Journal Publishing Company, 1965), pp. 308–9.

15. Elmer Bennett, "Federal Responsibility For Indian Resources," 26 September 1959 (Address by the Under Secretary of the Department of the Interior before the Federal Bar Association, Indian Affairs Committee, Washington, D.C.), box 12, Fred A. Seaton Papers, Dwight D. Eisenhower Presidential Library, Abilene, Kansas.

16. William Brophy to Chan Gurney, 3 May 1946, box 417, William Brophy Papers, Harry S. Truman Presidential Library, Independence, Missouri.

17. Jose Toledo, interview by James P. Romero, 1–2 March 1970, Jemez Pueblo, New Mexico, tape 446, side 1, Doris Duke Indian Oral History Collection, Special Collections, William Zimmerman Library, University of New Mexico, Albuquerque.

18. "So-Called Emancipation Bill Threatens American Indian Rights" (Statement by Association on American Indian Affairs, 1 April 1948), box 76, White House file, Philleo Nash Papers, Harry S. Truman Presidential Library.

19. David A. Baerreis, ed., "The Indian in Modern America," A Symposium at the Wisconsin State Historical Society (Madison, Wisconsin, 1956).

20. Harry S Truman to Julius A. Krug, 4 March 1949, box 154, Desk Files of William Brophy and John R. Nichols, accession number (hereafter cited as acc. no.) 67–A–721, Record Group (hereafter cited as RG) 75, Federal Archives and Records Center (hereafter cited as FARC), Suitland, Maryland.

21. "Abuse of Indians a Point of Attack in Reds' Propaganda," Adirondack *Daily Enterprise,* Saranac Lake, New York, 6 May 1948, box 16, William Brophy Papers.

22. "Indian Bureau Makes Progress," 30 June 1949, news release by the Department of Interior, box 43, White House file, Philleo Nash Papers.

23. "Brophy Lauded By President," Albuquerque *Tribune,* 5 June 1948.

24. Glenn L. Emmons, "U.S. Aim: Give Indians a Chance," *Nation's Business,* July 1955, p. 42.

25. Joseph Bruner to William Stigler, 3 September 1945, box 22, William G. Stigler Papers, Western History Collections (hereafter cited as WHC), University of Oklahoma, Norman.

26. U.S. Congress, House, "A House Resolution to provide for removal of restrictions on property of Indians who serve in the armed forces," H.R. 4196, 79th Cong., 1st sess., 1945.

27. Memorandum no. 68, Sophie D. Aberle and William Brophy to Senate Commission, "Discrimination against Indians," box 31, William Brophy Papers.

28. "To Remove Restrictions on Indian Property," 8 June 1944, Indian Rights

Association Papers, microfilm 182, series 3, reel 113, Newberry Library, Chicago.

29. "Indian Bureau Director Pays Denver Visit," news clipping, n.d., box 18, William Brophy Papers.

30. William A. Brophy to Pearce C. Rodney, 3 May 1945, box 1, ibid.

31. "Job Help Pledged to Indian Veterans," Milwaukee *Journal*, 25 November 1945.

32. Lester Oliver to Elmer Thomas, 5 May 1946, box 417, Elmer Thomas Papers, WHC, University of Oklahoma.

33. Statement by William A. Brophy in a meeting with William Zimmerman and Boyd Jackson, 6 May 1946, box 15, William Brophy Papers.

34. Reed Buzzard to George Schwabe, 22 June 1946, box 15, George Schwabe Papers, WHC, University of Oklahoma.

35. George Schwabe to Reed Buzzard, 16 July 1946, ibid.

36. U.S. Congress, Senate, Committee on Indian Affairs, Harry S Truman, *Aspects of Indian Policy,* S. Rept. 1945, 79th Cong., 1st sess., Report for the Committee on Indian Affairs. 92:7998–99.

37. House Resolution 2148, introduced in the House of Representatives, 80th Cong., 1st sess., 3 April 1947, box 21, William G. Stigler Papers.

38. Elmer Thomas to Jess Spring, 2 June 1947, box 420, Elmer Thomas Papers.

39. U.S. Congress, House, Committee on Public Lands, *Providing for the Removal of Restrictions on Property of Indians who served in the Armed Forces,* H. Rept. 1947, 80th Cong., 1st sess., 1947.

Chapter 2

1. Land Policies of the Department of the Interior, box 12, William Brophy Papers, Harry S. Truman Presidential Library.

2. Superintendent of Bureau of Indian Affairs to J. Bartley Miliam, 18 January 1944, Muskogee Area Office Correspondence, acc. no. 69–A–430, RG 75, FARC, Fort Worth.

3. Kenneth R. Philp, *John Collier's Crusade for Indian Reform, 1920–1954* (Tucson: University of Arizona Press, 1977), pp. 211–13.

4. "Zimmerman May Succeed Collier," Gallup *Independent,* 31 January 1945.

5. Farewell Message to Members of the Indian Service, Tribal Councils, and Other Indian Leadership, and Friends of the Indians' Cause, n.d., John Collier Papers, microfilm, reel 31, Newberry Library, Chicago.

6. News article in Gallup *Independent,* 31 January 1945.

7. "Indians Oppose Brophy Choice," Albuquerque *Tribune,* 27 February 1945.

8. Gid Graham to William G. Stigler, 18 March 1945, box 23, William G. Stigler Papers, WHC, University of Oklahoma.

9. "New Mexico Alumnus," vol. 22, April 1945, box 16, William Brophy Papers; and Warner W. Gardner, interview by Jerry Hess, 22 June 1972, Wash-

ington, D.C., Oral History Collection, Harry S. Truman Presidential Library, Independence, Missouri.

10. William Brophy to James Renville, 4 May 1945, William Brophy Papers.

11. William G. Stigler to LaWanna Henley, 13 July 1945, box 14, William G. Stigler Papers.

12. "Indian Policy Change Likely," Albuquerque *Journal,* 16 July 1945.

13. "Blackfeet Adopt Brophy, Call Him 'Mountain Eagle,'" Albuquerque *Journal,* 16 July 1945.

14. "Brophy Praises Indian Record," Albuquerque *Tribune,* 18 July 1945; and William Brophy to Jim McBroom, 13 December 1945, box 1, William Brophy Papers.

15. "Brophy Meets Officials, Indians," Albuquerque *Journal,* 24 August 1945.

16. "Brophy to Shake Up Indian Service," Gallup *Independent,* 25 August 1945.

17. U.S. Congress, House, "A Joint Resolution establishing a joint congressional committee to make a study of claims of Indian tribes against the United States and to investigate the administration of Indian affairs," H.R. 237, 79th Cong., 1st sess., 1945.

18. U.S. Congress, House, "A House Resolution to create an Indian Claims Commission, to provide for the powers, duties, and functions thereof, and for other purposes," H.R. 4497, 79th Cong., 1st sess., 1945.

19. Report by Congressman Henry M. Jackson, 10 December 1945, Indian Rights Association Papers, microfilm 182, series 3, reel 113, Newberry Library, Chicago.

20. Address by William A. Brophy to the Indian Rights Association, 17 January 1946, box 13, William Brophy Papers.

21. Harvey Smith to Harry S Truman, 21 February 1946, box 6–AA, Indian Claims Commission Papers, Harry S. Truman Presidential Library, Independence, Missouri.

22. Joseph O'Mahoney, "Creating an Indian Claims Commission," 15 July 1946, Indian Rights Association Papers, microfilm 182, series 3, reel 113.

23. Julius A. Krug to Harry S Truman, 1 August 1946, box 6–AA, Indian Claims Commission Papers.

24. A. K. Wiley to Harry S Truman, 6 August 1946, ibid.

25. Cross-Reference Report on H.R. 4386, Approved 8 August 1946, box 58, official file, Harry S. Truman Papers, Harry S. Truman Presidential Library, Independence, Missouri.

26. "An Act to Facilitate and Simplify the Administration of Indian Affairs," *Hearing before the Committee on Indian Affairs, U. S. Senate,* 79th Cong., 2d sess., Indian Rights Association Papers, microfilm 182, series 3, reel 113.

27. Philp, *John Collier's Crusade,* pp. 200–201; and S. Lyman Tyler, *A History of Indian Policy* (Washington: U.S. Department of the Interior–Bureau of Indian Affairs, 1973), p. 150.

28. Statement by the President upon Signing Bill Creating the Indian Claims Commission, 13 August 1946, *Public Papers of the Presidents of the United States, Harry S. Truman, 1946* (Washington: U.S. Government Printing Office, 1965), p. 414; and Nancy O. Lurie, "The Indian Claims Commission Act," *The*

Annals of the American Academy of Political and Social Science 311 (May 1957), pp. 56–70. Another useful article on the Claims Commission is John R. White, "Barmecide Revisited: The Gratuitous Offset in Indian Claims Cases," *Ethnohistory* 25 (Spring 1978), pp. 179–192.

29. "Brophy Maps New Program for Tribesmen," Oklahoma City *Times,* 21 August 1946.

30. Ibid.

31. William G. Stigler to Wilburn Cartwright, 23 August 1946, box 19, William G. Stigler Papers.

32. "Moore Hints Fight on Indian Bureau," Oklahoma City *Times,* 26 December 1946.

33. Statement of Senator E. H. Moore of Oklahoma before the Subcommittee on Indian Affairs of the Senate Public Lands Committee with Respect to S. 405, n.d., box 19, William G. Stigler Papers.

34. Blake Clarke, "Must We Buy America from the Indians All Over Again?" *Reader's Digest* 72 (March 1958), pp. 45–49.

35. Oscar L. Chapman to Harry S Truman, 22 August 1946, box 43, White House file, Philleo Nash Papers; and box 104, reading file, Oscar L. Chapman Papers, Harry S. Truman Presidential Library.

36. William T. Hagan, *American Indians* (Chicago and London: University of Chicago Press, 1961), p. 167; and William Coffer, *Phoenix: The Decline and Rebirth of the Indian People* (New York and London: Van Nostrand Reinholdt Company, 1979), p. 160.

37. Senate Bill 30 Introduced in 80th Cong., 1st sess., 6 January 1947, Indian Rights Association Papers, microfilm 182, series 3, reel 113.

38. Albert Aleck to George Malone, telegram, 10 June 1947, box 2, Pyramid Lake Paiute Indian Collection no. 16, Special Collections, University of Nevada Library, Reno.

39. Theodore Taylor, *The States and Their Indian Citizens* (Washington: U.S. Government Printing Office, 1972), pp. 51–52.

40. House Resolution 2858 Introduced in the House of Representatives, 80th Cong., 1st sess., 3 April 1947, box 21, William G. Stigler Papers.

41. U.S. Congress, House, Committee on Public Lands, "Emancipation of Indians," Hearings before the Subcommittee of the House Committee on Public Lands on H.R. 2958, H.R. 2165 and H.R. 1113, 80th Cong., 1st sess., 1947, pp. 79, 80, 84, and 104–6.

42. "Asks Rise for Indian Bureau," New York *Herald-Tribune,* 12 April 1947; and Alice Henderson Rossin, "Two Ways to Set the Indian Free" (Statement before the House Subcommittee on Indian Affairs, 11 April 1947), Elmer Thomas Papers, WHC, University of Oklahoma.

43. Joyn R. Provinse, "The Withdrawal of Federal Supervision of the American Indian" (Paper presented at the National Conference of Social Work, San Francisco, 15 April 1947), box P–S, Office Files of Assistant Commissioner Joyn R. Provinse, National Archives, Washington, D.C. The tribes listed for termination in the Zimmerman Plan are in Tyler, *History of Indian Policy,* pp. 163–64.

44. Oscar L. Chapman to Hugh Butler, 2 May 1947, box 106, reading file, Oscar L. Chapman Papers.

45. Senate Bill 1222 Introduced in the 80th Cong., 1st sess., 2 May 1947, box 21, William G. Stigler Papers.

46. U.S. Congress, House, Congressman Morse speaking for termination of the Klamath Indians, S. 1222, 80th Cong., 1st sess., 2 May 1947, *Congressional Record* 93:4458.

47. George Schwabe to Lawrence Birdsbill, 13 May 1947, box 12, George Schwabe Papers, WHC, University of Oklahoma.

48. Ibid.

49. Elmer Thomas to H. B. Reubelt, 19 May 1947, box 415, Elmer Thomas Papers.

50. U.S. Congress, House, Congresswoman Lusk speaking on withdrawal of Federal supervision over Indian Affairs, 80th Cong., 1st sess., 27 May 1947, *Congressional Record* 93:A3122.

51. Freddi Washington to Elmer Thomas, 11 July 1947, box 422, Elmer Thomas Papers.

52. U.S. Congress, Senate, Senator Butler speaking on removal of restrictions on certain Indian tribes, 80th Cong., 2d sess., 21 July 1947, *Congressional Record* 93:94665.

53. News release from the Department of Interior, box 494, Pierre Indian Agency Correspondence, no acc. no., no RG, FARC, Kansas City, Missouri.

54. William Brophy to Ruth M. Bronson, 20 September 1947, box 8, personal correspondence file 1947, William Brophy Papers.

55. "Indians Claim $7.5 Billion on Land Deals," *The Daily Oklahoman*, Oklahoma City, 21 September 1947.

56. William G. Stigler to Gibson R. Scott, 18 October 1947, box 15, William G. Stigler Papers.

57. Senate Bill 978 Introduced during 79th Cong., 1st sess., 10 May 1945, Indian Rights Association Papers, microfilm 182, series 3, reel 113.

58. Statement by the President Making Public a Report on the Needs of the Navajo Indians, 2 December 1947, *Public Papers of the Presidents of the United States, Harry S. Truman, 1947* (Washington: U.S. Government Printing Office, 1963), pp. 503–4; and "Statement by the President," box 6–AA, Indian Claims Commission Papers.

59. Ibid.

60. William Brophy to Harry S Truman, 31 December 1947, box 8, personal correspondence file 1947, William Brophy Papers.

61. William Brophy to Julius A. Krug, 31 December 1947, ibid.; William Brophy to Judge Bone, 8 March 1948, box 9, William Brophy Papers; and "Brophy Quits Indian Agency," New York *Herald-Tribune*, 17 January 1948.

62. Elmer Thomas to Fred Lookout, 29 January 1948, box 419, Elmer Thomas Papers.

63. Eugene L. Graves to Elmer Thomas, 2 February 1948, box 427, ibid.

64. Oscar L. Chapman to Wayne Morse, 7 May 1946, box 19, Wayne Morse Papers, Special Collections, University of Oregon Library, Eugene.

65. Veto of Bill for the Disposal of Submarginal Lands within Indian Reserva-

tions, 10 February 1948, Statement by Harry S Truman, *Public Papers of the Presidents of the United States, Harry S. Truman, 1948,* (Washington: U.S. Government Printing Office, 1964), p. 134.

66. Oscar L. Chapman to Hugh Butler, 11 March 1948, box 109, reading file, Harry S. Truman Papers.

67. Harry S Truman to Julius A. Krug, 29 March 1948, box 397, official file, ibid.

68. Memorandum from W. O. Roberts to Division Heads and Field Employees regarding Theodore Haas's report, "Trends and Portrends in the Indian Bureau," 4 January 1949, box 359701, Muskogee Area Office Correspondence, acc. no. 61–A–617, RG 79, FARC, Fort Worth.

69. "Ute Indians Hit a $31.7 Million Jackpot," *Life Magazine* 29 (24 July 1950), pp. 37–38; and "Indians Back Pay for the Utes," *Time* 56 (24 July 1950), p. 19.

70. Ibid.

71. "Ute Bill Bolsters Indians Faith in Democratic Government," news release by the Department of Interior, 10 September 1951, box 43, White House file, Philleo Nash Papers.

President Truman signed the Ute Claim Bill in August 1951, and funds for a per capita payment were included to pay three groups of the Southern Utes, Statement by President Truman, 21 August 1951, regarding approval of H.R. 3795, box 58, and Cross-Reference Report on House Resolution 3795, box 938, official file, Harry S. Truman Papers.

Chapter 3

1. "President Asked to End Discrimination Against Indians of New Mexico and Arizona," news release by the Association on American Indian Affairs, 13 January 1949, box 418, Elmer Thomas Papers, WHC, University of Oklahoma, Norman. Ruth M. Bronson, secretary of the National Congress of American Indians, wrote to all tribal chairmen and officials of the NCAI that she had consulted its attorneys about Senate Bill 691, which would set "the Indians off as a race apart under the Social Security Law" (31 January 1949), box 18, Wayne Morse Papers, Special Collections, University of Oregon Library, Eugene.

2. U.S. Congress, House, Congressman D'Ewart speaking on Indian populations and conditions in the United States, 81st Cong., 1st sess., 17 January 1949, *Congressional Record* 95:A232–33.

3. News statement by President Truman Asking for the End of Discrimination against Indians in New Mexico and Arizona, 13 January 1949, box 418, Elmer Thomas Papers.

4. Hollis Hampton to Carl Albert, 24 January 1949, box 418, Elmer Thomas Papers.

5. Harry J. W. Belvin to Robert S. Kerr, 29 January 1949, box 310, Robert S. Kerr Papers, WHC, University of Oklahoma, Norman.

6. Elmer Thomas to Hollis Hampton, 29 January 1949, box 418, Elmer Thomas Papers.

7. Harry Truman to Secretary of the Interior, 4 March 1949, box 937, official

file, Harry S. Truman Papers, Harry S. Truman Presidential Library, Independence, Missouri.

8. U.S. Congress, House, Congressman Poulson speaking in reference to Eleanor Roosevelt's statement on H.R. 2632 and Indian benefits, 81st Cong., 1st sess., 12 May 1949, *Congressional Record* 95:A2929.

9. Ibid.

10. U.S. Congress, Senate, Senator Langer speaking against the nomination of John R. Nichols to Commissioner of Indian Affairs, 81st Cong., 1st sess., 23 March 1949, *Congressional Record* 95:2929–96.

11. U.S. Congress, House, Congressman O'Neil speaking on Self-Government of American Indians, 81st Cong., 1st sess., 5 May 1949, *Congressional Record* 95:A2711–12.

12. "Indian Commissioner Sees Tribes Treated Like Other American Citizens," New York *Times*, 5 May 1949.

13. Robert Goombi to Elmer Thomas, 2 May 1949, box 421, Elmer Thomas Papers.

14. "Indian Bureau Makes Progress," 30 June 1949, news release by the Department of the Interior, box 43, White House file, Philleo Nash Papers, Harry S. Truman Presidential Library.

15. U.S. Congress, Senate, Senator McCarran speaking on Amendment of Constitution Relating to the Rights of the Indian Tribes, 81st Cong., 1st sess., 29 July 1949, *Congressional Record* 95:9745–46.

16. Faun Dixon, "Native American Property Rights: The Pyramid Lake Reservation Land Controversy" (Ph.D. diss., University of Nevada, Reno, 1980), pp. 124–25. An in-depth study of Paiute termination is Stanley J. Underdal, "On the Road toward Termination: The Pyramid Lake Paiutes and the Indian Attorney Controversy of the 1950s" (Ph.D. diss., Columbia University, 1977). On the political influence of Senator McCarran, see Jerome E. Edwards, *Patrick McCarran: Political Boss of Nevada* (Reno: University of Nevada Press, 1983).

17. Oliver La Farge to Joseph O'Mahoney, 22 June 1949, box 10/15/2, Patrick McCarran Papers, Nevada State Archives, Carson City, Nevada; and news release of NCAI, 5 January 1950, box 18, Wayne Morse Papers.

18. E. Resseman Fryer to Dillon Myer, 5 October 1950, box 2, Pyramid Lake Paiute Indian Collection no. 16, Special Collections, University of Nevada Library, Reno.

19. E. Resseman Fryer to Dillon Myer, 15 May 1950, ibid.

20. See n. 15.

21. U.S. Congress, Senate, Senator Malone speaking on Abolition of the Bureau of Indian Affairs—Introduction of a Bill, 81st Cong., 1st sess., 17 October 1949, *Congressional Record* 95:14778–79.

22. Address of Dr. John R. Nichols, Commissioner of Indian Affairs, to the Oklahoma-Kansas Superintendents' Association at Oklahoma, 17 November 1949, Muskogee Area Office Correspondence, box 455120, acc. no. 70–A–27, RG 75, FARC, Fort Worth.

23. U.S. Congress, Senate, Senator Wiley speaking on the Need for a Scrutiny of America's Indian Policy, 81st Cong., 2d sess., 28 March 1950, *Congressional Record* 96:4182.

24. U.S. Congress, Senate, Senator Butler Speaking on "Are Indians Wards of the Government?" 81st Cong., 2d sess., 30 March 1950, *Congressional Record* 96:1–2.

25. Theodore Taylor, *The States and Their Indian Citizens* (Washington: U.S. Government Printing Office, 1972), p. 56; and "Indians Might Do Better with Less Protection," Saturday Evening Post 223 (29 July 1950), p. 10.

26. Oscar L. Chapman to J. Hardin Peterson, 25 July 1950, box 155, Desk Files of Dillon S. Myer, acc. no. 67–A–721, RG 75, FARC, Suitland, Maryland.

27. Dillon S. Myer to Herbert H. Lehman, 2 October 1950, John Collier Papers, microfilm, series 3, reel 38, Newberry Library, Chicago.

28. "The Bosone Resolution," newspaper article in the New York *Herald*, box 9, Dale E. Doty Papers, Harry S. Truman Presidential Library.

29. Oscar L. Chapman to John Collier, 31 August 1950, box 25, Joel Wolfsohn Papers, Harry S. Truman Presidential Library.

30. "20 Indian Soldiers Killed in Korea," 27 December 1950, news release by the Department of Interior, box 43, White House file, Philleo Nash Papers.

31. Edward T. Follard, White House correspondent for the Washington *Post*, 1923–67, interview by Jerry N. Hess, 20 August 1970, Washington, D.C., Oral History Collection, Harry S. Truman Presidential Library.

32. "Commissioner Myer Condemns Action by Cemetery Officials," n.d., news release by the Department of Interior, box 43, White House file, Philleo Nash Papers.

33. "Indian G.I. Buried in Arlington Rites," New York *Times*, 6 September 1951; "Indian to be Buried in Arlington Sept. 5," Washington *Post*, 31 August 1951; "Indian's Widow Here: Hero's Burial Today," Washington *Post*, 5 August 1951; "Sergt. Rice Rests in Arlington After Full Military Honors," Washington *Post*, 6 September 1951.

34. Senator Hugh Butler Introduced Senate Bill 485 in the Senate's 1st session of the 82d Congress, 16 January 1951, box 21, William G. Stigler Papers, WHC, University of Oklahoma.

35. Address by W. O. Roberts, area director, on Individual Indian Money Regulations, Conference of District Agents, 10 August 1951, box 393335, Muskogee Area Office Correspondence, acc. no. 69–A–430, RG 75, FARC, Fort Worth.

36. Toby Morris to Harry S Truman, 19 October 1950, box 58, official file, Harry S. Truman Papers.

37. "The American Indian," *The Commonweal* 55 (16 November 1951), pp. 131–32.

38. U.S. Congress, House, Congressman Bow speaking about the Bureau of Indian Affairs, 82d Cong., 2d sess., 18 March 1952, *Congressional Record* 98:2485–92.

39. Ibid.

40. Reva Beck Bosone to R. D. Curry, 7 May 1952, box 17, Reva Beck Bosone Papers, Special Collections, Marriott Library, University of Utah, Salt Lake City.

41. U.S. Congress, House, Congressman Delaney speaking on Authorizing and Directing Secretary of the Interior to Study Respective Tribes, Bands And

Groups of Indians, 82d Cong., 2d sess., 1 July 1952, *Congressional Record* 98:8782–87.

42. Warner W. Gardner, Solicitor, U.S. Department of the Interior, 1941–43, and Assistant Secretary of the Interior, 1946–47, interview by Jerry N. Hess, 22 June 1972, Washington, D.C., Oral History Collection, Harry S. Truman Presidential Library.

Chapter 4

1. Oscar L. Chapman to Dwight D. Eisenhower, 16 March 1950, National Personnel Records Center, General Services Administration, St. Louis, Missouri; Oscar L. Chapman to Harry S Truman, 18 March 1950, official file, Harry S. Truman Papers, Harry S. Truman Presidential Library; and "Nichols to Make Territorial Study," 23 March 1950, news release by the Department of Interior, box 43, White House file, Philleo Nash Papers, Harry S. Truman Presidential Library. The Washington *Star* reported that Myer was named the new commissioner before Nichols was notified that he was replaced; "Myer Named to Indian Bureau Before Nichols Learns of Change," Washington *Star,* 23 March 1950.

2. James Curry to Avery Winnemucca, 24 March 1950, box 2, Pyramid Lake Paiute Indian Collection no. 16, Special Collections, University of Nevada Library.

3. Ibid.

4. "Nichols to Make Territorial Study," 23 March 1950, news release by the Department of the Interior, box 16, William Brophy Papers, Harry S. Truman Presidential Library.

5. Robert Pennington, Chief of the Tribal Government Services, Bureau of Indian Affairs, interview by Donald Fixico, 13 August 1979, Washington, D.C.; and William Zimmerman, Jr., "Role of the Bureau of Indian Affairs," *The Annals of the American Academy of Political and Social Science* 311 (May 1957), p. 40.

6. Harold Ickes, "Go East, Young Indian!" New Republic 125 (3 September 1951), p. 17.

7. "President Truman Acts to Protect Paiute Indians," Washington *Bulletin,* newspaper of the National Congress of American Indians, box 311, Robert S. Kerr Papers, WHC, University of Oklahoma.

8. "Tribal Trouble," Washington *Post,* 24 October 1951.

9. Dillon S. Myer to the Secretary of the Interior, 1 October 1951, box 9, Department of the Interior subject file, Dale E. Doty Papers, Harry S. Truman Presidential Library.

10. Harold Ickes, "The Indian Loses Again," *New Republic* 125 (24 September 1951), p. 16.

11. Dillon S. Myer, "The Needs of the American Indian" (Address to the Combined Assemblies of the Division of Christian Life and Work of the National Council of the Churches of Christ at Buck Hill Falls, Pennsylvania, 12 December 1951), box 393335, Muskogee Area Office Correspondence, acc. no. 69–A–430, RG 75, FARC, Fort Worth.

12. Statement by Dillon S. Myer before a subcommittee of the Senate Committee on Interior and Insular Affairs, 21 January 1952, box 2, Government Agencies file, Dillon S. Myer Papers, Harry S. Truman Presidential Library.

13. Speech by Dillon S. Myer before the annual meeting of the Association on American Indian Affairs, New York, 26 March 1952, Ibid.

14. "Indian Attorneys," Washington *Post*, 30 January 1952.

15. Dillon S. Myer to Theodore B. Hall, 1 February 1952, box 393336, Muskogee Area Office Correspondence, acc. no. 69–A–430, RG 79, FARC, Fort Worth.

16. Meeting of Dillon S. Myer and Red Lake Tribal Business Association, Red Lake Reservation, Minnesota, 8 July 1952, box 566814, Red Lake Area Office files, acc. no. 67–A–814, RG 75, FARC, Kansas City.

17. "Experiment in Immorality," *The Nation* 175 (26 July 1952), p. 61.

18. Excerpts from remarks by Dwight D. Eisenhower to thirty-five American Indian tribes at the 31st Inter-tribal Indian Ceremonial, Gallup, New Mexico, 10 August 1952, box 618, White House Central Files, Dwight D. Eisenhower Presidential Library.

19. Felix Cohen to John Collier, 23 July 1952, John Collier Papers, microfilm, series 3, reel 34, Newberry Library.

20. Memorandum, Dillon S. Myer to All Bureau Officials, 5 August 1952, box 566816, Minneapolis Area Office Correspondence, acc. no. 67–A–54, RG 75, FARC, Kansas City, Missouri.

21. Oliver La Farge, "Helping Elect the Great White Father," *The Reporter* (28 October 1952), pp. 31–33.

22. Special Meeting with Commissioner of Indian Affairs, 26 September 1952, box 2, Government Agencies file, Dillon S. Myer Papers.

23. Ibid.

24. Institute of Ethnic Affairs, "The Crisis in United States Indian Affairs," 9 October 1952, box 9, Department of Interior file, Dale E. Doty Papers.

25. Dillon S. Myer to All Tribal Council Members, 10 October 1952, box 2, Government Agencies file, Dillon S. Myer Papers.

26. Dillon S. Myer to Marion E. Gridley, 7 November 1952, box 393335, Muskogee Area Office Correspondence, acc. no. 69–A–430, RG 75, FARC, Fort Worth.

27. Dillon S. Myer, "Indian Administration: Problems and Goals," *Social Science Review* 27, (June 1953), pp. 193–200.

28. John Collier, "A Perspective on the United States Indian Situation of 1952 in Its Hemispheric and World-Wide Being," box 25, Joel H. Wolfsohn Papers, Harry S. Truman Presidential Library.

29. Commissioner Dillon S. Myer's Campaign Document, 15 December 1952, box 43, White House file, Philleo Nash Papers.

30. Juan de Jesús Romero, 6 December 1952, general file, White House Central Files, Dwight D. Eisenhower Presidential Library.

31. E. Morgan to BIA Commissioner, 24 June 1953, box 26, Portland Area Office Correspondence, no acc. no., RG 75, FARC, Seattle.

32. Juliet Saxon to Dwight D. Eisenhower, 9 February 1953, box 309, general file, White House Central Files, Dwight D. Eisenhower Presidential Library.

33. William Hudnut, Jr., to Dwight D. Eisenhower, 13 January 1953, box 310, ibid.

34. "Fair Plan for the Red Man," New York *Times*, 18 January 1953.

35. Telegram, Leo M. Kennerly to Dwight D. Eisenhower, 4 February 1953, box 310, general file, White House Central Files, Dwight D. Eisenhower Presidential Library.

36. Thomas E. Stephens to Douglas McKay, 20 February 1953, box 309, ibid.

37. John Collier, "Back to Dishonor?" *The Christian Century* 71 (12 May 1954), pp. 578–80.

38. "La Farge Charges U.S. Breaks Indian Trust," *The Christian Century* 71 (12 May 1954), pp. 604–5.

39. John Collier, "Indian Takeaway Betrayal of a Trust . . ." *The Nation* 179 (2 October 1954), pp. 290–91.

Chapter 5

1. "Transfer of Indian Hospitals and Health Facilities to Public Health Services" Hearing before the Senate Subcommittee on Indian Affairs, 29 May 1954, John Collier Papers, microfilm, series 3, reel 43, no. 862, Newberry Library.

2. House Concurrent Resolution 108 introduced by Senator Henry M. Jackson and passed during the 83d Congress, 1 August 1953, Indian Rights Association Papers, microfilm 182, series 3, reel 114, Newberry Library; H.C.R. 108 introduced in the House by William H. Harrison, 9 June 1953, box 120, Klamath Agency Files, no acc. no., RG 75, FARC, Seattle.

3. Ibid.

4. Gary Orfield, *A Study of the Termination Policy* (Denver: National Congress of American Indians, n.d.), p. 2. Members of the Senate Subcommittee on Indian Affairs who studied termination legislation during the 83d Congress were Arthur V. Watkins, Utah, Chairman; Henry C. Dworashak, Idaho; Thomas H. Kuchel, California; Clinton P. Anderson, New Mexico; and George Smathers, Florida; House Subcommittee members on Interior Affairs were E. Y. Berry, South Dakota, chairman; A. L. Miller, Nebraska; Wesley A. D'Ewart, Montana; John P. Saylor, Pennsylvania; William H. Harrison, Wyoming; J. Ernest Wharton, New York; Jack Westland, Washington; Clinton Young, Nevada; John J. Rhodes, Arizona; Clair Engle, California; Wayne Aspinall, Colorado; James Donovan, New York; James A. Haley, Florida; George A. Shufford, North Carolina; and E. L. Barlett, Alaska; Termination of Federal Supervision over Certain Tribes of Indians, "Joint Hearings Before the Subcommittee on Interior and Insular Affairs," U.S., Congress, 83d Cong., 2d sess., 1954, in John Collier Papers, microfilm, series 3, reel 44, no. 884, Newberry Library.

5. "'Menominees' Full Freedom Assured at General Council," Shawano *Journal*, Wisconsin, 22 June 1953.

6. Orfield, *Study of the Termination Policy*, p. 13.

7. Charles F. Wilkinson and Eric R. Briggs, "The Evolution of the Termination Policy," *American Indian Law Review* 5, no. 1 (Summer 1977), pp. 155–56.

8. Record of Menominee Indian Tribe Population, Minneapolis Area Office Correspondence, box 54, Keshena Indian Agency Correspondence, acc. no. 66–A–837, RG 75, FARC, Chicago.

9. Minutes of the General Council of the Menominee Indian Tribe, 20 June 1953, Keshena, Wisconsin, box 45, Minneapolis Area Office Correspondence, acc. no. 66–A–837, RG 75, FARC, Chicago.

10. Ibid.

11. Ibid.

12. Douglas McKay to Hugh Butler, 16 March 1953, box 2, Government Agencies file, Dillon S. Myer Papers, Harry S. Truman Presidential Library.

13. Patricia Ourada, *The Menominee Indians* (Norman: University of Oklahoma Press, 1979), pp. 283–84.

14. "Progress in Withdrawal," Muskogee Area Office, 30 June 1953, box 393335, Muskogee Area Office Correspondence, acc. no. 69–A–430, RG 75, FARC, Fort Worth.

15. "Reduced Federal Participation in Indian Affairs Reported," news release by the Department of Interior, box 43, White House file, Philleo Nash Papers, Harry S. Truman Presidential Library.

16. "House Concurrent Resolution 108," *U.S. Statutes at Large,* vol. 67 (1953), p. B132; and U.S. Congress, House, *Termination of Federal Supervision, Concurrent Resolution 108,* 83d Cong., 1st sess., 1 August 1953 (Washington: U.S. Government Printing Office, 1953).

17. Glenn L. Emmons, "The Problem Stated," *Rotarian* 84–85 (August 1954), pp. 26–29.

18. Concurrent Resolution 108 and Treaties, box 368, Desk Files of William Brophy and John R. Nichols, acc. no. 68–A–245, RG 75, FARC, Suitland, Maryland; and Orfield, *Study of the Termination Policy,* p. 6.

19. Minutes of General Council of the Menominee Indian Tribes, 17 July 1953, Keshena, Wisconsin, box 45, Minneapolis Area Office Correspondence, acc. no. 66–A–837, RG 75, FARC, Chicago.

20. Minutes of General Council of the Menominee Indian Tribe, 12–14 September 1953, Keshena, Wisconsin, ibid.

21. Harold E. Fey, "Our National Indian Policy," *The Christian Century* 72 (30 March 1955), pp. 395–97.

22. "House Concurrent Resolution 108," *U.S. Statutes at Large,* vol. 67 (1953), pp. 588–90.

23. Petition of Turtle Mountain Indians to House of Representatives and the Senate of the Congress of the United States, and to the Secretary of the Interior of the United States, 22 October 1953, White House file, Philleo Nash Papers.

24. S. Lyman Tyler, *A History of Indian Policy,* (Washington: U.S. Department of the Interior–Bureau of Indian Affairs, 1973), p. 176; see, also, David P. Delorme, "'Emancipation' and the Turtle Mountain Chippewas," *American Indian* 7 (Spring 1954), pp. 11–20.

25. Orfield, *Study of the Termination Policy,* p. 13.

26. Annual Budget Message to the Congress: Fiscal Year 1954, Statement by Harry S. Truman, 9 January 1953, *Public Papers of the Presidents of the United States, Harry S. Truman, 1953* (Washington: U.S. Government Printing Office, 1966), p. 1128.

27. The congressional schedule for terminating tribes included:

Bills	Tribe
S. 2670, H.R. 7390	Indians of Utah (Paiute and Shoshone)
S. 2744, H.R. 6382, H.R. 6547	Indians of Texas
S. 2746, H.R. 7317	Indians of Western Oregon
S. 2743, H.R. 7318	Sac & Fox and Iowa of Kansas and Nebraska, and the Kickapoo and Potawatomi of Kansas
S. 2745, H.R. 7320	Klamaths of Oregon
S. 2750, H.R. 7319	Flatheads of Montana
S. 2747, H.R. 7321	Seminoles of Florida
S. 2748, H.R. 7316	Turtle Mountain Chippewas of North Dakota
S. 2749, H.R. 7322	Indians of California
S. 2813, H.R. 7135	Menominees of Wisconsin

Memorandum from Arthur Lazarus, Jr., and Richard Schifter to Clients, 2 February 1954; Orme Lewis to Dwight Eisenhower, January 1954; Orme Lewis to Richard Nixon, 4 January 1954; and Orme Lewis to Joseph W. Martin, 4 January 1954, box 77, Philleo Nash Papers.

28. Orme Lewis to Joseph W. Martin, 4 January 1954, ibid.

29. S. 2746 passed as Public Law 58 for the termination of federal supervision over the property of certain tribes and bands of Indians located in Western Oregon, box 32, bill file, Dwight D. Eisenhower Presidential Library.

30. Alexander Lesser to Philleo Nash, 1 February 1954; and Oliver La Farge to Alexander Lesser, 2 February 1954, box 77, Philleo Nash Papers.

31. Memorandum concerning H.R. 1381 to promote the rehabilitation of the Five Civilized Tribes and other Indians of eastern Oklahoma, Marie L. Hayes to Indian Leaders, 4 February 1954, box 455120, Muskogee Area Office Correspondence, acc. no. 70–A–27, RG 75, FARC, Fort Worth.

32. John Collier, "'Terminating' The American Indian," 13 February 1954, box 43, White House file, Philleo Nash Papers.

33. Homer B. Jenkins to William O. Roberts, 25 March 1954, box 393333, Muskogee Area Office Correspondence, acc. no. 69–A–430, RG 75, FARC, Fort Worth.

34. Glenn L. Emmons to Walter King, 8 April 1954, ibid.

35. Summary of Meeting with Members of the Quapaw Tribe held in Muskogee, Oklahoma, 7 May 1954, Muskogee Area Office Correspondence, acc. no. 70–A–27, RG 75, FARC, Fort Worth.

36. "Should the American Indian be given full Citizenship Responsibility" (Debate between Senator George Smathers and Senator Arthur Watkins, 22 April 1954, Dumont Television Station, Washington D.C.), box 49416, Pierre Indian Agency Correspondence, no acc. no., no RG, FARC, Kansas City.

37. Ibid.

38. Ibid.

39. Memorandum, H. Rex Lee to Assistant Commissioner, Branch Chiefs, Area Directors, Superintendents, and Tribal Councils, 24 September 1954, box

55, Denver Area Office Correspondence, acc. no. 72–A–289, RG 75, FARC, Denver. A copy of the memorandum is also in box 566816, Minnesota Agency Correspondence, acc. no. 67–A–54, RG 75, FARC, Kansas City.

40. Sherman Adams to N. B. Johnson, 1 November 1954, box 618, official file, White House Central Files, Dwight D. Eisenhower Presidential Library.

41. Paul L. Fickinger to Members of the Inter-Tribal Council of the Five Civilized Tribes, Executive Committee of the Cherokee Nation, Chickasaw Indian leaders, and Seminole Indian Leaders, 27 January 1955, box 455120, Muskogee Area Office Correspondence, acc. no. 70–A–27, RG 75, FARC, Fort Worth.

42. James C. Hagerty to Ms. E. J. Harrigan, 25 February 1955, box 1164, general file, White House Central Files, Dwight D. Eisenhower Presidential Library.

43. Hubert H. Humphrey to Oveta Culp Hobby, 17 March 1955, box 36, Oveta Culp Hobby Papers, Dwight D. Eisenhower Presidential Library.

44. Indian Health Program, U.S. Public Health Service Report (August 1972), DHEW Publication No. (ASM) 73–12,003, pp. 1–36.

45. H.R. 5566 introduced during the 84th Congress, 1 August 1955, to terminate the existence of the Indian Claims Commission, box 209, official file, White House Central Files, Dwight D. Eisenhower Presidential Library.

46. Paul L. Fickinger to Guy Froman, 15 February 1956, box 393333, Muskogee Area Office Correspondence, acc. no. 69–A–430, RG 75, FARC, Fort Worth.

47. Statement on Current Issues in Indian Affairs, April 1956, box 9, William Brophy Papers, Harry S. Truman Presidential Library. Another copy of the statement is in box 12, Fred A. Seaton Papers, Dwight D. Eisenhower Presidential Library.

48. Fred Seaton to Walter Christenson, 1 August 1956, box 7, personal correspondence, Fred A. Seaton Papers.

49. Ibid.

50. Frank Church to B. W. Davis, n.d., box RN–12, Richard L. Neuberger Papers, Special Collections, University of Oregon Library, Eugene.

Chapter 6

1. Carole E. Goldberg, "Public Law 280: The Limits of State Jurisdiction over Reservation Indians," *UCLA Law Review* 22 (Fall 1975), p. 541.

2. Telegram, Edward J. Thye to Dwight D. Eisenhower, 15 August 1953, box 628, official file, White House Central Files, Dwight D. Eisenhower Presidential Library.

3. Statement by President Eisenhower, released by James C. Hagerty, Press Secretary to the President, 15 August 1953, box 618, ibid.

4. Dwight D. Eisenhower to Hugh Butler, 17 August 1953, ibid.

5. Principal Recommendations of Survey Team to Bureau of Indian Affairs, 26 January 1954, box 115, official file, White House Central Files, Dwight D. Eisenhower Presidential Library.

6. Survey Report on the Bureau of Indian Affairs (26 January 1954), printed for the use of the Committee on Interior and Insular Affairs (Washington: U.S. Government Printing Office, 1954).

7. Memorandum, Douglas McKay to Indian leaders, 7 April 1954, box 455120, Muskogee Area Office Correspondence, acc. no. 70–A–27, RG 75, FARC, Fort Worth.

8. Oliver La Farge to Alexander Lesser, 23 February 1954, box 76, White House file, Philleo Nash Papers, Harry S. Truman Presidential Library.

9. Statement by President Eisenhower, released by James C. Hagerty, Press Secretary to the President, box 121, official file, White House Central Files, Dwight D. Eisenhower Presidential Library; and Statement by the President upon Signing Bill Concerning Termination of Federal Supervision over the Menominee Indian Tribe, 17 June 1954, *Public Papers of the Presidents of the United States, Dwight D. Eisenhower, 1954* (Washington: U.S. Government Printing Office, 1960), p. 582.

10. "Turned Down by Bureau, Indians Ask State for Help," Shawano *Evening Leader,* Wisconsin, 6 October 1954.

11. Roger D'Ewart to James Murray, 11 July 1957; and Hatfield Chilson to Clair Engle, 11 July 1957, box 18, Bureau of Indian Affairs Records, no acc. no., RG 75, National Archives, Washington, D.C. Pertinent articles on Menominee termination are Nancy O. Lurie, "Menominee Termination from Reservation to Colony," *Human Organization* 31 (Fall 1972), pp. 257–70; David W. Ames and Burton R. Fisher, "The Menominee Termination Crisis: Barriers in the Way of a Rapid Cultural Transition," *Human Organization* 18 (Fall 1959), pp. 101–11; and Robert B. Edgertown, "Menominee Termination: Observation on the End of a Tribe," *Human Organization* 21 (Spring 1962), pp. 10–16.

12. Statement of the Department of the Interior on Potential Legislative Trouble Spots—Menominee Indian Termination Act Amendment, 4 December 1957, box 16, subject file, Fred A. Seaton Papers, Dwight D. Eisenhower Presidential Library.

13. Oliver La Farge, "Termination of Federal Supervision: Disintegration of the American Indians," *The Annals of American Political and Social Science* 311 (May 1957), p. 45.

14. Orme Lewis to Rowland R. Hughes, 10 August 1954, box 12, bill file, Dwight D. Eisenhower Presidential Library.

15. William P. Rogers to Rowland R. Hughes, 10 August 1954, ibid.

16. Roger W. Jones to Dwight D. Eisenhower, 12 August 1954, ibid.

17. Harold B. Anthony to John Collier, 13 July 1954, John Collier Papers, microfilm, series 3, reel 33, Newberry Library.

18. J. P. Kinney, "Will the Indian Make the Grade?" *American Forests* 60 (December 1954), pp. 24–27 and 52–53.

19. Harold E. Fey, "The Indian and the Law," *The Christian Century* 72 (9 March 1955), pp. 297–99.

20. "Three Prominent Oregonians Named as Management Specialists for the Klamath Indian Termination Program," news release by the Department of the Interior, 26 January 1955, William Kelly Papers, folder A–545, Arizona State Museum, University of Arizona, Tucson.

21. "Must Indian Injustices Go to the President?" *The Christian Century* 72 (1 June 1955), p. 643.

22. Thomas E. Connolly, "The Future of the American Indian," *Catholic World* 181 (July 1955), pp. 246–51.

23. Glenn L. Emmons to Joseph McCarthy, 6 June 1955, box 54, Keshena Indian Agency Correspondence, acc. no. 66–A–837, RG 75, FARC, Chicago.

24. "Consultation or Consent?" *The Christian Century* 73 (25 January 1956), pp. 103–4.

25. Allan Baris, "Washington's Public Law 280 Jurisdiction on Indian Reservations," *Washington Law Review* 53 (October 1978), pp. 703 and 712.

26. Report on Audit of Administration of Indian Lands by Bureau of Indian Affairs, Department of the Interior, January 1956, box 117, official file, White House Central Files, Dwight D. Eisenhower Presidential Library; and the President's News Conference of 15 January 1956, *Public Papers of the Presidents of the United States, Dwight D. Eisenhower, 1956* (Washington: U.S. Government Printing Office, 1958), p. 202.

27. Statement on Current Issues in Indian Affairs, April 1956, box 9, William Brophy Papers, Harry S. Truman Presidential Library; another copy of the statement is in box 12, Fred A. Seaton Papers.

28. Excerpts of Testimony of Wade Crawford before Senate Appropriations Committee, 15 March 1956, box RN–12, Richard L. Neuberger Papers, Special Collections, University of Oregon Library.

29. Cover Statement of Senator Richard L. Neuberger of Oregon to House Interior Subcommittee on Indian Affairs, n.d., ibid.

30. Richard L. Neuberger to G. H. Bertrand, 24 March 1956, ibid.

31. Paul L. Fickenger to Ed Edmondson, 6 June 1956, box 393333, Muskogee Area Office Correspondence, acc. no. 69–A–S30, RG 75, FARC, Fort Worth.

32. Field Trip Report, Homer B. Jenkins to Glenn Emmons, 30 September 1954, box 393333, Muskogee Area Office Correspondence, acc. no. 69–A–430, RG 75, FARC, Fort Worth.

33. Report of Consultation with Indians Concerning Legislation to Readjust Trust Relationship Existing between the Government and Eight Tribes Comprising the Quapaw Jurisdiction in Northeastern Oklahoma, ibid.

34. Homer B. Jenkins to Ed Edmondson, 9 December 1954, box 393333, Muskogee Area Office Correspondence, acc. no. 69–A–430, RG 75, FARC, Fort Worth.

35. Report of Meeting with Members of the Quapaw Tribe, 9 January 1955, Miami, Oklahoma, ibid.

36. "Federal Supervision over Texas Indians to Be Terminated July 1, 1955," news release by the Department of Interior, box RN–12, Richard L. Neuberger Papers.

37. Marie L. Hayes to Paul L. Fickinger and C. C. Marrs, 23 July 1956, box 393324, Muskogee Area Office Correspondence, acc. no. 69–A–430, RG 75, FARC, Fort Worth.

38. "Question Validity of Klamath Plan," *The Christian Century* 73 (25 July 1956), pp. 882–83; and Susan Hood, "Termination of the Klamath Tribe in Oregon," *Ethnohistory* 19 (Fall 1972), pp. 379–92.

39. Senate Bill 469 was sponsored by Senators Richard L. Neuberger and Wayne Morse, H.R. 258 was introduced by Senator Albert Ullman, and H.R. 2471 was introduced by Congressman Miller, Statement by Senator Richard Neuberger, October 1956, box RN–12, Richard L. Neuberger Papers.

40. Minutes of Meeting between Commissioner of Indian Affairs and Old and New Members of Klamath Tribe Executive Committee, Portland, Oregon, 29 October 1956, box 2, Klamath Agency Files, no acc. no., RG 75, FARC, Seattle.

41. "Postponement of Sales of Klamath Tribal Lands Recommended by Seaton," news release by the Department of Interior, 7 January 1957, box RN–12, Richard L. Neuberger Papers.

42. Richard L. Neuberger to Editor of *The Oregonian*, 26 February 1957, ibid.

43. Richard L. Neuberger to Al McCready, 26 February 1957, ibid.

44. Report of Conference, Commissioner of Indian Affairs with Cherokee Tribal Delegates, Dallas, Texas, 11 December 1956, box 3, Glenn L. Emmons Papers, Special Collections, William Zimmerman Library, University of New Mexico, Albuquerque.

45. Fred A. Seaton to Sherman Adams, 27 May 1957, box 618, official file, White House Central Files, Dwight D. Eisenhower Presidential Library.

46. Sherman Adams to Elmo Smith, 29 May 1957, ibid.

47. Mrs. Wade Crawford, "An Indian Talks Back," *American Forests* 63 (July 1957), pp. 4, 48–50.

48. "Basic Needs of Indian People," special report prepared by school administrators, June 1957, box 1, Aberdeen Area Office Correspondence, acc. no. 75–A–457, RG 75, FARC, Denver.

49. Data on Termination of Federal Supervision over the Klamath Indian Reservation, compiled by Rex Putnam, 31 December 1956, box 110, Bureau of Indian Affairs Correspondence, acc. no. 68–A–4937, RG 75, FARC, Suitland.

50. William Dean, "Klamath Hearings in Oregon," *American Forests* 63 (November 1957), pp. 12, 65–67.

51. Ibid.

52. Statement of the Department of Interior on Potential Legislative Trouble Spots—Klamath Indian Forest Bill, 4 December 1957, box 16, subject file, Fred A. Seaton Papers.

53. C. E. Nash to Richard L. Neuberger, 6 December 1957, box RN–12, Richard L. Neuberger Papers.

54. Fred A. Seaton to Dwight D. Eisenhower, 13 January 1958, box 618, official file, White House Central Files, Dwight D. Eisenhower Presidential Library; "Secretary Seaton Asks Congress to Protect Conservation Features of Klamath Indian Forest," news release by the Department of Interior, 13 January 1958, box 12, Fred A. Seaton Papers; and Senator Richard L. Neuberger Speaking on Administration Recommendations Regarding Klamath Indian Reservation at Klamath Falls, Oregon, 16 January 1958, box 16, subject file, Fred A. Seaton Papers.

55. Statement of Under Secretary of the Interior Hatfield Chilson on Senate Bill 3051 and Senate Bill 2047, 3 February 1958, box 17, Fred A. Seaton Papers; and Fred A. Seaton, "Seaton Outlines Klamath Indian Proposal to Congress," *American Forests* 64 (February 1958), pp. 12–13, 38–39.

56. Combined Statement before Senate Indian Subcommittee Considering S. 2047 and S. 3051 by Sheldon E. Kirk, Chairman of Klamath General Council; Jesse L. Kirk, Sr., Vice-Chairman of Klamath General Council and Vice-Chairman of Klamath Executive Committee; Dibbon Cook, Secretary of Klamath General Council and Acting Secretary of Klamath Executive Committee; and Boyd Jackson, Treasurer of Klamath Tribe, 4 February 1958, Box RN–13, Richard L. Neuberger Papers.

57. Richard L. Neuberger, "Solving the Stubborn Klamath Dilemma," *American Forests* 64 (April 1958), pp. 20–22, 40–42.

58. Telegram, Robert Holmes to Richard Neuberger, 15 July 1958, box RN–13, Richard L. Neuberger Papers.

59. Report of Meeting Held with the Modoc Tribe of Indians, Miami, Oklahoma, 6 February 1958, box 393333, Muskogee Area Office Correspondence, acc. no. 69–A–430, RG 75, FARC, Fort Worth.

60. Report of Special Meeting Held with the Modoc Tribe of Indians, southwest of Wyandotte, Oklahoma, 6 February 1958, ibid.

61. Paul L. Fickinger to E. E. Lamb, 31 March 1958, ibid.

62. "Klamath Indian Lands Reappraised," news release by the Department of Interior, 14 January 1959, box 393331, Muskogee Area Office Correspondence, acc. no. 69–A–430, RG 75, FARC, Fort Worth; and Roger Ernst to Richard L. Neuberger, 13 January 1959, box RN–13, Richard L. Neuberger Papers.

63. "Portland Bank Takes over Trusteeship of Residual Klamath Indian Estate," news release by the Department of Interior, 4 March 1959, box 393331, Muskogee Area Office Correspondence, acc. no. 69–A–430, RG 75, FARC, Fort Worth.

64. L. B. Staver to Fred A. Seaton, 12 March 1959, box 27, Fred A. Seaton Papers.

65. Richard L. Neuberger to Lawrence E. Slater, 29 June 1959, box 7, Richard L. Neuberger Papers, Oregon Historical Society, Portland, Oregon.

66. "Interior Department Proposes Bill Authorizing Special Loan Program Withdrawing Klamath Indians," news release by the Department of Interior; and "Change in Regulations Will Permit Indian Bureau Loans to Withdrawing Klamath Members Regardless of Degree of Indian Blood," news release by the Department of Interior, 16 July 1959, box 393331, Muskogee Area Office Correspondence, acc. no. 69–A–430, RG 75, FARC, Fort Worth. An in-depth study of the termination policy affecting the Klamaths and other tribes of the Pacific Northwest is Larry J. Hasse, "Termination and Assimilation: Federal Indian Policy, 1943–1961" (Ph.D. diss., Washington State University, 1974).

67. Mrs. Thomas Dewey to Clair Engle, 15 January 1959, box CE–66, Clair Engle Papers, California State Archives, Sacramento.

68. Arthur Lazarus, Jr., to Philleo Nash, 7 March 1958, box 111, Philleo Nash Papers.

69. Melvin L. Robertson, "Report of the Menominee," 24 March 1958, box 52, Keshena Indian Agency Correspondence, acc. no. 66–A–837, RG 75, FARC, Chicago.

70. Menominee Indian Study Committee, Wisconsin Legislative Council, 18 April 1959, Keshena, Wisconsin, box 53, Keshena Indian Agency Correspondence, acc. no. 66–A–837, RG 75, FARC, Chicago.

71. Menominee Coordinating and Negotiating Committee to Fred A. Seaton, 16 January 1959, box 111, Philleo Nash Papers.

Chapter 7

1. Barton Greenwood to Robert S. Kerr, n.d., box 320, Robert S. Kerr Papers, WHC, University of Oklahoma.

2. James O. Palmer, "A Geographical Investigation of the Effects of the Bureau of Indian Affairs' Employment Assistance Program upon the Relocation of Oklahoma Indians, 1967–1971" (Ph.D. diss., University of Oklahoma, 1975), pp. 42–44; and Elaine Neils, "The Urbanization of the American Indian and the Federal Program of Relocation and Assistance" (Master's thesis, University of Chicago, 1969), p. 53 (this work was published by the University of Chicago, Department of Geography under the title *Reservation to City: Indian Migration and Federal Relocation* in 1971).

3. Charles F. Wilkinson and Eric R. Briggs, "The Evolution of Termination Policy," *American Indian Law Review* 5, no. 1 (Summer 1977), pp. 155–56.

4. Summary Proceedings Conference of Area Directors, Washington, D.C., 8–10 January 1951, box 155, Desk Files of Dillon S. Myer, acc. no. 67–A–721, RG 75, FARC, Suitland.

5. D'Arcy McNickle, *They Came Here First: The Epic of the American Indian* (New York, Hagerstown, San Francisco and London: Harper and Row, 1949), p. 253.

6. Elaine M. Neils, *Reservation to City: Indian Migration and Federal Relocation* (Chicago: University of Chicago, Department of Geography, 1971), p. 61.

7. Theodore Stern, *The Klamath Tribe: A People and Their Reservation* (Seattle and London: University of Washington Press, 1965), pp. 186–87.

8. Memorandum no. 34, Sophie D. Aberle to the Commission, 26 December 1957, box 67, William Brophy Papers, Harry S. Truman Presidential Library.

9. Alan Sorkin, *American Indians and Federal Aid* (Washington, D.C.: The Brookings Institute, 1971), p. 107.

10. Neils, *Reservation to City,* p. 135.

11. Report of the Chicago Field Employment Assistance Office, 1 November 1951, box 154, Philleo Nash Papers, Harry S. Truman Presidential Library.

12. S. Lyman Tyler, *A History of Indian Policy* (Washington: U.S. Department of the Interior–Bureau of Indian Affairs, 1973), p. 159.

13. "Administration of Withdrawal Activities," Report of the Bureau of Indian Affairs, by the Comptroller General of the United States, March 1958, box 117, official file, White House Central Files, Dwight D. Eisenhower Presidential Library.

14. Neils, *Reservation to City,* p. 69; Palmer, "Geographical Investigation," p. 49; and Dillon S. Myer, "Indian Administration: Problems and Goals," *Social Science Review* 27 (June 1953), pp. 193–200.

15. *Annual Report of the Commissioner of Indian Affairs, 1953* (Washington, D.C.: U.S. Government Printing Office, 1953), pp. 39–40.

16. Bureau of Relocation, Fiscal Year 1954, Report, box RN–12, Richard L. Neuberger Papers, University of Oregon Library.

17. This twenty-two page report was one of the most comprehensive studies on relocation; the investigators were Dr. Mary Hayes, chairperson; Dr. Angie Debo; Miss La Verne Madigan; Dr. Charles Russell; and Mr. William Zimmerman. See La Verne Madigan, "The American Indian Relocation Program" a report undertaken with the assistance of the Field Foundation, based upon the findings of a Relocation Survey Team under the direction of Dr. Mary H. S. Hayes (New York: Association on American Indian Affairs, 1956), p. 5.

18. O. K. and Marjorie Armstrong, "The Indians are Going to Town," *Reader's Digest* 66 (January 1955), pp. 38–43; and Rex Lee to Victor Wickersham, 9 March 1955, no box no., Victor Wickersham Papers, WHC, University of Oklahoma.

19. Jack D. Forbes, *The Indian in America's Past* (Englewood Cliffs: Prentice-Hall, 1964), p. 123.

20. Branch of Relocation Annual Report of Fiscal Year 1955, box RN–12, Richard L. Neuberger Papers, University of Oregon Library.

21. Speech by Commissioner of Indian Affairs Glenn L. Emmons at a luncheon meeting of the Muskogee Chamber of Commerce, 6 January 1955, Muskogee, Oklahoma, box 618, official file, White House Central Files, Dwight D. Eisenhower Presidential Library.

22. Memorandum, Glenn L. Emmons to Secretary of the Interior, 20 May 1955, ibid.

23. "Indian Bureau to Launch New Audit Education Program with Five Tribal Groups," news release by the Department of the Interior, 25 October 1955, box 15, acc. no. 67–A–721, Bureau of Indian Affairs Correspondence, RG 75, FARC, Suitland.

24. Madelon Golden and Lucia Carter, "New Deal for America's Indians," *Coronet* 38 (October 1953), pp. 74–76.

25. Memorandum to Commissioner of Indian Affairs and Assistant Commissioners, 1 December 1955, box 455120, Muskogee Area Office Correspondence, acc. no. 70–A–27, RG 75, FARC, Fort Worth. Studies of the status of Oklahoma Indians during the mid-1950s include Angie Debo, "Termination and the Oklahoma Indians," *American Indian* 7 (Spring 1955), pp. 17–23; and Susan Work, "The 'Terminated' Five Tribes of Oklahoma: The Effect of Federal Legislation and the Administrative Treatment on the Government of the Seminole Nation," *American Indian Law Review* 6, no. 1 (Summer 1978), pp. 81–143.

26. Madigan, "American Indian Relocation Program," p. 12.

27. "Relocation Benefitting Indians and Oklahoma," news release by Muskogee Area Office of the Bureau of Indian Affairs, box 393335, Muskogee Area Office Correspondence, acc. no. 69–A–430, RG 75, FARC, Fort Worth.

28. Kimmis Henderick, "U.S. Helps Indians Move," *Christian Science Monitor*, Boston, 6 March 1956.

29. Ruth Mulvey Harmer, "Uprooting the Indians," *Atlantic Monthly* 197 (March 1956), pp. 54–57.

30. Statement on Current Issues in Indian Affairs, April 1956, box 12, Fred A. Seaton Papers, Dwight D. Eisenhower Presidential Library.

31. Branch of Relocation Services Annual Report Fiscal Year 1956, box RN-12, Richard L. Neuberger Papers, University of Oregon Library.

32. Madigan, "American Indian Relocation Program," p. 3.

33. Ibid.; and "Voluntary Relocation Program of Indian Bureau to be Greatly Enlarged in New Fiscal Year," news release by the Department of Interior, 27 June 1956, box 12, Fred A. Seaton Papers.

34. Minutes of Tribal Council Conference at Omaha, Nebraska, 19–21 June 1956, box 36, Billings Indian Agency Correspondence, acc. no. 72–A–289, RG 75, FARC, Denver.

35. Ibid.

36. Report by the Comptroller General, "Administration of Withdrawal Activities," March 1958, official file, White House Central Files, Dwight D. Eisenhower Presidential Library.

37. U.S. Congress, Senate, Senator Langer speaking on Bulova Plant at Rolla, North Dakota, 85th Cong., 1st sess., 13 August 1957, *Congressional Record* 103:14475–76.

38. "Approval Announced of Navajo Action in Appropriating $300,000 Tribal Funds for Industrial Development Program," news release by the Department of Interior, 17 December 1956, box 12, Fred A. Seaton Papers.

39. Alan Sorkin, *American Indians and Federal Aid* (Washington: The Brookings Institute, 1971), p. 109.

40. Palmer, "Geographical Investigation," p. 50.

41. Madigan, "American Indian Relocation Program," p. 5; and Minutes of Meeting of Keweenaw Bay Indian Community Tribal Council, 23 July 1957, box 1, Minneapolis Area Office Correspondence, acc. no. 73–A–489, RG 75, FARC, Chicago.

42. "On-the-Job Training Opportunities Provided for Nearly 700 Indians," news release by the Department of Interior, 24 July 1957, box 12, Fred A. Seaton Papers.

43. E. Y. Berry to Glenn Emmons, 19 October 1957, box 4, Glenn L. Emmons Papers, Special Collections, William Zimmerman Library, University of New Mexico.

44. Report, "The Program of Relocation Services," 28 October 1957, Phoenix, Arizona, box 4, Phoenix Area Office Correspondence, acc. no. 66–A–194, RG 75, FARC, Denver.

45. Homer B. Jenkins to Area Directors (Portland, Phoenix, Minneapolis, and Muskogee) and Field Officers (Oakland, St. Louis, and Chicago), 1 November 1957, box 2, ibid.

46. Edith R. Mirrielees, "The Cloud of Mistrust," *Atlantic Monthly* 199 (February 1957), pp. 55–59.

47. Memorandum, Relocation Specialist to Area Director at Phoenix Area Office, 3 December 1957, box 3, Phoenix Area Office Correspondence, acc. no. 66–A–194, RG 75, FARC, Denver.

48. S. D. Aberle to the Commission on the National Conference on American Indian Youth, 26 December 1957, box 67, William Brophy Papers.

49. "Additional Progress in Indian Education and Economical Opportunity Reported for Fiscal 1957," news release by the Department of Interior, 31 January 1957, box 12, Fred A. Seaton Papers.

50. William Zimmerman, Jr., "The Role of the Bureau of Indian Affairs," *The*

Annals of the American Academy of Political and Social Science 311 (May 1957), p. 39; and Neils, *Reservation to City*, p. 109.

51. Forbes, *Indian in America's Past*, p. 122; William Kelly, "The Basis of Indian Life," *The Annals of the American Academy of Political and Social Science* 311 (May 1957), p. 79; and "Indian Reservations May Some Day Run Out of Indians," *Saturday Evening Post* 230 (23 November 1957), p. 10.

Relocations and Related Costs, Fiscal Years 1952–1957

Fiscal Year	Number of Relocatees	Total Dollars	Cost Per Person
1952	868	$ 576,413	$664
1953	1,470	566,093	385
1954	2,553	579,431	227
1955	3,459	690,525	200
1956	5,119	973,475	190
1957	6,964	2,806,687	403
Totals	20,433	$6,192,624	$303

Source: "Administration of Withdrawal Activities Report," March 1958, by the Comptroller General, official file, White House Central Files, Dwight D. Eisenhower Presidential Library.

52. "Indians Lift on Own Bootstraps," *The Christian Century* 75 (26 March 1958), p. 366.

53. Peter Donner, "The Economic Position of American Indians," box 78, William Brophy Papers.

54. Report, "Administration of Withdrawal Activities," March 1958, official file, White House Central Files, Dwight D. Eisenhower Presidential Library.

55. Louis Cioffi to Dwight D. Eisenhower, 24 October 1958, box 754, President's Personal File, Dwight D. Eisenhower Presidential Library.

56. Joseph C. Vasquez, interview by Floyd O'Neil, 27 January 1971, Los Angeles, California, Interview no. 1009, box 53, acc. no. 24, Doris Duke Indian Oral History Collection, Special Collections, Marriott Library, University of Utah, Salt Lake City.

57. Sorkin, *American Indians and Federal Aid*, p. 121; Joan Ablon, "American Indian Relocation: Problems of Dependency and Management in the City," *Phylon*, Vol. 26, (winter, 1965), pp. 365–66 and Neils, "Reservation to City," p. 90.

58. Sorkin, *American Indians and Federal Aid*, p. 125.

59. Wilkinson and Briggs, "Evolution of Termination Policy," *American Indian Law Review*, p. 162; and Madigan, "American Indian Relocation Program," pp. 12 and 15.

60. Madigan, "American Indian Relocation Program," p. 17; Palmer, "Geographical Investigation," p. 104; and U.S. Congress, Senate, discussion on the success of the Relocation Program, 85th Cong., 1st sess., 14 March 1957, *Congressional Record* 103:3643.

61. Douglas Thorson, "Report on the Labor Force and the Employment

Conditions of the Oneida Indians," October 1958, box 3, Great Lakes Indian Agency File, acc. no. 73–A–489, RG 75, FARC, Chicago.

62. Howell Raines, "American Indians: Struggling for Power and Identity," *New York Times Magazine,* 11 February 1979, Section VI, p. 28.

63. John Dressler, "Recollections of a Washo Statesman," Oral History Project, Special Collections, University of Nevada Library, Reno.

64. Madigan, "American Indian Relocation Program," pp. 8–9.

65. Louis Cioffi to Dwight D. Eisenhower, 17 December 1958, box 754, President's Personal File, Dwight D. Eisenhower Presidential Library.

66. Del Barton to Sarah McClendon, 23 March 1959, box 4, Glenn L. Emmons Papers.

67. Memorandum, Superintendent of Fort Apache Indian Agency to F. M. Haverland, 9 November 1959, box 5, Phoenix Area Office Correspondence, acc. no. 66–A–194, RG 75, FARC, Denver.

68. John C. Dibbern to F. M. Haverland, 17 November 1959, ibid.

69. Ibid.

70. Sophie D. Aberle to Commissioner, Assistant Commissioners of Indian Bureau, and Dr. Virgil K. Whitaker, 25 November 1959, box 31, William Brophy Papers.

71. "Emmons Claims Indian Relocation Big Success," Phoenix *Republic,* 29 February 1960 and "Relocation of Indians Proclaimed Success," Phoenix *Gazette,* 28 February 1960.

72. "Emmons Cites Evidence of Indian Success in Relocation," news release by the Department of the Interior, 29 February 1960, box 4, Phoenix Area Office Correspondence, acc. no. 66–A–194, RG 75, FARC, Denver.

73. Speech delivered by Assistant Commissioner Thomas M. Reid at a meeting of the delegates of the Province of the Midwest of the Episcopal Church, Cincinatti, Ohio, 29 February 1960, ibid.

74. Angie Debo to La Verne Madigan, 27 August 1956, Personal Papers of Angie Debo, Marshall, Oklahoma.

75. William Metzler, "Relocation of the Displaced Worker," *Human Organization* 22 (Summer 1963), pp. 142–45.

76. Prafulla Neog, Richard G. Woods and Arthur M. Harkins, "Chicago Indians: The Effects of Urban Migration," a report compiled in conjunction with the Training Center for Community Programs in coordination with the Office of Community Programs Center for Urban and Regional Affairs, Chicago, January, 1970.

77. Marie Streeter, interview by Floyd O'Neil, 5 March 1971, San Jose, California, interview number 1036, box 54, acc. no. 24, Doris Duke Indian Oral History Collection, Special Collections, Marriott Library, University of Utah.

78. Timothy G. Baugh, "Urban Migration and Rural Responses: The Relocation Program among the Kiowa, Comanche and Plains Apache, 1950–1973," (Paper presented at the 37th Plains Conference, Kansas City, Missouri, November 1979).

79. George Woodward, interview by Floyd O'Neil, Gerald Huntley, and Judith Kilpatrick, 2 March 1971, Oakland, California, interview no. 1003, box 54, acc. no. 24, Doris Duke Indian Oral History Collection, Special Collections, Marriott Library, University of Utah.

Chapter 8

1. Memorandum, Area Director to Commissioner of Indian Affairs and Assistant Commissioners, 14 January 1957, box 564255, Minneapolis Area Office Correspondence, acc. no. 62–A–400, RG 75, FARC, Kansas City.

2. "Loan Regulations Broadened to Aid Indian Tribes in Attracting Industry," news release by the Department of Interior, 21 February 1957, box 12, Fred A. Seaton Papers, Dwight D. Eisenhower Presidential Library.

3. "Indian Bureau Industrial Program Emphasis with Creation of New Branch and Appointment of Consultant," news release by the Department of Interior, 17 August 1957, box RN–12, Richard L. Neuberger Papers, University of Oregon Library.

4. Meeting of Commissioner of Indian Affairs and His Staff with Menominee Indian Study Committee of Wisconsin Legislative Council, 28 March 1957, box 53, Keshena Indian Agency Correspondence, acc. no. 66–A–837, RG 75, FARC, Chicago.

5. "Glenn Emmons Among 45 to Receive Awards from Interior Department," Washington *Post*, 26 April 1957; and "Indian Commissioner's Achievements Are Listed," Albuquerque *Journal*, 26 April 1957.

6. "Termination of the American Indian Wardship Status," report compiled by Glenn L. Emmons and William Ulman, 14 February 1958, box 16, subject file, Fred A. Seaton Papers.

7. "Action Needed for Indian Rights," *The Christian Century* 74 (29 May 1957), p. 676.

8. Dwight D. Eisenhower to Arthur B. Stewart, 7 September 1957, box 618, official file, White House Central Files, Dwight D. Eisenhower Presidential Library.

9. Dwight D. Eisenhower to Flora E. Shirah, 28 September 1957, ibid.

10. Lawrence E. Lindley, "Why Indians Need Land," *The Christian Century* 74 (6 November 1957), pp. 1316–18.

11. James Murray to Fred A. Seaton, 27 November 1957, box RN–12, Richard L. Neuberger Papers, University of Oregon Library.

12. Oliver La Farge to Mrs. Reed, 16 December 1957, ibid.

13. William Dean, "Klamath Hearings in Oregon," *American Forests* 63 (November 1957), pp. 12, 65–67.

14. Memorandum, P. T. LaBreche to Chief, Branch of Tribal Programs, 11 December 1957, box 393333, Muskogee Area Office Correspondence, acc. no. 69–A–430, RG 75, FARC, Fort Worth.

15. Memorandum, Herschel Schooley to Albert Toner, 28 March 1958, box 11, Records of White House Staff Research Group, Dwight D. Eisenhower Presidential Library.

16. Memorandum, Paul L. Fickinger to All Area Directors, 21 May 1958, box 393324, Muskogee Area Office Correspondence, acc. no. 69–A–430, RG 75, FARC, Fort Worth.

17. U.S. Congress, House, Congressman Hemphill speaking on the Catawba Indian Nation, 86th Cong., 1st sess., 7 April 1958, *Congressional Record* 105:5462.

18. Memorandum, Homer B. Jenkins to H. Rex Lee, concerning termination

of Catawba Indian Reservation, 31 March 1959, box 103, Bureau of Indian Affairs Correspondence, acc. no. 67–A–721, RG 75, FARC, Suitland.

19. U.S. Congress, House, Congressman Berry Speaking on An Exceptional Statement on Free Enterprise, 86th Cong., 1st sess., 11 August 1959, *Congressional Record* 105:15583.

20. Ann Hood to Clair Engle, 19 July 1959, "Indian Affairs—General" Folder, Clair Engle Papers, Tehama County Library, Red Bluff, California.

21. "The Current Government Programs for Indian Development," address by Commissioner of Indian Affairs Glenn L. Emmons, 3 July 1958, Estes Park, Colorado, 3 July 1958, box 12, Fred A. Seaton Papers.

22. "More Indian Tribes Sending Children to College," news release by the Department of Interior, ibid.

23. The following forty-one *rancherías* were terminated by Public Law 671 on 18 August 1958 during the 85th Congress: Alexander Valley, Auburn, Big Sandy, Big Valley, Blue Lake, Buena Vista, Cache Creek, Chicken Ranch, Chico, Cloverdale, Clod Springs, Elk Valley, Guidiville, Gratona, Greenville, Hopland, Indian Ranch, Lytton, Mark West, Middleton, Montgomery Creek, Mooretown, Nevada City, North Fork, Paskenta, Picayune, Pinoleville, Potter Valley, Quartz Valley, Redding, Redwood Valley, Robinson, Rohnerville, Ruffeys, Scotts Valley, Smith River, Strawberry Valley, Table Bluff, Table Mountain, Upper Lake, and Wilton, Public Law 85–671, box 417599, Sacramento Area Office Correspondence, acc. no. 69–A–537, RG 75, FARC, San Bruno, California.

24. Glenn L. Emmons to Leonard Hill, 7 August 1958, ibid.

25. "Remarks by Secretary of the Interior Fred A. Seaton, Broadcast September 18, 1958, over Radio Station KCLA," Flagstaff, Arizona, ibid.

26. "Indians Still Losing Their Land," *The Christian Century* 75 (1 October 1958), pp. 1102–03.

27. Ibid.

28. John F. Baldwin to Dwight D. Eisenhower, 25 November 1958, box 117, official file, White House Central Files, Dwight D. Eisenhower Presidential Library.

29. "Statement by the Department of the Interior Concerning the 'Kaleidoscope' Television Program of November 16, 1958, on the American Indian," Box 12, Fred A. Seaton Papers.

30. Report to the Congress of the United States, Review of Programming, Budgeting, Accounting, and Reporting Activities of the Bureau of Indian Affairs, Department of Interior, November 1958, box 117, official file, White House Central Files, Dwight D. Eisenhower Presidential Library.

31. Roger Ernst to Gerald D. Morgan, 22 December 1958, box 430, ibid.

32. Arthur S. Flemming, "They Are Winning War on Disease among Indians," Box 383326, Muskogee Area Office Correspondence, acc. no. 69–A–430, RG 75, FARC, Fort Worth.

33. Ibid.

34. U.S. Congress, Senate, Senator Mansfield speaking on Federal Responsibility toward Indians, 86th Cong., 1st sess., 5 March 1959, *Congressional Record* 105:3309–10.

35. "Department Supports Choctaw Termination Bill Introduced in Con-

gress at Request of Tribal Representatives," news release by the Department of Interior, 13 April 1959, box 393326, Muskogee Area Office Correspondence, RG 75, FARC, Fort Worth.

36. Address by Glenn L. Emmons, Commissioner of Indian Affairs, before a Conference on Industrial Development Sponsored by the Navajo Tribe, Gallup, New Mexico, 21 May 1959, box 12, Fred A. Seaton Papers.

37. Seminole Indians Plan Ceremony at Interior Department, 26 February 1959, box 16, subject file, ibid.

38. U.S. Congress, House, Congressman Berry speaking on Indian Self-Help Bill, 86th Cong., 1st sess., 12 June 1959, *Congressional Record* 105:10714–16.

39. Roger Ernst to Richard M. Nixon, 29 June 1959, box 16, subject file, Fred A. Seaton Papers.

40. "Interior Department Proposes Legislation Adding 350,000 Acres to Indian Tribal Holdings," news release by the Department of Interior, 8 July 1959, ibid; and Senate Bill 2345 introduced by Senator James Murray, 86th Cong., 1st sess., Senate, Box RN–12, Richard L. Neuberger Papers, University of Oregon Library.

41. U.S. Congress, Senate, Senator Murray speaking on Indian Land and Credit Policy, 86th Cong., 1st sess., 10 September 1959, *Congressional Record* 105:18889–90.

42. Glenn L. Emmons to Max Gubatayo, 8 October 1957, box 3, Pyramid Lake Paiute Indian Collection no. 16, Special Collections, University of Nevada Library.

43. Robert W. Fenwick, "Program of Self-Help Can Ease Sioux Hardship," Denver *Post*, 6 January 1960.

44. Robert W. Fenwick, "Indians Hope to Survive White 'Folly,'" ibid.

45. Robert W. Fenwick, "Time and Progress Pass These Indians By," Denver *Post*, 7 January 1960.

46. Robert W. Fenwick, "Indian Slum Poses Big Problem to Rapid City," ibid.

47. Robert W. Fenwick, "U.S. Bureau Apparently Would End Trusteeship," Denver *Post*, 15 January 1960.

48. Report on Branch of Relocation Services Financial Program, Fiscal Year 1960, box 436248, Anadarko Area Office Correspondence, 30 June 1960; and Kiowa Area Field Office Correspondence, acc. no. 70–A–27, RG 75, FARC, Fort Worth.

49. Robert W. Fenwick, "U.S. Efforts to Aid Indians Clumsy and Costly," Denver *Post*, 15 January 1960.

50. Oliver L. Farge, "The Enduring Indian," *Scientific American* 202 (February 1960), pp. 37–45.

51. James G. Frechette to Fred A. Seaton, 19 April 1960, box 16, subject file, Fred A. Seaton Papers.

52. John Bear, John K. Papkee, and Jean A. Wanatee to E. J. Riley, 2 May 1960, box 4, Minneapolis Area Office Correspondence, acc. no. 71–A–1221, RG 75, FARC, Kansas City.

53. Ed Vieham to Fred Seaton, 11 May 1960, box 31, personal correspondence, Fred A. Seaton Papers.

54. Statement on American Indians by Frank George, Member of Na-

tionalities Division (American Indians), Democratic National Committee, before the Democratic Platform Committee, Denver, Colorado, 27 May 1960, box 138, Personal File, Philleo Nash Papers, Harry S. Truman Presidential Library.

55. Memorandum, Sophie D. Aberle to Commissioner of Indian Affairs and Assistant Commissioners, 18 August 1960, box 31, William Brophy Papers, Harry S. Truman Presidential Library.

56. Ibid.

57. Roger Ernst to Fred A. Seaton, 23 August 1960, box 16, subject file, Fred A. Seaton Papers.

58. La Verne Madigan to William A. Brophy, 30 August 1960, William Brophy Papers.

59. Robert Yellowtail to Fred A. Seaton, 3 September 1960, box 34, Fred A. Seaton Papers.

60. Ibid.

61. Oliver La Farge to William Brophy, 18 October 1960, box 10, William Brophy Papers.

62. Resolution of Menominee General Council Meeting, Keshena, Wisconsin, 12 December 1960, box 48, Keshena Indian Agency Correspondence, acc. no. 66–A–837, RG 75, FARC, Chicago.

63. Glenn L. Emmons, Panel Discussion held by the Indian Law Committee of the Federal Bar Association, Chicago, Illinois, 17 September 1960, box 2, Glenn L. Emmons Papers, Special Collections, William Zimmerman Library, University of New Mexico.

64. "Indian Land Trust Restrictions Expiring in 1961 Extended Five Years," news release by the Department of Interior, 22 December 1960, box 393326, Muskogee Area Office Correspondence, RG 75, FARC, Fort Worth.

65. William A. Brophy and Sophie D. Aberle, *The Indian: America's Unfinished Business* (Norman: University of Oklahoma Press, 1966), p. 187.

66. Glenn L. Emmons to Dwight D. Eisenhower, 23 December 1960, box 117, official file, White House Central Files, Dwight D. Eisenhower Presidential Library.

67. Report on United States Indian Population and Land, 1960, box 149, Philleo Nash Papers; and Charles F. Wilkinson and Eric R. Briggs, "The Evolution of Termination Policy," *American Indian Law Review* 5 (Summer 1977), p. 151.

Chapter 9

1. Stanley D. Lyman, interview by Floyd O'Neil and Gregory Thompson, n.d., Pine Ridge Agency, South Dakota, interview no. 1031, box 54, acc. no. 24, Doris Duke Indian Oral History Collection, Special Collections, Marriott Library, University of Utah.

2. George Pierre, *American Indian Crisis* (San Antonio: The Naylor Company, 1971), p. 39.

3. See n. 1.

4. Psychosocial problems of Indian residents in Klamath County after termi-

nation are discussed in Charles C. Brown, "Identification of Selected Problems of Indians Residing in Klamath County, Oregon—An Examination of Data Generated since Termination of the Klamath Reservation" (Ph.D. diss., University of Oregon, 1973).

5. Harvey D. Rosenthal, "Their Day in Court: A History of the Indian Claims Commission" (Ph.D. diss., Kent State University, 1973).

An early study of the Indian Claims Commission Act is Thomas Le Duc, "The Work of the Indian Claims Commission under the Act of 1946," *Pacific Historical Review* 26 (February 1957), pp. 1–16. A discussion of the end of the commission, and information on Arthur Watkins as the chief commissioner, is in the "Post-Senate, Claims Commission" folder, Arthur V. Watkins Papers, Special Collections, Archives and Manuscripts, Harold B. Lee Library, Brigham Young University, Provo, Utah.

6. Robert Bennett, interview by Joe B. Frantz, 13 November 1968, Washington, D.C., Oral History Collection, Lyndon B. Johnson Presidential Library, Austin, Texas; a similar interview with Bennett, no. 836, is in the Doris Duke Indian Oral History Collection, Special Collections, William Zimmerman Library, University of New Mexico, Albuquerque.

7. Philip Cassadore, interview by J. Bell, 14 October 1970, Arizona, folder A–647, Doris Duke Indian Oral History Collection, Arizona State Museum, University of Arizona, Tucson.

8. Lenora DeWitt, interview by Gerald Wolf, 25 August 1971, Lower Brule, South Dakota, interview no. 39, pt. 1, tape 786s, microfiche, American Indian Research Project–Doris Duke Indian Oral History Collection, University of South Dakota, Vermillion.

9. Moses Big Crow, interview by Herbert Hoover, 31 August 1971, Vermillion, South Dakota, interview no. 50, pt. 2, tape 745, ibid.

10. Lena Haberman, interview by Georgia Brown, 12 June 1971, La Mirada, California, interview no. O.H. 639, Doris Duke Indian Oral History Collection, Oral History Collection, California State University, Fullerton.

11. Memorandum, Stewart Udall to Lyndon B. Johnson, 20 January 1964, executive file FG, box 203, Lyndon B. Johnson Presidential Library.

12. The Indian Health Program, U.S. Public Health Service Report (August 1972), DHEW Publication no. (ASM) 73–12,003, pp. 1–36.

13. For a discussion of Indian–white differences in perceptions of space, time, matter, energy, and causality, see Vine Deloria, Jr., *The Metaphysics of Modern Existence* (New York: Harper and Row, 1979). Differences of perceptions are also explained in Jamake Highwater, *The Primal Mind: Vision and Reality in Indian America* (New York: Harper and Row, 1980).

14. Stewart Udall, interview (no. 3) by Joe B. Frantz, 29 July 1969, Washington, D.C., tape 1, Oral History Collection, Lyndon B. Johnson Presidential Library.

15. See n. 6. Robert Bennett commented on the Indian reluctance to accept P.L. 280 because of the limitations and restrictions of the law, which are covered in the following articles: Linda Cree, "Extension of County Jurisdiction over Indian Reservations in California, Public Law 280 and the Ninth Circuit," *Hastings Law Journal* 25, no. 3 (May 1974), pp. 535–94; Joel E.

Gurthals, "State Civil Jurisdiction over Tribal Indians—A Re-Examination," *Montana Law Review* 35, no. 2 (Summer 1974), pp. 340–47; and Louis D. Persons II, "Jurisdiction: Public Law 280—Local Regulation of Protected Indian Lands," *American Indian Law Review* 6, no. 2 (Winter 1978), pp. 403–15.

16. Arthur V. Watkins, interview by Ed Edwin, 14 January 1968, Washington, D.C., Oral History Collection, Dwight D. Eisenhower Presidential Library.

17. Jenkins L. Jones, "Time for Indians to Join U.S.," Washington *Star*, 27 August 1962.

18. Joseph J. S. Feathers to Alan Bible, 9 December 1964, box 245, Alan Bible Papers, Special Collections, University of Nevada Library, Reno.

19. Harold T. Johnson to Clair Engle, 23 April 1964, "Indian Affairs—General folder," Clair Engle Papers, Tehama County Library, Red Bluff, California.

20. "Three California Rancherias Terminated by the Bureau of Indian Affairs," 1 September 1965, news release by the Department of the Interior; and "Four More California Rancherias Terminated," 25 February 1966, news release by the Department of the Interior, box 34, Records of the Department of the Interior, Lyndon B. Johnson Presidential Library.

21. "Federal Supervision Terminated at Greenville Rancheria, California," 15 December 1966, news release by the Department of Interior; and "Federal Supervision Terminated at Quartz Valley Rancheria, California," 27 January 1967, news release by the Department of Interior, ibid.

22. Adeline Croswell to Lyndon B. Johnson, 26 August 1964, box 74, Gen LE–IN, White House Central Files, Lyndon B. Johnson Presidential Library. A study that disagrees with the suggestion that the Colvilles were ready for termination is Susanna A. Hayes, "The Resistance to Education for Assimilation by the Colville Indians, 1872–1972" (Ph.D. diss., University of Michigan, 1973). Hayes contends that the Colvilles retained many sociocultural traditions despite the effects of government policy, including termination, over a hundred year period.

23. U.S. Congress, Senate, H.R. 10911, "to provide for preparation of a roll of persons of California Indian descent and the distribution of certain judgement funds," 90th Cong., 2d sess., 4 June 1968; a copy of this bill, which was urged by many California Indians, is in box 76, Wayne Morse Papers, Special Collections, University of Oregon Library.

24. Wilfred P. Schoenberg to Lyndon B. Johnson, 8 May 1966, Gen–IN 2, White House Central Files, Lyndon B. Johnson Presidential Library.

25. See n. 14; John Carver, Jr., interview (no. 5) by William Moss, 7 October 1969, Washington, D.C., Oral History Collection, John F. Kennedy Presidential Library, Waltham, Massachusetts; this interview substantiates the poor relationship between Udall and Nash. Udall's views on Indian affairs are clarified in Stewart L. Udall, "The State of the Indian Nation—An Introduction," *Arizona Law Review* 10 (Winter 1968), pp. 554–57.

26. See n. 6.

27. Ibid.

28. Allen Rowland, interview by Al Spang, 5 March 1971, Lame Deer,

Montana, interview no. 864, Doris Duke Indian Oral History Collection, Special Collections, William Zimmerman Library.

29. Panel Discussion on "Termination" for the television show, "The Advocates," 24 January 1970, taped by Michael B. Husband, interview no. 450, ibid.

30. John Dressler, "Recollections of a Washo Statesman," p. 134, Oral History Project, Special Collections, University of Nevada Library.

Epilog

1. Excerpts from a talk by Philleo Nash, Commissioner of Indian Affairs, before a Joint Meeting of the Pawnee, Kaw, and Otoe-Missouria tribes of Oklahoma and the Potawatomi, Sac and Fox, Iowa, and Kickapoo tribes of Kansas, Ponca City, Oklahoma, 4 March 1962, box 143, Philleo Nash Papers, Harry S. Truman Presidential Library. A clearer statement of Nash's views on Indian affairs is in Philleo Nash, "Indian Administration in the United States: Address, December 6, 1962," *Vital Speeches* 29 (15 February 1963), pp. 278–83.

2. Inter-Tribal Council of Nevada, Inc., to Stewart L. Udall, 24 January 1967, box BE232, Walter S. Baring Papers, Nevada State Archives, Carson City.

3. David H. Getches, Daniel M. Rosenfelt and Charles F. Wilkinson, *Cases and Materials on Federal Indian Law* (St. Paul: West Publishing Company, 1979), pp. 334–46. No judicial procedures were listed in the law to enforce Indian civil rights; see Cliff A. Jones, "Remedies: Tribal Deprivation of Civil Rights: Should Indians Have A Cause of Action under 42 U.S.C. 1983?" *American Indian Law Review* 3, no. 1 (Summer 1975), pp. 183–95.

For further legal limitations of the Indian Civil Rights Act, see *American Indian Civil Rights Handbook* (Washington: U.S. Government Printing Office, March 1972); Donald L. Burnett, Jr., "Historical Analysis of the 1968 'Indian Civil Rights Act,'" *Harvard Journal on Legislation* 9 (May 1972), pp. 557–626; Arthur Lazarus, *North Dakota Law Review* 45, no. 3 (Spring 1969), pp. 337–52; Joseph de Raismes, "Indian Civil Rights Act of 1968 and the Pursuit of Responsible Tribal Self-Government," *South Dakota Law Review* 20, no. 1 (Winter 1975), pp. 59–106; and Alvin J. Ziontz, "In Defense of Tribal Sovereignty, An Analysis of Judicial Error in Construction of the Indian Civil Rights Act," *South Dakota Law Review* 20, no. 1 (Winter 1975), pp. 1–58.

4. Wendall Chino to Lyndon B. Johnson, 27 December 1967, Gen LE–IN, box 74, White House Central Files, Lyndon B. Johnson Presidential Library, Austin, Texas.

5. Paul Harvey, "Why Does the Indian Say 'Ugh'?" news commentary, 22 May 1965, box 2, Robert Leland Papers, Special Collections, University of Nevada Library, Reno.

6. Richard Nixon, "Special Message to the Congress on Indian Affairs," 8 July 1970, *Public Papers of the Presidents of the United States, Richard Nixon, 1970* (Washington: U.S. Government Printing Office, 1971), p. 565.

7. For a discussion of the Blue Lake Land Claims, see William Schaab, interview by Dennis Stanford, 27 March 1969, interview no. 439, Doris Duke

Indian Oral History Collection, Special Collections, William Zimmerman Library, University of New Mexico.

The intention of the Alaska Native Claims Settlement Act is addressed as an effort to assimilate Alaska indigenous people into the dominant society in Lauren L. Fuller, "Alaska Native Claims Settlement: Analysis of the Protective Clauses of the Act through A Comparison with the Dawes Act of 1887," *American Indian Law Review* 4, no. 2 (Winter 1976), pp. 269–78.

A comprehensive study of the Menominee restoration is Stephen J. Herzberg, "The Menominee Indians: Termination to Restoration," *American Indian Law Review* 6, no. 1 (Summer 1978), pp. 143–86. See, also, Joseph F. Preloznik and Steven A. Felsenthal, "The Menominee Struggle to Maintain Their Tribal Assets and Protect Their Treaty Rights Following Termination," *North Dakota Law Review* 51 (Fall 1974), pp. 53–71; and Nicholas C. Peroff, *Menominee Drums: Tribal Termination and Restoration, 1954–1974* (Norman: University of Oklahoma Press, 1982).

Russel Barsh and Ronald Trosper contend that the act will cause no significant changes for Indian people; Barsh and Trosper, "Title I of the Self-Determination and Education Assistance Act of 1975," *American Indian Law Review* 3, no. 1 (Summer 1975), pp. 361–95. See also Robert Ericson and D. Rebecca Snow, "Indian Battle for Self-Determination," *California Law Review* 58, no. 1 (March 1970), pp. 445–90.

8. Gerald R. Ford, "Remarks at a Meeting With American Indian Leaders," 16 July 1976, *Public Papers of the Presidents of the United States, Gerald R. Ford, 1976–77*, vol. 3 (Washington: U.S. Government Printing Office, 1977), pp. 2020–23.

9. "The Reagan Budget," Nations: The Native American Magazine 1, no. 1 (1981), pp. 21–25.

Bibliography

Manuscript Collections

Arizona State Museum, University of Arizona, Tucson, Arizona.
  William Kelly Papers.
California State Archives, Sacramento, California.
  Clair Engle Papers.
Dwight D. Eisenhower Presidential Library, Abilene, Kansas.
  Elmer Bennett Papers.
  Bill Files.
  Oveta Culp Hobby Papers.
  President's Personal File.
  Records of White House Staff Record Group.
  Fred A. Seaton Papers.
  White House Central Files.
Lyndon B. Johnson Presidential Library, Austin, Texas.
  Records of the Department of the Interior
  White House Central Files
National Archives, Washington, D.C.
  Bureau of Indian Affairs Records.
  Office Files of Assistant Commissioner Joyn R. Provinse.
  Office Records of Assistant Commissioner William Zimmerman.
Nevada State Archives, Carson City, Nevada.
  Walter S. Baring Papers.
  Patrick McCarran Papers.
Newberry Library, Chicago, Illinois.
  John Collier Papers, Microfilm.
  Indian Rights Association Papers, Microfilm.
Oregon Historical Society, Portland, Oregon.
  Richard L. Neuberger Papers.
Special Collections, Marriott Library, University of Utah, Salt Lake City, Utah.
  Reva Beck Bosone Papers.
Special Collections, University of Nevada Library, Reno, Nevada.
  Alan Bible Papers.
  Robert Leland Papers.
  Pyramid Lake Paiute Indian Collection no. 16.

Special Collections, University of Oregon Library, Eugene, Oregon.
Richard L. Neuberger Papers.
Wayne Morse Papers.
Special Collections, Archives and Manuscripts, Harold B. Lee Library, Brigham Young University, Provo, Utah.
Arthur V. Watkins Papers.
Special Collections, William Zimmerman Library, University of New Mexico, Albuquerque, New Mexico.
Glenn L. Emmons Papers.
Tehama County Library, Red Bluff, California.
Clair Engle Papers.
Harry S. Truman Presidential Library, Independence, Missouri.
William Brophy Papers.
Oscar L. Chapman Papers.
Dale E. Doty Papers.
Indian Claims Commission Papers.
Dillon S. Myer Papers.
Philleo Nash Papers.
Harry S. Truman Papers.
Joel Wolfsohn Papers.
Western History Collections, University of Oklahoma, Norman, Oklahoma.
Robert S. Kerr Papers.
George Schwabe Papers.
William G. Stigler Papers.
Elmer Thomas Papers.
Victor Wickersham Papers.

Personal Papers Collections

Personal Papers of Angie Debo, Marshall, Oklahoma.

Records of the Bureau of Indian Affairs

Annual Report of Commissioner of Indian Affairs, 1953. Washington, D.C.: U.S. Government Printing Office, 1953.
Annual Report of Commissioner of Indian Affairs, 1962. Washington, D.C.: U.S. Government Printing Office, 1962.
Branch of Relocation Annual Fiscal Year 1955 Report. Bureau of Indian Affairs, Washington, D.C.
Branch of Relocation Annual Fiscal Year 1956 Report. Bureau of Indian Affairs, Washington, D.C.
Federal Archives and Records Center, Chicago, Illinois.
Great Lakes Indian Agency Files.
Keshena Indian Agency Correspondence.
Minneapolis Area Office Correspondence.
Federal Archives and Records Center, Denver, Colorado.
Aberdeen Area Office Correspondence.

Billings Indian Agency Correspondence.
Phoenix Area Office Correspondence.
Federal Archives and Records Center, Fort Worth, Texas.
Anadarko Area Office Correspondence.
Kiowa Area Office Field Correspondence.
Miami Area Office Correspondence.
Muskogee Area Office Correspondence.
Federal Archives and Records Center, Kansas City, Missouri.
Minneapolis Area Office Correspondence.
Minnesota Agency Correspondence.
Pierre Indian Agency Correspondence.
Red Lake Area Office Files.
Federal Archives and Records Center, San Bruno, California.
Sacramento Area Office Correspondence.
Federal Archives and Records Center, Seattle, Washington.
Colville Agency Correspondence.
Klamath Agency Files.
Portland Area Office Correspondence.
Federal Archives and Records Center, Suitland, Maryland.
Bureau of Indian Affairs Correspondence.
Desk Files of William Brophy and John R. Nichols.
Desk Files of Dillon S. Myer.
Muskogee Area Office, Bureau of Indian Affairs, Muskogee, Oklahoma.
Files of Tribal Operations.
National Personnel Records Center, General Services Administration, St. Louis, Missouri.
Sacramento Area Office, Bureau of Indian Affairs, Sacramento, California.
Files of Reality Department.

U.S. Government Documents

American Indian Civil Rights Handbook. Washington: U.S. Government Printing Office, March 1972.

Emmons, Glenn L. "Readjustment with Security for the American Indian." In *Toward Economic Development for Native American Communities.* Washington: U.S. Government Printing Office, 1969.

"House Concurrent Resolution 108," *U.S. Statutes at Large.* Vol. 67. 1953.

Indian Health Program. U.S. Public Health Service Report. August 1972. DHEW Publication No. (ASM) 73–12,003.

Public Papers of the Presidents of the United States, Dwight D. Eisenhower, 1953. Washington: U.S. Government Printing Office, 1960.

Public Papers of the Presidents of the United States, Dwight D. Eisenhower, 1954. Washington: U.S. Government Printing Office, 1960.

Public Papers of the Presidents of the United States, Dwight D. Eisenhower, 1956. Washington: U.S. Government Printing Office, 1958.

Public Papers of the Presidents of the United States, Dwight D. Eisenhower, 1958. Washington: U.S. Government Printing Office, 1959.

Public Papers of the Presidents of the United States, Gerald Ford, 1976–77. Vol. 3. Washington: U.S. Government Printing Office, 1977.

Public Papers of the Presidents of the United States, Richard Nixon, 1970. Washington: U.S. Government Printing Office, 1971.

Public Papers of the Presidents of the United States, Harry S. Truman, 1946. Washington: U.S. Government Printing Office, 1965.

Public Papers of the Presidents of the United States, Harry S. Truman, 1947. Washington: U.S. Government Printing Office, 1963.

Public Papers of the Presidents of the United States, Harry S. Truman, 1948. Washington: U.S. Government Printing Office, 1964.

Public Papers of the Presidents of the United States, Harry S. Truman, 1953. Washington: U.S. Government Printing Office, 1966.

Survey Report on the Bureau of Indian Affairs. 26 January 1954. Printed for the use of the Committee on Interior and Insular Affairs. Washington: U.S. Government Printing Office, 1954.

U.S. Congress. House. "A House Resolution to create an Indian Claims Commission to provide for the powers, duties, and functions thereof, and for other purposes." H.R. 4497, 79th Cong., 1st sess., 1945.

U.S. Congress. House. "A House Resolution to provide for removal of restrictions on property of Indians who serve in the armed forces." H.R. 4196, 79th Cong., 1st sess., 1945.

U.S. Congress. House. "A Joint Resolution establishing a joint congressional committee to make a study of claims of Indian tribes against the United States and to investigate the administration of Indian affairs." H.R. 237, 79th Cong., 1st sess., 1945.

U.S. Congress. House. Committee on Public Lands. "Emancipation of Indian Hearings" before the Subcommittee on Indian Affairs of the Committee on Public Lands, House of Representatives on H.R. 2958, H.R. 2165 and H.R. 1113. 80th Cong., 1st sess., 1947.

U.S. Congress. House. Congresswoman Lusk speaking on withdrawal of Federal supervision over Indian Affairs, 80th Cong., 1st sess., 27 May 1947. *Congressional Record,* vol. 93.

U.S. Congress. House. Committee on Public Lands. *Providing for the Removal of Restrictions on Property of Indians who served in the Armed Forces.* H. Rept., 1947. 80th Cong., 1st sess., 1947.

U.S. Congress. House. Congressman Morse speaking for termination of the Klamath Indians, S. 1222, 80th Cong., 1st sess., 2 May 1947. *Congressional Record,* vol. 93.

U.S. Congress. House. Congressman D'Ewart speaking on Indian populations and conditions in the United States, 81st Cong., 1st sess., 17 January 1949. *Congressional Record,* vol. 95.

U.S. Congress. House. Congressman D'Ewart speaking in reference to Eleanor Roosevelt's statement on H.R. 2632 and Indian benefits, 81st Cong., 1st sess., 12 May 1949. *Congressional Record,* vol. 95.

U.S. Congress. House. Congressman O'Neil speaking on Self-Government of American Indians, 81st Cong., 1st sess., 5 May 1949. *Congressional Record,* vol. 95.

U.S. Congress. House. Congressman Poulson speaking in reference to Eleanor

Roosevelt's statement on H.R. 2632 and Indian benefits, 81st Cong., 1st sess., 12 May 1949. *Congressional Record,* vol. 95.

U.S. Congress. House. Congressman Bow speaking on Table of Population, Income, and Educational Statistics on Individual Indian Tribes, 82d Cong., 1st sess., 14 August 1951. *Congressional Record,* vol. 97.

U.S. Congress. House. Congressman Bow speaking about the Bureau of Indian Affairs, 82d Cong., 2d sess., 18 March 1952. *Congressional Record,* vol. 98.

U.S. Congress. House. Congressman Delany speaking on Authorizing and Directing Secretary of the Interior to study Respective Tribes, Bands and Groups of Indians, 82d Cong., 2d sess., 1 July 1952. *Congressional Record,* vol. 98.

U.S. Congress. House. Congressman Delany speaking on Investigation of the Bureau of Indian Affairs, 82d Cong., 2d sess., 1 July 1952. *Congressional Record,* vol. 98.

U.S. Congress. House. *Termination of Federal Supervision, Concurrent Resolution 108.* 83d Cong., 1st sess., 1 August 1953. Washington. U.S. Government Printing Office. 1953.

U.S. Congress. House. Congressman Hemphill speaking on the Catawba Indian Nation, 86th Cong., 1st sess., 7 April 1958. *Congressional Record,* vol. 105.

U.S. Congress. House. A Bill to be the policy of Congress, as rapidly as possible, to make Indians within the territorial limits of the United States subject to the same laws and entitled to the same privileges and responsibilities as are applicable to other citizens of the United States and that Indians should assume their full responsibilities as American citizens. H.C.R. 169, 87th Cong., 1st sess., 1959.

U.S. Congress. House. Congressman Berry speaking on Indian Self-Help Bill, 86th Cong., 1st sess., 12 June 1959. *Congressional Record,* vol. 105.

U.S. Congress. House. Congressman Berry speaking on An Exceptional Statement on Free Enterprise, 86th Cong., 1st sess., 11 August 1959. *Congressional Record,* vol. 105.

U.S. Congress. House. George H. Dunne, "The Indian's Dilemma." 85th Cong., 1st sess., 1957. *Congressional Record,* vol. 103.

U.S. Congress. House. A Bill to provide for the acquisition of and the payment for individual Indian and tribal lands of the lower Brule Sioux Reservation in South Dakota, required by the United States for Big Bend Dam and Reservoir project on the Missouri River, and for the rehabilitation of social and economic development of the members of the tribe, and for other purposes. H.R. 5144, 87th Cong., 2d sess., 1961.

U.S. Congress. House. Statement by Dr. Philleo Nash on Kinzua Dam Controversy, 88th Cong., 1st sess., 1963. *Congressional Record,* vol. 109.

U.S. Congress. Senate. Committee on Indian Affairs. Harry S Truman, *Aspects of Indian Policy.* S. Rept., 1945. 79th Cong., 1st sess., 1945. *Congressional Record,* vol. 92.

U.S. Congress. Senate. Senator Butler speaking on removal of restrictions on certain Indian tribes, 80th Cong., 2d sess., 21 July 1947. *Congressional Record,* vol. 93.

U.S. Congress. Senate. Senator Langer speaking against the nomination of John

R. Nichols to Commissioner of Indian Affairs, 81st Cong., 1st sess., 23 March 1949. *Congressional Record,* vol. 95.

U.S. Congress. Senate. Senator Malone speaking on Abolition of the Bureau of Indian Affairs—Introduction of a Bill, 81st Cong., 1st sess., 17 October 1949. *Congressional Record,* vol. 95.

U.S. Congress. Senate. Senator McCarran speaking on Amendment of Constitution Relating to Rights of Indian Tribes, 81st Cong., 1st sess., 29 July 1949. *Congressional Record,* vol. 95.

U.S. Congress. Senate. Senator Butler speaking on "Are Indians Wards of the Government?" 81st Cong., 2d sess., 30 March 1950. *Congressional Record,* vol. 96.

U.S. Congress. Senate. Senator Wiley speaking on the Need for a Scrutiny of America's Indian Policy, 81st Cong., 2d sess., 28 March 1950. *Congressional Record,* vol. 96.

U.S. Congress. Senate. Senator Malone speaking on the Indian and the Indian Bureau—Equal Rights for Indians, 82d Cong., 1st sess., 22 September 1951. *Congressional Record,* vol. 97.

U.S. Congress. Senate. Senator Anderson speaking on Proposed Termination of Federal Supervision over Indian Affairs in California, 82d Cong., 2d sess., 10 April 1952. *Congressional Record,* vol. 98.

U.S. Congress. Senate. Senator Watkins speaking on Proposed Termination of Federal Supervision over Affairs of Certain Indians of Oregon, 82d Cong., 2d sess., 19 April 1952. *Congressional Record,* vol. 98.

U.S. Congress. Senate. Senator Mansfield speaking on Federal Responsibility toward Indians, 86th Cong., 1st sess., 5 March 1959. *Congressional Record,* vol. 105.

U.S. Congress. Senate. Report of Amending "An Act Relative to Employment for Certain Adult Indians on or near Indian Reservations." S. Doc. 134. 87th Cong., 1st sess., 1956.

U.S. Congress. Senate. Discussion on the success of the Relocation Program, 85th Cong., 1st sess., 14 March 1957. *Congressional Record,* vol. 103.

U.S. Congress. Senate. Senator Langer speaking on Bulova Plant at Rolla, North Dakota, 85th Cong., 1st sess., 13 August 1957. *Congressional Record,* vol. 103.

U.S. Congress. Senate. Senator Murray speaking on Indian Land and Credit Policy, 86th Cong., 1st sess., 10 September 1959. *Congressional Record,* vol. 105.

U.S. Congress. Senate. "To provide for preparation of a roll of persons of California Indian descent and the distribution of the certain judgement funds." H.R. 10911, 90th Cong., 2d sess., 4 June 1968.

Books

Brophy, William A., and Sophie D. Aberle. *The Indian: America's Unfinished Business.* Norman: University of Oklahoma Press, 1966.

Chapman, Berlin B. *The Otoes and Missourias: A Study of Indian Removal and the Legal Aftermath.* Oklahoma City: Times Journal Publishing Company, 1965.

Coffer, William. *Phoenix: The Decline and Rebirth of the Indian People.* New York and London: Van Nostrand Reinholdt Company, 1979.

Deloria, Vine, Jr. *The Metaphysics of Modern Existence.* New York: Harper and Row, 1979.

Edwards, Jerome E. *Patrick McCarran: Political Boss of Nevada.* Reno: University of Nevada Press, 1983.

Forbes, Jack D. *The Indian in America's Past.* Englewood Cliffs: Prentice-Hall, 1964.

Getches, David H., Daniel M. Rosenthal, and Charles F. Wilkinson. *Cases and Materials on Federal Indian Law.* St. Paul: West Publishing Company, 1979.

Hagan, William T. *American Indians.* Chicago and London: University of Chicago Press, 1961.

Highwater, Jamake. *The Primal Mind Vision and Reality in Indian America.* New York: Harper and Row, 1980.

Indians in the War, 1945. Chicago: Department of the Interior–Bureau of Indian Affairs, 1945.

Johnson, Broderick H. ed. *Navajos and World War II.* Tsaile: Navajo Community College Press, 1977.

McNickle, D'Arcy. *They Came Here First: The Epic of the American Indian.* New York, Hagerstown, San Francisco, and London: Harper and Row, 1949.

Neils, Elaine. *Reservation to City: Indian Migration and Federal Relocation.* Chicago: University of Chicago, Department of Geography, 1971.

Orfield, Gary. *A Study of the Termination Policy.* Denver: National Congress of American Indians, n.d.

Ourada, Patricia. *The Menominee Indians.* Norman: University of Oklahoma Press, 1979.

Peroff, Nicholas C. *Menominee Drums: Tribal Termination and Restoration, 1954–1974.* Norman: University of Oklahoma Press, 1982.

Philp, Kenneth R. *John Collier's Crusade for Indian Reform, 1920–1954.* Tucson: University of Arizona Press, 1977.

Pierre, George. *American Indian Crisis.* San Antonio: The Naylor Company, 1971.

Prucha, Francis Paul, ed. *Documents of United States Indian Policy.* Lincoln and London: University of Nebraska Press, 1975.

Sorkin, Alan. *American Indians and Federal Aid.* Washington: The Brookings Institute, 1971.

Steiner, Stan. *The New Indians.* New York: Dell Publishing Company, 1968.

Stern, Theodore. *The Klamath Tribe: A People and Their Reservation.* Seattle and London: University of Washington Press, 1965.

Taylor, Theodore. *The States and Their Indian Citizens.* Washington: U.S. Government Printing Office, 1972.

Tyler, S. Lyman. *A History of Indian Policy.* Washington: U.S. Department of the Interior–Bureau of Indian Affairs, 1973.

Underhill, Ruth. *The Navajos.* Norman: University of Oklahoma Press, 1956.

Articles

Ablon, Joan. "American Indian Relocation: Problems of Dependency and Management in the City." *Phylon* 66 (Winter 1965).
"Action Needed for Indian Rights." *The Christian Century* 74 (29 May 1957).
Adair, John, and Evon Vogt. "Navajo and Zuni Veterans: A Study of Contrasting Modes of Culture Change." *American Anthropologist* 51 (1949).
"The American Indian." *The Commonweal* 55 (16 November 1951).
Ames, David W., and Burton R. Fisher. "The Menominee Termination Crisis: Barriers in the Way of a Rapid Cultural Transition." *Human Organization* 18 (Fall 1959).
Armstrong, O.K., and Marjorie Armstrong. "The Indians are Going to Town." *Reader's Digest* 66 (January 1955).
Baris, Allan. "Washington's Public Law 280 Jurisdiction on Indian Reservations." *Washington Law Review* 53 (October 1978).
Barsh, Russel, and Ronald Trosper. "Title I of the Indian Self-Determination and Education Assistance Act of 1975." *American Indian Law Review* 3 (Summer 1975).
Burnett, Donald L., Jr. "Historical Analysis of the 1968 'Indian Civil Rights Act.'" *Harvard Journal on Legislation* 9 (May 1972).
Clarke, Blake. "Must We Buy America from the Indians All Over Again?" *Reader's Digest* 72 (March 1958).
Collier, John. "Back to Dishonor?" *The Christian Century* 71 (12 May 1954).
———. "Indian Takeaway Betrayal of a Trust . . ." *The Nation* 179 (2 October 1954).
Connolly, Thomas E. "The Future of the American Indian." *Catholic World* 181 (July 1955).
"Consultation or Consent?" *The Christian Century* 73 (25 January 1956).
Crawford, Mrs. Wade. "An Indian Talks Back." *American Forests* 63 (July 1957).
Cree, Linda. "Extension of County Jurisdiction over Indian Reservations in California, Public Law 280 and the Ninth Circuit." *Hastings Law Journal* 25 (May 1974).
Dean, William. "Klamath Hearings in Oregon." *American Forests* 63 (November 1957).
Debo, Angie. "Termination of the Oklahoma Indians." *American Indian* 7 (Spring 1955).
Delorme, David P. "'Emancipation' and the Turtle Mountain Chippewas." *American Indian* 7 (Spring 1954).
De Raismes, Joseph. "Indian Civil Rights Act of 1968 and the Pursuit of Responsible Tribal Self-Government." *South Dakota Law Review* 20 (Winter 1975).
Edgerton, Robert B. "Menominee Termination: Observation on the End of a Tribe." *Human Organization* 21 (Spring 1962).
Emmons, Glenn L. "The Problem Stated." *Rotarian* 84–85 (August 1954).
———. "U.S. Aim: Give Indians a Chance." *Nation's Business* (July 1955).
Ericson, Robert, and D. Rebecca Snow. "Indian Battle for Self-Determination." *California Law Review* 58 (March 1970).

"Experiment in Immortality." *The Nation* 175 (26 July 1952).

Fey, Harold E. "Our National Indian Policy." *The Christian Century* 72 (30 March 1955).

———. "The Indian and the Law." *The Christian Century* 72 (9 March 1955).

"First Americans are Last; Pro and Con Discussion." *Senior Scholastic* 62 (4 March 1953).

Fuller, Lauren L. "Alaska Native Claims Settlement: Analysis of the Protective Clauses of the Act through A Comparison with the Dawes Act of 1887." *American Indian Law Review* 4 (Winter 1976).

Goldberg, Carole. "Public Law 280: The Limits of State Jurisdiction over Reservation Indians." *UCLA Law Review* 22 (Fall 1975).

Golden, Madelon, and Lucia Carter. "New Deal for America's Indians." *Cornet* 38 (October 1953).

Gurthals, Joel E. "State Civil Jurisdiction over Tribal Indians—A Re-Examination." *Montana Law Review* 35 (Summer 1974).

Harmer, Ruth Mulvey "Uprooting the Indians." *Atlantic Monthly* 197 (March 1956).

Herzberg, Stephen J. "The Menominee Indians: Termination to Restoration." *American Indian Law Review* 6 (Summer 1978).

Holm, Tom. "Fighting a White Man's War: The Extent and Legacy of American Indian Participation in World War II." *Journal of Ethnic Studies* 9 (Summer 1981).

Hood, Susan. "Termination of the Klamath Tribe in Oregon." *Ethnohistory* 19 (Fall 1972).

Ickes, Harold. "Go East Young Indian!" *New Republic 125* (3 September 1951).

———. "The Indian Loses Again." *New Republic* 125 (24 September 1951).

———. "Justice in a Deep Freeze." *New Republic* 126 (21 May 1951).

"Indian Reservations May Some Day Run Out of Indians." *Saturday Evening Post* 230 (23 November 1957).

"Indians—Criminal Procedure: Habeus Corpus as an Enforcement Procedure under the Civil Rights Act of 1968." *Washington Law Review 46* (May 1971).

"Indians Back Pay for the Utes." *Time* 56 (24 July 1950).

"Indians Lift on Own Bootstraps." *The Christian Century* 75 (26 March 1958).

"Indians Might Do Better with Less Protection." *Saturday Evening Post* 223 (29 July 1950).

"Indians Still Losing Their Land." *The Christian Century* 75 (1 October 1958).

Jones, Cliff A. "Remedies: Tribal Deprivation of Civil Rights; Should Indians Have A Cause of Action under 42 U.S.C. 1983?" *American Indian Law Review* 3 (Summer 1975).

Kelly, William. "The Basis of Indian Life." *The Annals of the American Academy of Political and Social Science* 311 (May 1957).

Kinney, J. P. "Will the Indian Make the Grade?" *American Forests* 60 (December 1954).

"La Farge Charges U.S. Breaks Indian Trust." *The Christian Century* 71 (12 May 1954).

La Farge, Oliver. "The Enduring Indian." *Scientific American* 202 (February 1960).

———. "Helping Elect the Great White Father." *The Reporter* (28 October 1952).

———. "Termination of Federal Supervision: Disintegration of the American Indians." *The Annals of the American Academy of Political and Social Science* 311 (May 1957).

———. "They Were Good Enough for the Army." *Reader's Digest* 52 (February 1948).

Lazarus, Arthur, Jr. "Title II of the 1968 Civil Rights Act: An Indian Bill of Rights." *North Dakota Law Review* 45 (Spring 1969).

Le Duc, Thomas. "The Work of the Indian Claims Commission under the Act of 1946." *Pacific Historical Review* 26 (February 1957).

Lindley, Lawrence E. "Why Indians Need Land." *The Christian Century* 74 (6 November 1957).

Lurie, Nancy O. "The Indians Claims Commission Act." *The Annals of the American Academy of Political and Social Science* 311 (May 1957).

———. "Menominee Termination from Reservation to Colony." *Human Organization* 31 (Fall 1972).

Metzler, William. "Relocation of the Displaced Worker." *Human Organization* 22 (Summer 1963).

Mirrielees, Edith R. "The Cloud of Mistrust." *Atlantic Monthly* 199 (February 1957).

"Must Indian Injustices Go to the President?" *The Christian Century* 72 (1 June 1955).

Myer, Dillon S. "Indian Administration: Problems and Goals." *Social Science Review* 27 (June 1953).

Nash, Philleo. "Indian Administration in the United States: Address, December 6, 1962," *Vital Speeches* 29 (15 February 1963).

Neuberger, Richard L. "Solving the Stubborn Klamath Dilemma." *American Forests* 64 (April 1958).

Persons, Louis D. II. "Jurisdiction: Public Law 280—Local Regulation of Protected Indian Lands." *American Indian Law Review* 6 (Winter 1978).

Peterson, Helen. "American Indian Political Participation." *The Annals of the American Academy of Political and Social Science* 311 (May 1957).

Preloznik, Joseph F., and Steven A. Felsenthal. "The Menominee Struggle to Maintain Their Tribal Assets and Protect Their Treaty Rights Following Termination." *North Dakota Law Review* 51 (Fall 1974).

"Question Validity of Klamath Plan." *The Christian Century* 73 (25 July 1956).

Raines, Howell. "American Indians: Struggling for Power and Identity." *New York Times Magazine* (11 February 1979), Section VI.

"The Reagan Budget." *Nations: The Native American Magazine* 1 (1981).

Reichert, Bert. "Wisconsin's New Indian Country." *American Mercury* 90 (May 1960).

"Ruffled Feathers." *Time* (11 November 1957).

Seaton, Fred A. "Seaton Outlines Klamath Indian Proposal to Congress." *American Forests* 64 (February 1958).

Udall, Stewart L. "The State of the Indian Nation—An Introduction." *Arizona Law Review* 10 (Winter 1968).

"Ute Indians Hit a $31.7 Million Jackpot." *Life Magazine* 29 (24 July 1950).

Van de Mark, Dorothy. "The Raid on Reservations." *Harper's Magazine* 212 (March 1956).

Watkins, Arthur V. "Termination of Federal Supervision: The Removal of Restrictions over Indian Property and Person." *The Annals of the American Academy of Political and Social Science* 311 (May 1957).

White, John R. "Barmecide Revisited: The Gratuitous Offset in Indian Claims Cases." *Ethnohistory* 25 (Spring 1978).

Wilkinson, Charles F., and Eric R. Briggs. "The Evolution of the Termination Policy." *American Indian Law Review* 5 (Summer 1977).

Work, Susan. "The 'Terminated' Five Tribes of Oklahoma: The Effect of Federal Legislation on the Government of the Seminole Nation." *American Indian Law Review* 6 (Summer 1978).

Zimmerman, William, Jr. "The Role of the Bureau of Indian Affairs." *The Annals of the American Academy of Political and Social Science* 311 (May 1957).

Ziontz, Alvin J. "In Defense of Tribal Sovereignty, An Analysis of Judicial Error in Construction of the Indian Civil Rights Act." *South Dakota Law Review* 20 (Winter 1975).

Newspapers

Adirondack *Daily Enterprise,* Saranac Lake, New York. 6 May 1948.

Albuquerque *Journal,* New Mexico. 16 July and 24 August 1945; 18 July 1953; 26 April 1957.

Albuquerque *Tribune,* New Mexico. 27 February, 13 and 18 July 1945; 5 June 1948.

Christian Science Monitor, Boston. 6 March 1956.

The Daily Oklahoman, Oklahoma City, Oklahoma. 21 September 1947.

Denver *Post,* Colorado. 6, 7, and 15 January 1960.

Gallup *Independent,* New Mexico. 31 January 1945.

Milwaukee *Journal,* Wisconsin. 25 November 1945.

New York *Herald-Times.* 12 April 1947; 17 January 1948.

New York *Times.* 8 September 1945; 5 May 1949; 6 September 1951; 18 January 1953.

Oklahoma *Times,* Oklahoma City. 21 August 1946.

Phoenix *Gazette,* Arizona. 28 February, 1960.

Phoenix *Republic,* Arizona. 28 February 1960.

Shawano *Evening Leader,* Wisconsin. 6 October 1954.

Shawano *Journal,* Wisconsin. 22 June 1953.

Washington *Post,* Washington, D.C. 5 and 31 August, 6 September, and 24 October 1951; 30 January 1952; 26 April 1957.

Washington *Star,* Washington, D.C. 23 March 1950; 27 August 1962.

Dissertations and Theses

Brown, Charles C. "Identification of Selected Problems of Indians Residing in Klamath County Oregon—An Examination of Data Generated since Termination of the Klamath Reservation." Ph.D. diss., University of Oregon, 1973.

Burt, Larry W. "United States Expansion and Federal Policy toward Native Americans, 1953–1960." Ph.D. diss., University of Toledo, 1979.

Dixon, Faun. "Native American Property Rights: The Pyramid Lake Reservation Land Controversy." Ph.D. diss., University of Nevada, 1980.

Hasse, Larry J. "Termination and Assimilation: Federal Indian Policy, 1943–1961." Ph.D. diss., Washington State University, 1974.

Hayes, Susanna A. "The Resistance to Education for Assimilation by the Colville Indians, 1872–1972." Ph.D. diss., University of Michigan, 1973.

Neils, Elaine. "The Urbanization of the American Indian and the Federal Program of Relocation and Assistance." Master's thesis, University of Chicago, 1969.

Palmer, James O. "A Geographical Investigation of the Effects of the Bureau of Indian Affairs' Employment Assistance Program upon the Relocation of Oklahoma Indians, 1967–1971." Ph.D. diss., University of Oklahoma, 1975.

Rosenthal, Harvey D. "Their Day in Court: A History of the Indian Claims Commission." Ph.D. diss., Kent State University, 1976.

Underdal, Stanley J. "On the Road toward Termination: The Pyramid Lake Paiutes and the Indian Attorney Controversy of the 1950s." Ph.D. diss., Columbia University, 1977.

Miscellaneous Papers

Baerris, David A., ed. "The Indian in Modern America." Collection of papers presented at the symposium of the Wisconsin State Historical Society, Madison, 1956.

Baugh, Timothy G. "Urban Migration and Rural Responses: The Relocation Program among the Kiowa, Comanche and Plains Apache, 1950–1973." Paper presented at the 37th Plains Conference, Kansas City, Missouri, November 1979.

Madigan, La Verne. "The American Indian Relocation Program." Report undertaken with the assistance of the Field Foundation, Inc., New York, 1956, New York: Association on American Indian Affairs, 1956.

Neog, Prafulla, Richard G. Woods, and Arthur M. Harkins. "Chicago Indians: The Effects of Urban Migration." Report compiled in conjunction with the Training Center for Community Programs, in coordination with the Office of Community Program Center for Urban and Regional Affairs, Chicago, January 1970.

Provinse, Joyn R. "The Withdrawal of Federal Supervision of the American Indian." Paper presented at the National Conference of Social Work, San Francisco, 15 April 1947.

Tyler, S. Lyman. "Indian Affairs: A Work Paper on Termination, with an Attempt to Show Its Antecedents." Institute on American Indian Studies, Brigham Young University, Provo, Utah, 1964.

Interviews and Oral Histories

Bennett, Robert. Commissioner of Indian Affairs. Interview by Joe B. Frantz. Washington, D.C., 13 November 1968. Oral History Collection, Lyndon B. Johnson Presidential Library, Austin, Texas.

Bennett, Robert. Commissioner of Indian Affairs. Interview no. 836. Doris Duke Indian Oral History Collection, Special Collections, William Zimmerman Library, University of New Mexico, Albuquerque.

Big Crow, Moses. Interview by Herbert Hoover. Vermillion, South Dakota, 31 August 1971. Interview no. 50, pt. 2, tape 745. American Indian Research Project–Doris Duke Indian Oral History Collection, University of South Dakota, Vermillion.

Carver, John A., Jr. Assistant Secretary of the Department of Interior. Interview by William Moss. Washington, D.C., 7 October 1969. Interview no. 5. Oral History Collection, John F. Kennedy Presidential Library, Waltham, Massachusetts.

Cassadore, Philip. Interview by J. Bell. 14 October 1970. Folder A–647. Doris Duke Indian Oral History Collection, Arizona State Museum, University of Arizona, Tucson.

DeWitt, Lenora. Interview by Gerald Wolf. Lower Brule, South Dakota, 25 August 1971. Interview no. 39, pt. 1, tape 786s. American Indian Research Project–Doris Duke Indian Oral History Collection, University of South Dakota, Vermillion.

Dressler, John. "Recollections of a Washo Statesman." Oral History Project, Special Collections, University of Nevada Library, Reno.

Emmons, Glenn L. Commissioner of Indian Affairs. Interview by Mary Lu Moore. Albuquerque, New Mexico, 15 April 1974. Special Collections, William Zimmerman Library, University of New Mexico, Albuquerque.

Follard, Edward T. White House Correspondent for the Washington *Post*. Interview by Jerry N. Hess. Oral History Collection, Harry S. Truman Presidential Library, Independence, Missouri.

Gardner, Warner W. Assistant Secretary of the Interior. Interview by Jerry N. Hess. Washington, D.C., 22 June 1972. Oral History Collection, Harry S. Truman Presidential Library, Independence, Missouri.

Haberman, Lena. Interview by Georgia Brown. La Mirada, California, 12 June 1971. Interview no. O.H. 639. Doris Duke Indian Oral History Collection, Oral History Collection, California State University, Fullerton.

Lyman, Stanley D. Relocation Officer of the Bureau of Indian Affairs. Interview by Floyd O'Neil and Gregory Thompson. Pine Ridge Agency, South Dakota, n.d. Interview no. 1031, acc. no. 24, box 54, Doris Duke Indian Oral History Collection, Special Collections, Marriott Library, University of Utah, Salt Lake City.

Myer, Dillon S. Commissioner of Indian Affairs. 1970. Regional Oral History Collection, Bancroft Library, University of California, Berkeley.

Panel Discussion on "Termination" for the television show, "The Advocates." Taped by Michael B. Husband. 24 January 1970. Interview no. 450. Doris Duke Indian Oral History Collection, Special Collections, William Zimmerman Library, University of New Mexico, Albuquerque.

Pennington, Robert. Chief of the Tribal Government Services, Bureau of Indian Affairs. Interview by Donald Fixico. Washington, D.C., 13 August 1979.

Rowland, Allen. Interview by Al Spang. Lame Deer, Montana, 5 March 1971. Interview no. 864. Doris Duke Indian Oral History Collection, Special Collections, William Zimmerman Library, University of New Mexico, Albuquerque.

Schaab, William. Special Attorney for the Taos Pueblo. Interview by Dennis Stanford. 27 March 1969. Interview no. 439. Doris Duke Indian Oral History Collection, Special Collections, William Zimmerman Library, University of New Mexico, Albuquerque.

Streeter, Marie. Relocation Officer of the Bureau of Indian Affairs. Interview by Floyd O'Neil. San Jose, California, 5 March 1971. Interview no. 1036, acc. no. 24, box 54. Doris Duke Indian Oral History Collection, Special Collections, Marriott Library, University of Utah, Salt Lake City.

Toledo, Jose. Interview by James P. Romero. Jemez Pueblo, New Mexico, 1–2 March 1970. Tape 446, side 1. Doris Duke Indian Oral History Collection, Special Collections, William Zimmerman Library, University of New Mexico, Albuquerque.

Udall, Stewart. Secretary of the Department of the Interior. Interview by Joe B. Frantz. Washington, D.C., 29 July 1969. Interview no. 3. Oral History Collection, Lyndon B. Johnson Presidential Library, Austin, Texas.

Vasquez, Joseph C. Interview by Floyd O'Neil. Los Angeles, California, 27 January 1971. Interview no. 1009, acc. no. 24, box 53. Doris Duke Indian Oral History Collection, Special Collections, Marriott Library, University of Utah, Salt Lake City.

Watkins, Arthur V. Senator of Utah and Chief Commissioner of Indian Claims Commission. Interview by Ed Edwin. Washington, D.C., 14 January 1968. Oral History Collection, Dwight D. Eisenhower Presidential Library, Abilene, Kansas.

Wicks, Chaske F. Interview by Bea Medicine. Little Rock, California, 15 February 1969. Microfiche, tape 356, pt. 2. American Indian Research Project–Doris Duke Indian Oral History Collection, University of South Dakota, Vermillion.

Woodward, George. Interview by Floyd O'Neil, Gerald Huntley, and Judith Kilpatrick. Oakland, California, 2 March 1971. Interview no. 1033, acc. no. 24, box 54. Doris Duke Indian Oral History Collection, Special Collections, Marriott Library, University of Utah, Salt Lake City.

Index